MW01037226

TELL ME THE TRUEST THING YOU KNOW

DAN O'HARE

Copyright © 2022 Dan O'Hare
Cover design by Caroline O'Hare
Edited by Mark Decker
Design by Aaron Rosenberg
ISBN 978-1-892544-17-9
All rights reserved.
No part of this work covered by the copyright herein may be reproduced or
distributed in any form or by any means, except as permitted by U.S. copy-
right law, without the prior written permission of the copyright owner.
First edition

For Dan Crotty and Kevin McNulty

Thank you for showing my father true friendship until the end.

CONTENTS

Letter to Olive

When I started writing this book I didn't know why I was writing it, or for whom this book was being written. At first I was pretty sure it was just for me, as some sort of therapy. I guess I also thought in some way it was for my father, to keep his story alive.

As I continued to write I began to think it may actually be for you, my dear sweet daughter Olive. Almost every decision I make is with you in mind. This is not a platitude or exaggeration. Even the simple habitual choices, such as the food I eat, are made with you in mind. It has become my central preoccupation, to try and extend my life just a little longer, so I can witness one more of your many accomplishments. I am not sure why I have developed this obsession, but perhaps it is because I am an older parent – I was almost thirty-nine when you were born – or perhaps it is because you were born just a few months before I lost my own father to a stroke, and my regret for you not getting to know him weighs on me more than I have admitted to myself. Or perhaps it is because I always felt I was going to die young, and have long been twisted in an endless conversation with my psyche about death. But because of some—or *all*—of these reasons, I have looked at this book as a way to leave something behind for you when I'm not around to express what I learned in my lifetime. Like all parents, I hope life will be easier for you than it was for me. I have no idea what challenges you will face in your life, only that you are likely to struggle with many things, and you should know this is to be expected. Struggle is what makes us human, it makes us who we are. That, and our mistakes. Though by the time you are reading this, I'm sure you will already have accepted these platitudes.

I don't know if my father ever allowed himself to explore who he was and why he acted the way he did. If he had made that exploration, he never let me know. He wasn't honest with his children about his mental or physical health, and because of that my brother and I were left to navigate these inherited waters without so much as a hand-drawn chart. And it's not like my father got help from his parents, either. We all know mental health wasn't really discussed by those generations. I want to end that cycle.

Before you were born I was drinking myself to death. Not quickly, but every day I would drink a little more than I did the day before, until I was drinking a full liter of whiskey each night while also smoking two to four packs of cigarettes daily. It wasn't a conscious decision, it just happened slowly. I would often drink alone in the back yard of our Astoria apartment and just think. I would talk to myself. I imagined random future events, like giving a graduation commencement speech. I created entire speeches in my head and spoke them softly to myself while pacing, smoking, and drinking. To our poor neighbors I must have looked like such a madman. Ironically, I was so lost and yet all I thought about was giving advice. It never occurred to me that I might have been lost because I didn't have anyone on whom to impart guidance. In those days I had no idea what my purpose was in this life, and I was certain I would never be a father. Your mother, my dear wife Caroline, had endured many fertility treatments and miscarriages, and even the doctors had given up on us having a child. We couldn't afford adoption. I told myself this was fine, but it clearly wasn't. Either I never gave myself the space to understand how important having a child was for me, or I'm now using that as an excuse for my unhealthy habits. Either way, your mother and I had come to the hard conclusion that, contrary to our wishes, we would not become parents. Yet less than a year after we had finally let go of the dream, you came into our lives. I quit smoking and heavy drinking the day I found out your mother was pregnant.

After suffering miscarriages, it was hard to believe that things could go right. Throughout most of your mother's pregnancy we were waiting for the bad news, steeling ourselves for the impending defeat of our dream. But when this tiny new life was suddenly brought into our world, my own life became a constant mix of fear, excitement, exhaustion, joy, hope, and unexpected sadness.

Your maternal grandfather died suddenly when you were three months old. Your paternal grandfather went into the nursing home when you were eleven months old and took three and a half years to die, but practically speaking he was already dead when he got there. You never knew either of them, and I wish you had, as they were two truly interesting characters. You would have loved both of them, and I know you would have been a bright shining light in their lives.

So part of why I wrote this book was to find a way for you to know my father—or maybe for you to know me, in case I'm not around. Better yet, when you are older and I am gone, perhaps you can use this book to understand a little something about yourself, and understand that you are not alone in this world. Art has always made me feel connected to something more, made me feel like I am a part of an unnamable thing which is much bigger than myself. Maybe this is what is meant by the term "culture?" I have a hard time with this word, because the larger the crowd I am in, the more I feel alone. Culture just feels so big. Perhaps that's why I love books. Reading connects me to another person without any crowd noise or distractions. Each book I read is an intense and intimate conversation with the author, and the rest of the world just needs to wait until we are done talking. I am hoping that this book—or any book—will do that for you.

But perhaps this isn't for you, either. Maybe it's for no one. There was a time in my younger days when I used to write a poem each day and then burn it, as I had read somewhere that JD Salinger did this. My goal was to eliminate the arrogance in my writing, but instead my writing became far more arrogant, since I knew no one would read it. Still, a part of me wants to burn this when I am done. I can't fathom anyone who doesn't know me wanting to read this book, and I assume anyone who does know me will either be upset or disappointed by my words. So the temptation to watch these pages burn is real, and it's only the thought of you someday reading this that stays my hand.

Now that I am done with this book and have come back to the beginning, I realize there is something important you need to know: you have permission to not grieve for me. You don't owe me a single day of sadness. All I want for you is to live your life with your eyes, heart, and mind open, seeking your own experiences. My life changed when I found certain poets, certain artists, and certain philosophers. Find your own Gwendolyn Brooks. Find your own Cicero. Find your own Amanda Palmer, your own John Grant. Find your own Clarissa Pinkola Estes, your own Robin Wall Kimmerer, and your own Langhorne Slim. Find whatever is out there for you. Or don't. It's not my life, it's yours, and you owe none of it to me.

Don't ever let the thought that I missed out on something make you sad. Don't think, *Dad would have loved this song, this play, this film, this story, or this joke.* I did love it, I loved it through you. That's more than enough.

I hope to see you grow into the incredible human I know you will become. And I hope to share with you at least some of your failures, your mistakes, and your losses. But if I don't, if I am not able to be with you, please know that it is okay to forget me. It is okay to let me go. It is okay to live your life and find your own way and no matter what way that is, it is yours and yours alone. You owe me nothing.

You already saved my life once, and that's enough. All I ask is that you laugh, free and easy. I promise I will not haunt you.

I love you forever.

FOR OLIVE
(written when she was three months old)

This is the voice of an angry sea
a tempest of promise
through which I hold my breath
the jubilation and horror of every possibility
lurk
she stole all the magic I once claimed
she gathers my ghosts and
whispers of some distant thunder
a mystery I will never solve

was I a stone cast aside?
skipped into a slow muddy river
as time tore through tomorrow
the waters had grown deep and more still
every day I would drown with my spirits,
quieting the madness of doubt
fearless, embracing sleep

but now I have never sang and danced more
for she can carry these notes where I cannot
far past my horizon
into the sunsets I shall never see.
I can teach her only to hear trees breathe
how to listen to their singing
and that stillness can set one free

how am I no longer dead?
her tiny lungs are mighty
they cry to me, remind me to breathe
in the brown world of which I had hidden
they echo all the way down
distorted thunder becomes a promise
I will not drown
I will not drown

BECOMING BIFF LOMAN

My father used to say, "When my son was fifteen years old I cast him as Biff Loman, and he never stopped being in character." That's pretty much all you need to know about me and my father, but here's a book about it anyway.

That was Matt O'Hare at his best, when he was honest. His sense of humor was his only way to be sort-of, half-heartedly, and still-guardedly, honest. To the best of my recollection he never told the full truth about anything, preferring to either gently tease, embellish enough to add a little humor, or rely heavily on sarcasm. He was a strong believer in the old cliché, "If you get them laughing you can tell them anything." Those that knew him well might say he had a hard time being honest without either screaming or joking—usually in public joking, in private screaming. Don't worry, I'm not going to talk much about the private screaming. Like so many of his Baby Boomer generation, he had undiagnosed mental illnesses which came out as violence. This book is not really about that, even though it's important. This book is about the other times, the public dad, and the stories that he told. This book is an attempt to keep alive the creation of my father, his own persona, a larger-than-life jokester who was passionate about a few things and rarely honest about anything, especially his own feelings. This book is also about helping myself to understand the last three-and-a-half years of his life, which should really be referred to as his death, for it certainly should not be included in any definition of "life."

Matt O'Hare's passions were primarily theater and sports, but his best talent was creating a public person who would make people smile and was pleasant to be around. His game was simply to be well-liked, just like Willy Loman. This was my father's craft and art, which I guess can be described as "charm." Until I was roughly fourteen or fifteen years old, I was pretty good at playing that game, too. I was smart enough, good enough at sports, and friendly enough to be well-liked. However, when I became a teenager that changed. Like many teenagers before me, I started to question many of the systems and institutions that make up our society. I started to question the game it seemed we were all playing. I felt trapped in a life that was not my own, and eventually became certain that almost everything I knew to be true was actually a manufactured lie. I hungered for something real, something solid, something untainted by the machine of our culture. Just like Biff.

What really happened in my early teen years is probably too much story for any one book that—let's be honest—no one wants to read anyway. Maybe my dad recognized I was like Biff in more ways than even I knew, and maybe that's why he chose to direct *Death of a Salesman* for my tenth grade Drama Elective play. Maybe deep down he thought casting me as Biff would help me understand something about myself, or maybe it's not deep at all. It could be that I just reminded him of Biff because I was tall and played sports, I don't know. I never got a chance to ask him, because I never thought of that until just now.

My father and I had lots of ups and downs, like most sons and fathers do. One night when I was twenty and at the movie theater seeing *Multiplicity* with the then love of my life, my mother left my father. My mother actually left my father for the man who was, at that time, my boss. During my parents' divorce, my father strangely decided to blame me for everything that went wrong in his life, and as a result we decided not to speak to each other for a few years. Eventually we did speak again, largely because of baseball, Notre Dame football, and Thanksgiving.

About twenty years after the night of *Multiplicity*, when my daughter was just eleven months old, my father suffered a massive hemorrhagic stroke. It took him three-and-a-half years to die from it. I was there for him, from the first night in the hospital to his last breath in the nursing home, literally holding his hand as he passed. My father was never the same after the stroke, as his mind was not just damaged, it was ruined. He could not read, watch TV, or follow sports, and he rarely made sense in conversation. He was not in a vegetative state, but he had lost his intelligence, his humor, and most of his personality. He became something like a doppelganger that had cobbled together some old memories of my father, but could learn nothing new, and could make sense of little from the past. Various doctors who never conferred with one another did what they could to treat his many symptoms, but in effect they medicated away his humanity.

In his very rare lucid moments after the stroke, between certain medications wearing off and others not yet kicking in, he would ask me to kill him. I started to dread these "good" days, when he seemed to find a small spark of the intelligence which once defined him, when he was actually capable of understanding where he was; the request would usually come for me to get him a knife, or a gun, or push him off a bridge. It was often right when I would muster up a modicum of hope that he might be getting better when he would motion to me to get close and whisper his request to die. The worst part is, that these requests were simultaneously the most honest my father ever was with me, and the most helpless I have ever felt.

At first, I would stop by and see my father every day in the nursing home, but that got to be too taxing on me. I then went three or four times a week. Finally, I settled on twice a week. For the last three years of his life I spent at least a half hour, usually more, with this shell of a man I once loved. I started to hate seeing my father, hate the relationship dynamic I had developed with him, and hate what we had become.

Before we get into all of that, you need to know just a little more about me. I was the first person born to permanent residents of Ocean Pines, Maryland. Ocean Pines is an enormous Home Owners Association nestled on the western shore of the confluence of the St. Martin River and Assawoman Bay, and is separated from Ocean City, Maryland by the latter. Initially used primarily for retirement and vacationers, it did not become the year-round populated community it is today until sometime after I left for college in 1994. When I was young, Ocean Pines was almost barren of year-round homes and only had a population to speak of in the summer months, when it would swell from the five hundred or so full-time residents to over ten thousand vacationers. I grew up on the water, in the woods, and exploring the life that existed between these two realms. I was a three-sport athlete at Worcester Country School in Berlin Maryland, starting every varsity game in all three sports all four years of high school. I was also class president for four years, preformed in theater (in case you forgot I was Biff in *Death of a Salesman*), and was sort-of engaged to my childhood sweetheart, who I believed was the love of my life. I had a slew of good friends, never did homework but got okay grades, was generally well-liked, and never whistled in elevators. Basically, I was the typical cisgendered, straight, white-privileged, golden boy asshole. I went to college briefly, supposedly to play sports. When my parents divorced, I dropped out of college, broke up with the love of my life, became a bartender, traveled throughout Europe, moved to Ireland for a little while, then became a wanderer in the United States for about a year before settling in New York City. I have never been comfortable in my skin, even before I played Biff Lowman. Like Biff, I was a good athlete until I gave it all up and disappeared from sports for quite a while. Like Biff, I have had thirty some jobs in my life, including being a cowboy and a carpenter. Like Biff (and Happy) I drank too much scotch. From 1999 to 2014 I mostly lived in New York, while chiefly working in film and television, largely for MTV and Comedy Central. In 2014, my pregnant wife Caroline and I moved to our vacation home in Salisbury,

MD, which we had purchased in September 2012, right in the midst of the Baltimore Orioles' improbable—but predictable—playoff run.

A few months after my father passed I began having health problems. First, I thought I was having a heart attack, which turned out to be a panic attack. Then I thought I was having a stroke, but this also turned out to be a panic attack. Then I developed a chronic headache that I believed was located at the exact place my father had his stroke. I felt the pain where I knew his stroke was, even though I knew the brain does not have pain receptors that would "feel" pain there. This turned out to be chronic sinusitis, or allergies, or poor nutrition, or maybe anxiety. Possibly all four. Shortly after that, in March of 2020 I got COVID-19. After COVID I had chronic pain in my chest, left arm, and left jaw, which was diagnosed as heartburn, arthritis, a pinched nerve, Premature Ventricular Contractions (PVCs), or possibly anxiety.

It took many doctor visits before I began to realize that I was dealing with—or perhaps more accurately, *not* dealing with—unchecked anxiety and grief. While I thought I was fine and seemed fine to the outside world, my body was telling me a different story. For me, grief and anxiety manifested physically. Of all the things I have spent too much time thinking about, grief and anxiety were never high on the list. Honestly, at this point I'm not sure I'm even able to tell them apart.

In many ways I'm just another son writing another book about another father because he's having a hard time accepting his dad's death. I am aware this is a common trope. In the novel *American Pastoral*, Philip Roth's alter ego Nathan Zuckerman is approached by Seymour "The Swede" Levov asking for help to write a tribute to his father. Zuckerman does not help him of course, but he meets with Levov, which starts a whole different story. While it's clear I am not Philip Roth, what started out as a kind of tribute to my father became a different story. A story about mental health.

Just like Biff Lowman, I am built in a way that needs to get to the guts of things. Even though Biff was a huge disappointment to his father, he forced the whole family to face the truth. All those years spent drinking and "thinking" in solitude were of no help to me now. To get healthy, I needed to be truly honest. Like a cliché machine, I needed to look back to move forward, I needed to face my past to understand my present, I needed to finally be okay with being my failures. At the end of the play, Biff knew who he was. Maybe, just maybe, my father saw far ahead into my future and knew he needed to cast me as Biff. Maybe he saw something in me that reminded him of that character. More likely though, he just cast me as Biff because I was tall.

I Am Not My Father

When walking down the street in Berlin, Maryland I inevitably run in to people who knew my dad. They will stop me and innocuously ask, "Are you Matt O'Hare's son?" The reason this happens is twofold: first is that Berlin is a small town and my dad was well-known there. Second, I look like my father. It's more than just a passing resemblance.

I know that people mean well when they say things like that. They liked my dad. They want to say, *I knew your dad, and he was a great guy, and since you are related to him you must be lucky to be related to a nice guy,* or something to that effect. What I hear when they say, "you look just like your dad" is, *you are going to have a stroke and your daughter is going to see some pale version of you while she takes care of you for years until you finally stop breathing and you leave her with nothing but grief and unanswered questions.* Okay, so maybe that's a little dark, but that's the truth. That is really how my brain processes the words "You look like your dad."

Am I my father? If he was writing this book, he would have tried to make everything nice and funny. I would prefer to make people cry. My flippancy aside, I clearly am a very different person from my father, it's just that we have some similarities. My anxiety seems to have amplified those similarities until they took on an oversized importance.

Once you start looking for similarities you are going to find them. My dad had a torn rotator cuff, I have a torn rotator cuff. My dad had bad knees, I have a root tear in my right knee. How anxiety conflates the information of *both my father and I have bad knees* to *I am going to have a stroke* is one of the first things I had to come to terms with about anxiety.

Children look like their parents, and they inherit their parents' genes. Children pick up their parents' mannerisms and they blame them for their shortcomings. James Hillman (who may have been the last Jungian psychologist to actually know Jung in his lifetime) told a great story in his book *A Souls Code* about identical twins separated at birth and raised in different countries by different adoptive families. Both of the twins, who were interviewed when they were in their fifties, were extraordinarily neat and tidy, fastidious in their manner of dress, and exceptionally organized. When asked why they believed he was this way, the first one said, "Without a doubt it was because of my mother. She kept the house spotless. She had twelve clocks in the living room, and all twelve had to chime noon at exactly the same time. She's certainly the reason I am this way." When the psychologist asked the other twin why he was this way, he answered, "No question it is because of my mother. She was a total slob."

We put an oversized amount of blame on our parents for our shortcomings, just as our parents might get a little too much credit for our successes. That does not mean there is nothing to learn from understanding their lives, however. Doctors will be the first to tell you that knowing a patient's history is the only way to start to treat them effectively, and a large part of their history is knowing their family history.

One of my all-time favorite interviews was in 2008 when Dan Carlin interviewed the luminary James Burke on Carlin's *Hardcore History* podcast. Carlin asked Burke if he thought there was any validity in all the comparisons made between ancient Rome and the current United States. Burke gave a well-reasoned and typically involuted response that "Rome is in one out of twenty-seven zillion ways similar to the United States of America, and in twenty-seven zillion ways minus one it is not like America." Building on this, he explained that it is worth studying the similarities between the two because you can always glean insight into your current state by looking at your collective past. Similarly, us knowing our parents means we will know more about ourselves. We still need to recognize that in twenty-seven zillion ways minus one we are not like them.

Likewise, by hiding who we truly are from our children, we steal a valuable tool from their lives. I do not blame parents for this either conscious or unconscious theft; I think everyone is just stumbling through life as best as they can. But if I recognize this "fact" then I certainly need to do something about it. Did my grandfather have anxiety? I don't know, he never told me, and I doubt he ever told his son. Did my father have anxiety? I think it is evident that he did, but he labored to hide it from everyone, usually by trying to be funny or by being well-liked.

Well, I'm not that funny. I don't need to be well-liked; in fact, I don't even want to be liked at all. I find far more entertainment in love and hate. In our short existence we might as well be entertained. But my feelings aside, in my father's obituary I did ask others to honor him by telling a good story. So, I might as well oblige.

MY FIRST STORY
or
I Had a Plant Growing Out of My Arm

My dad didn't like nature. He always seemed frustrated or uncomfortable in any sort of natural environment. That did not mean he disliked being outside; in fact, he loved being outside, as long as outside meant being in the bleachers or stands or on the sideline of a game somewhere. He was also okay with the beach, as he liked walking on a clean sandy beach, right by the shoreline. However, being in the woods frightened my father. He would never go hiking or camping or fishing, even though both of his sons loved those activities, and he wanted nothing to do with gardens.

My father only had a couple of stories about being outdoors that he liked to tell. One was about the time he was trying to earn a merit badge for Boy Scouts, when he was trying to learn how to start a fire. He was with two of his friends and they had built a circle of rocks and broken concrete they had gathered from a parking lot which was at the edge of a hay field near a park. They collected a bunch of pine needles and sticks from the park and were trying to start the fire using a flint and steel. It was a dry, windy day, so every time he and his friends would almost get the fire going, the wind would whip up and blow it out. At least that's what they thought, until his friend turned around and noticed one of the sparks from the fire had set the entire field behind them ablaze. While he technically succeeded in starting a fire, understandably no merit badge was awarded.

The other story he liked to tell was about how as a teenager he worked one summer for a farmer picking beans, strawberries, and melons. He spent the morning picking the produce, and then worked the afternoon at the produce stand. I think he only worked there a month or two. One day a woman came by and acted pretty rude to my dad and his teen coworkers. She kept bossing them around without saying please or thank you.

While she was paying she said, "And get me a watermelon. Carry it to the car and put it in the trunk."

So my dad chose the watermelon that was on display and had been sitting in the hot sun for at least five hours. He probably did not know what was going to happen, but he knew it was the worst watermelon to give her.

A half hour after the rude lady drove away, her car came flying back into the parking lot. She got out of the car in a furious state, her dress stained red—she was noticeably wet and had bits of watermelon and seeds still clinging to her matted hair. Apparently the moment she put a knife in the watermelon it exploded. At least that's the story my dad told, but I have never tried to recreate the experiment. To my knowledge, that one summer is the extent of my dad's experience with farming.

My dad had farmers on his side of the family perhaps going as far back as the Celt conquest of Ireland, but he just never had the itch. Dad always wanted to be around people, so fields, pastures, gardens, and nature in general just didn't really appeal to him. His mother, Mary, grew up on a farm, and that side of the family still farms in Delavan, Illinois. They are pretty wonderful people, but I have only spent time with them at funerals. Unfortunately, we were never close to them, and once my grandmother moved off the farm, her branch of the family seemed to lose any connection to the soil. In fact, none of my dad's siblings had any interest in gardening or farming at all, with one tiny exception.

My father had four siblings: my Aunt Peggy got Multiple Sclerosis (MS) in her twenties and was bedridden for the rest of her life, my grandma taking care of her the whole time; my Aunt Bonnie taught special education and was a school administrator, and always seemed to live in cities; my Uncle Harry never left home, coached a little, worked for UPS, and for a while claimed to be a professional lottery player; and then there was my Uncle Mike.

Uncle Mike was always a bit of a mystery to me because he and my dad had a falling out before I was born, so I never got to know him. Mike sometimes lived with my grandparents in their basement, and sometimes had his own place, but always lived nearby their Dyer, Indiana home. On very rare occasions Tom and I would catch a glimpse of him, walking from the kitchen to the basement, or quickly out the door when we came to visit, but he never stopped to talk. He was tall, but walked with a kind of hunch, like he was holding something heavy slung over his shoulders. My dad used to say, "Mike would be six foot five if he ever stood up straight." My dad and Mike stopped speaking to each other when my dad was in college, but their mother always kept Dad informed of what Mike was up to. Mike had a ton of different jobs, though the most consistent was as a wedding photographer. He was one of those people that often had some side hustle going. Without a doubt, his most memorable such hustle was being a professional Abraham Lincoln impersonator.

One day, my dad was visiting Peggy and Grandma. Dad was sitting in the living room with Grandma; they were probably drinking diet soda and eating Chicago dogs from Bozo's. As always, Peggy was in her bed in the adjoining room, but she could hear what they were saying, and they could hear her if she yelled, which she always did. Peggy had a high-pitched and quavering voice which might have been a symptom of MS, or might have been a product of yelling all the time. My grandmother on the other hand, had a calm, unassuming manner that was always trying to level out and make peace between her children. On this particular day while on his way into the house, my dad had noticed two dead plants that were right in the middle of the back yard, so once a lull in the conversation happened, he remembered them and asked my grandmother what they were.

"Oh, I don't know," Grandma said.

"Yes you do!" Peggy called from the other room. "They're cotton!"

"Cotton?" My dad was thoroughly confused, as anyone would be. "Why are you growing cotton?"

"Well Mike is," my grandmother answered.

"Why is Mike growing two cotton plants?"

"Oh, I don't know."

"Yes you do!" Peggy chimed in again. "He's growing cotton because Abraham Lincoln grew cotton!"

"Abraham Lincoln grew cotton?"

"Oh yes," my grandmother quickly confirmed. "Mike knows all about Abraham Lincoln now. He's one of the more popular Abraham Lincoln impersonators in the northern Indiana area."

"Are there a lot of Abraham Lincoln impersonators in the northern Indiana area?"

"Oh I don't know."

"There's only two! Mike and the good one!" Peggy yelled while most likely smiling.

"So why is he actually trying to grow cotton?"

"Oh, well, he thinks it will help set him apart from the other impersonators."

My dad tried to imagine how his estranged brother would use two crappy cotton plants at his mother's house to outcompete the only other Abraham Lincoln impersonator in the northern Indiana area.

"Well, they don't look very good. Is that what cotton is supposed to look like?"

"Oh, they're doing fine."

"No they're not! They're dying, like all of us!"

Like most of his stories, I heard my dad tell this one at least twenty times. It changed a little every time, because stories are supposed to do that, and it changed depending on to whom dad was telling the story. He relished a great story, and great stories are pointless unless there is someone to tell it to. I guess this is why he loved being around people, especially people that would laugh at his stories. Perhaps the reason he didn't like being alone in nature was just because there was no one there to laugh.

My mom, on the other hand, always seemed far more at peace in nature than around people. Don't get me wrong, my mom loves being around people too, but she has a different energy in social situations, and is much more relaxed with plants and wildlife. While my mom loves nature, she also likes to control it. She loves to garden, and as far as I know she always had this trait. Her father, my Grandpa Guarino, had a huge garden on the side lot by his house in Dalton Illinois, where he grew tomatoes, cucumbers, onions, squash, and even kept a chicken or two. I'm sure mom inherited this passion for gardening from him, and not long after I was born she began a thriving garden at our rented Ocean Pines home. Mom always grew tomatoes, and she taught me at an early age that there's really nothing like a home-grown, vine-ripened tomato. She also grew cucumbers, chives, peas, beans, squash, and rhubarb. We even had some fruit trees. She grew flowers too—she loved her flowers, especially her roses.

Because I was around my mom one hundred percent of the time from birth to age five, and because she loved to garden, I spent a good deal of time playing outdoors in the dirt. Apparently I liked finding things in the dirt, like worms, bugs, rocks, more dirt, and so on. In those days we lived on a canal, so I liked finding stuff in the water too, especially blue crabs (in case you forgot we were in Maryland). Mom could keep a better eye on me if I was not leaning over the bulkhead with a crab net, so I spent most of the time sitting on the dirt somewhere near her garden. To this day I can remember my mom telling me what a good helper I was in the garden, even though I would pick and eat everything I could, then go dig a random hole somewhere. Or I'd find a weed and make friends with it, proclaiming that this weed was the most important plant in the garden, if not the known universe, and should be protected at all costs. I know this is what I did because when I tell my mom this is exactly how

Olive "helps" me in the garden, she laughs and says, "Just like you did!"

It was on one of those endless summer garden days when I was four years old that I managed to pick up a lifelong scar on my arm. It was my first great story and I got pretty good at telling it, although I've never written it down before. But to honor my dad I'll give it a shot. Like all good stories it needs an audience, and this one usually required a visual aid, which I don't have because this isn't a picture book.

By the time I was in college, this is how I told it: first, it had to be late at night. Stories are better late at night when there's no rush to be anywhere and the time seems stolen anyway. Plus, I believe it's easier to focus on the plot at night, when the mystery inherent in the surrounding shadows helps suspend disbelief. Second, I had to let others tell some stories first, the appetizer stories. You never want to lead off with a great story. With a great story you need people to already be in a storytelling mood. Let them get their familiar stories out of the way, the ones about car accidents, getting drunk the first time, or perhaps something with humorous partial nudity or pubescent fumbling. These were the typical stories that college freshmen in the 1990s were familiar hearing, ones that didn't involve near death interspecies contagion. Then I would pull up my left sleeve.

"You see this scar?"

They would always say: "What is that, a burn?" (People say that because it looks exactly like a burn.)

"Nope. It was from a plant growing out of my arm."

Now you have to remember, in the 1990s the internet was not easily accessible, smart phones hadn't been invented yet and there were no cell phones among my peers. But there were urban legends; everyone both knew how to tell them and was pretty sure they weren't real. The best ones, the ones with that little un-popped kernel or two of truth could really get people second guessing their own doubt. However, being the contrarian that I was, I took the opposite tack. My theory was that when you started with a statement that was ridiculous, no one would believe you. Which is exactly what I wanted, because they then let down their defenses.

"Bullshit."

"No, it's true. When I was four years old I had a bug bite and I kept scratching it. It was just this open wound, and kept getting bigger and bigger. Finally my mom took me to the doctor, and they had no idea what it was, but said they would cut it out if my mom wanted. So then she took me to a dermatologist, and he had no idea what it was, and suggested I go to the hospital. My mom then took me to the local hospital, and they said they didn't know what it was, but they would cut it out if my mom wanted."

"After two days it had doubled in size, and my parents started freaking out. They flew me up to Johns Hopkins in Baltimore and the first doctors there looked at it and had no idea what it was, but instead of suggesting they cut it out they called in a specialist. The Hopkins dermatologist—who was like the top dermatologist in the country or world or something—came in, took one look at my arm, raised his eyebrows, nodded, and then looked at my mom and said, 'Do you have a rose garden?'

"My mom confirmed she did, and so the dermatologist turned to the other doctor and said to grab everyone who wasn't busy and bring them in to look at my arm. He said it was likely they would never see such a thing again, but just in case they should see what it looks like. He explained I had an incredibly rare condition called *sporotrichosis*, which comes from the thorn of a rose. Obviously it had pricked me and this disease had gotten in and started to grow. If left untreated, it would have *killed* me."

At this point, I had them. Their jaws would be on the floor, and their disbelief swept away by the credible details, my commitment to describing the lengthy progression of events, the Latin of the medical name of the disease, and the physical evidence of the rather large scar. Sometimes they would ask to see the scar again, and sometimes they asked if it hurt, or if I remembered the pain, or if I was scared. Some asked to call my parents to get corroboration. But they always asked the next question.

"What did they do? Did they cut it out?"

"They couldn't, it was in my blood stream. If they tried to cut it out I would have died."

"So what did they do?"

Here I would pause and smile. This is what I had been working for from the moment I started telling the story, and there was only going to be one way to end it.

"They injected me with Weed-B-Gon."

Most of my friends still do not know if this story is true.

Ocean Pines was a very different place when I was a kid. There are about 7,500 buildable lots in Ocean Pines, and as of 2020 there were less than 500 of those lots vacant. Most people now consider Ocean Pines to be suburban, even though there is no real urban center nearby. When I was a kid it felt much more rural; there were probably only about 500 homes built in all of Ocean Pines and most of those were used as vacation homes. Everything else was wild or empty. Like most kids of that era living in a rural area, we were kicked out of the house during the day, rain or shine until dinner time.

My brother Tom and I usually spent our days exploring the woods, swamp, marsh, and lagoon that surrounded White Horse Park and the Ocean Pines Boat Ramp. Back then there were no paths through those woods other than an old logging road, and there were no houses between our cul de sac street (Crows Nest Lane) and the campground, so it was essentially our own private wilderness to explore. During various expeditions, armed with a crab net, a cast net, a seine net, a butterfly net, a machete, a hatchet, or just a pocketknife sharpened stick, Tom and I chased every poor living creature in those woods and the surrounding waters.

We especially like going "marshmucking," which is what it sounds like. As a kid, there was something satisfying about stomping around in two-foot-thick marsh mud for no discernable reason. While I don't mind marshmucking now, I at least need a reason. In those days, I needed a reason *not* to go marshmucking.

My parents would occasionally take us to the beach in Ocean City, but usually if we were going to the beach, that meant going to Assateague Island. Assateague is this magical barrier island just south of Ocean City where wild ponies still roam. The legend of where the wild ponies came from, was that of a huge storm and a shipwrecked Spanish galleon where all the sailors perished, but the ponies swam to shore. The internet will tell you a more mundane story of a farmer releasing his horses on the island, but don't believe what you read on the internet. Assateague was once part of the same barrier island as Ocean City, but a hurricane tore an inlet between the two in 1933. The ocean side of the island is widely considered one of the cleanest beaches in the United States, and the bayside is made up of marshes, tidal pools, mosquito lakes, and the occasional pine tree. My brother and I liked the beach, but if my dad was not with us we always found a way to make it to the bayside of Assateague, to the marsh, and the mud, and the shallows.

Whether in Ocean Pines or on Assateague, my brother and I found endless fascination in the place between worlds, the swamp, the marsh, the tidal pools, and lagoon by the boat docks. Those are the places where the world is most alive, humming with the untamed mayhem of existence. We hunted frogs, lizards, snakes, bees, clams, mussels, minnows, fiddler crabs, and blue crabs... so many blue crabs. While it's a cliché, kids in Maryland really do take this shit seriously.

In fact, when my Aunt Peggy came out to visit (the only time she was ever able to do so before MS took her ability to walk), we took her crabbing to show her what all the fuss was about. She innocently came up to four-year-old me while I was inching in a chicken neck and asked me what I was doing. Apparently I just said:

"Leave me alone. I'm crabbing."

I don't remember saying that of course, but everyone else in the family is hell bent on ensuring I never forget it.

Tom and I would both eventually leave the Eastern Shore to live in New York City. We explored Europe, went to Mexico and the Caribbean, and traveled through the United States for work together, but the first places we explored were the wilds of Ocean Pines, and the bayside of Assateague. We spent the summers barefoot. We spent those long afternoons in the sun, chasing, harassing, and catching those poor tiny creatures that make up our world. When I was seven or eight years old, I used to wade in the water on the beach and herd the minnows in front of me, and then run up and smack the water knocking them to the shore. My brother said I looked like a baby bear learning how to fish. I wouldn't do anything with the minnows, I just wanted to hold them in my hands before letting them go. The same was true for pretty much everything we caught. We just wanted to hold them for a second or two, and then we would release them. Except for the crabs, we ate those.

Recently I read a book by John Waldman called *Running Silver*, which is about all the issues migrating fish on the Eastern Seaboard are facing. At the end of the book, Waldman has ten suggestions on what could be done to improve things, including dams having an existential crisis. This should happen, dams are often pointless and we are addicted to them. Plus, I am for everything having an existential crisis. However, the easiest suggestion in his book was for kids to get their feet wet. Something about being in that salty water, exploring those marshes, and getting muddy formed a connection to the world outside our manufactured and organized human society, a connection I couldn't shake if I tried. Not that I have ever tried, as I have always felt healthier in nature. If Waldman is correct, this is most likely because of the time spent with my brother getting muddy in the madness of the wild. Maybe my father never had this. I am so thankful I did.

It's one of the great joys of my life that Tom and Mom now take Olive to the tidal pools and marshes of the bayside of Assateague. Olive doesn't like to crab, but she loves exploring the bayside just as much as Tom and I did. I know these will be some of Olive's best memories of her family, some of her cleanest memories. They certainly are for me.

After my father was cremated my brother and I scattered some of his ashes at Assateague...but on the ocean side, of course. We're not monsters.

NATURE WALK

new red bayberry stems reach
into brown needled sand path
through mosquito lakes and razor grass
and pony dung with pointed laugh
brothers stomp and crouch and scream

fiddler crabs and bull minnows scatter
wild ponies watch warily
while tail-swatting greenheads
late afternoon on Assateague
tanned arms, burnt cheeks and bellies full
the adventure of a bold exploration through bay marshes

these tiny worlds of tidal gems
were mad with the chaos of hunger and desire
the first fevered city they wandered together
these hunters, these explorers, these rare brothers
made mighty in nature's dominion over man
two legends of secret Assateague
two kings who held the marsh in their hands
the gulls still echo their gray and golden laughter.

Taking the First Step

While I had depression since I was at least fourteen years old, anxiety was new to me only manifesting shortly after my father's death. What I know now, which I didn't know when I started experiencing anxiety, is that I have something similar to Somatic System Disorder. This means that I focus too much on physical symptoms of undiagnosed maladies, to the point where the focus becomes debilitating. For instance, if I have a sudden headache, I focus on that headache until I think I am having a stroke. Or when I have chest, arm, and shoulder pain all at the same time I focus on it until I am convinced I am having a heart attack. The mind fuck here is that if you are having chest, shoulder, and arm pain you need to go to the emergency room, and don't let this book be the reason you don't go. Often it will turn out that you are having a heart attack and you don't know unless a doctor tells you one way or another. Take the book with you, you can read it while you wait to find out if you have anxiety.

As I said before I was not having a heart attack, but I did have esophageal ulcers, PVCs, a torn rotator cuff, a torn bicep, and significant arthritis in my shoulder. In order to treat those issues, I had a choice of going on a bunch of medications, or changing my diet and exercising more. Because of my experience with seeing my father overmedicated, I chose the second option.

The easiest thing to do is exercise, as our bodies want to move. The problem is that, when we stop moving because of injury or because we allow our overscheduled lives to take priority over our health, we feel bad. When we feel bad, we don't want to exercise, and we get locked into a negative feedback loop. Then some of us gain weight, and the more weight we gain, the more pressure is put on our joints, and the harder it becomes to exercise since everything hurts even more.

I tore a bicep and my rotator cuff doing the 100-pushup challenge back in 2011, but I never went to the doctor or did any physical therapy for it, because I am an idiot. Over the next few years the pain in my arm and shoulder would occasionally flare up, but in 2018 it became a daily discomfort. In December 2019 I finally went to the doctor and got an MRI on my shoulder, where I found out the torn bicep went along with a torn rotator cuff. My bicep muscle would occasionally wrap around my shoulder joint, causing the severe pain. According to my surgeon, I needed surgery on both my shoulder and my bicep, and also the root tear I had in my knee. But before surgery he wanted me to do physical therapy.

I've always had a bad history with physical therapy. Either my insurance ran out before I completed it, or my PT office was shut down after being raided by the U.S. Marshals for running a Medicare scam (ahh, Queens, NY). This time, however, I got great PT, at POA Physical Therapy. My physical therapist, Robert Dawson, took the time to really listen to me, and understand my physical abilities and limitations. He got me moving, got me limber, and gave me exercises that encouraged me to get back into the gym. Once I was back in the gym, I started with cardio and light weight resistance training. It was only 30 minutes a day, but it was a start. Every couple of days I added in a new exercise until I was spending about an hour a day mixing cardio and strength training.

After two months I had lost twenty pounds and graduated from physical therapy. I went back to the surgeon, who examined me and said I no longer needed surgery. By developing my bicep and shoulder muscles, my bicep no longer slid overtop the shoulder joint. I wouldn't say I'm totally healed, but the pain is gone and my range of motion is mostly back.

It took a while for me to notice, but once I started to exercise regularly, my anxiety became much less severe. It did not disappear completely, but the daily exercise seems to mitigate some of the triggers. The less shoulder and bicep pain I have, the less opportunity my anxiety has to flare up. I also think the daily endorphins and the meditative repetition of exercise broke the chain of anxious thoughts.

Exercise is not a panacea, however. It didn't solve my ulcer issue (which at first I didn't even know I had, I just knew I was having chest pains). It didn't get rid of the headaches either. Robert suggested I should see a dietician. That surprised me, because I think of myself as someone who is pretty smart, and feeding myself has never been a challenge, so why would I need help to know what to eat? I would read the occasional article about nutrition, so I felt I was pretty well informed on the subject. But Robert had done such a good job with my PT that I took his advice.

This turned out to be a much bigger step than I realized at the time. My dietician had me keep a food journal for five days and then she sat down with me and went through what I ate item by item. She determined what I had never considered before: my diet was not nearly varied enough. The reason I felt bad was because I was not getting enough vitamins and nutrients in my food, and because I was not eating enough throughout the day. I would have a big breakfast after exercising, but usually just drink coffee until late afternoon, and by that time my blood sugar was low and I was dehydrated. Also, by eating a limited diet and not getting the vitamins I needed, that was affecting my nervous system, causing strange pains and weird feelings. For instance, I was not getting enough magnesium, which was causing my eye to twitch, which would trigger my anxiety.

She gave me some very simple advice: if I made certain to eat lots of different colors on my plate, I would most likely start getting the vitamins and nutrients I needed. Obviously this did not mean different color potato chips or sugared cereals, but rather foods that were naturally different colors. This was a simple idea that was admittedly challenging at first to follow.

In the last year I have also added ginger for inflammation, artichoke hearts for vitamins A and C and antioxidants, non-microwaved broccoli for flavonoids, almonds for magnesium, blueberries for superfoodness, free-range eggs for the omega 3 fatty acids, yogurt, chick peas, black beans, salmon, spinach, red and orange bell peppers—the list goes on. I have constantly changed and revised my diet, by finding things I love to eat that are also healthy. I basically backed into a Mediterranean diet. It takes time to research and learn—as we are bombarded with advertisements for unhealthy food, dedication is needed to rewire our brains and balance our food choices. Eating healthy in America is a never-ending process of learning new things and changing our habits. The world does not make this easy, but I know if I am going to get a grip on my mental health, this is a step I cannot skip. Besides, I love learning, and I love eating, so this combines two of my passions.

I have no interest in writing a self-help book, but diet and exercise were the first steps to getting healthy. It wasn't until after I had taken these steps that I was able to really start the exploration that became this book, so I felt I should include it. I know my father exercised occasionally to lose weight, but he did that with weird crash diets like eating nothing but cabbage soup, or consuming nothing but diet soda all day long. He was also heavily medicated. I have nothing against medication, but I don't think medication alone could treat my anxiety.

One crazy effect of this diet and exercise thing is that I'm now completely off the blood pressure medication that I had been on since my early twenties, and my cholesterol medication went from 60 mg of statin to 5 mg. Since my current total cholesterol is now below 100, I most likely will soon be off the statin as well. I lost 80 pounds, and have kept off the weight for over a year. In my quest for mitigating anxiety, I ended up just getting really healthy.

Seeing a competent physical therapist was huge. Seeing a competent dietician was huge, too. It's almost like these people trained in their selected fields know more than I do about these matters. Go figure! Looking back, this journey seems like such an obvious step, yet one I believed I was smart enough not to need for the first forty-four years of my life. I was wrong.

Matt O'Hare–The Man

My dad was a large man. He was six feet tall, but he told everyone he was six feet and ¾ inches because he thought that sounded better. His weight bounced around between 230 to 350 pounds, but for most of my formative years it was probably around 290 pounds. For most of his life he rarely exercised, and when he did, he would swim laps or go walk on the beach at Assateague.

While he loved sports, he was never an athlete. He once told me a story about trying out for Pop Warner football when he was eight years old. He practiced with his dad and really wanted to be a running back, but the weight requirement maxed out at seventy-five pounds for skill positions, and needless to say my dad weighed more than that. He worked hard to lose weight, but he was still over the limit. Tryouts were after school, so my grandpa told him not to eat breakfast or lunch, and to not drink any water all day; if he was thirsty he was just supposed to take a sip, swish it around his mouth and spit it out[1]. My dad weighed in at seventy-six pounds.

He did not stay at that weight for the whole season. While his weight meant he was relegated to being a lineman, the weight restriction on any player in his league was 104 pounds, and he was most likely over that by a week after tryouts. During practice his coach kept yelling at him (when he was most likely dogging it in some drill that required running) that he was going to be booted out of the league if anyone brought out the scale again. They never did, probably because he was not a good enough athlete for anyone to care that he was too big.

To the best of my recollection, that and little league baseball was the entirety of my dad's athletic career. He coached baseball and football at Wawasee Prep in Indiana, his alma matter and the first school where he taught. Once he became athletic director he coached the occasional team at Worcester Country School, but only when he could not find coaches, which was pretty rare. He always preferred finding a coach

---

1 Do not do this. In fact, take this as a warning that nothing in this book constitutes medical advice.

over coaching himself, and he would never coach the varsity teams. This wasn't due to laziness on my dad's part; he honestly felt the kids deserved the attention only a dedicated coach could provide, something he could not provide while also serving as an AD.

Even though he once coached baseball, I'm not sure he ever played competitive baseball after little league. Later in life he claimed he tore his rotator cuff pitching for some baseball team, but both Tom and I are convinced that he actually tore it while driving and trying to hit us while we were goofing off in the backseat of the car. The latter is far more likely than the former.

So while he was not an athlete, he was large and very physical. He had presence, which he cultivated and accentuated with his voice. Now, my father's voice changed throughout the years, so depending on when you knew him, you would know a different voice. But one thing remained consistent; he annunciated every single word, which gave him the effect of speaking confidently; and in public he always spoke from the diaphragm to project his voice.

When he first came to Berlin, Maryland in 1975 he had a pretty thick midwestern accent. In those days, accents from different regions were a bit more pronounced then they are today, as was the colloquial lexicon. As he told it, the first time he walked onto the bus was for the soccer team's first away game. Apparently he said: "Settle down, settle down! Now I don't want any pop on this bus, do you hear me?" Kids on the eastern shore of Maryland in the 1970s had never heard the term "pop" for soda before, but they all knew the term "pot" for weed, and that single moment of confusion was the only time in the 1970s any teenager considered my dad cool. *Like he would be okay with pot off the bus, just not on the bus? Alright...*

Depending on who you asked, my dad was either a great or terrible storyteller. For the most part I loved my dad's stories, but my brother couldn't stand them. My father did not have a linear storytelling style, as he meandered and connected lots of tangents. My brother used to say, "Dad, beginning, middle, end. That's how you tell a story!" My father found that funny, but never changed his style.

After Dad passed I was listening to a lecture series called *The Celtic World* by one of my favorite lecturers, Dr. Jennifer Paxton who relates how the traditional Celtic storytellers never told a story with just a beginning, middle, and end; rather, they pulled in many different tangential characters and scenes. The more tangents the bard could connect, the better the story. I called my brother right away to tell him that. Dad would have loved to know he was just carrying on the ancient tradition of his people.

I don't think my dad could have ever written a book, as there was a physicality to how he told stories that just would not have translated to the page. To him, a story was not just words, it was hand gestures, knowing looks, long sighs, pregnant pauses, and overall body language. He also intentionally developed a lot of affectations in his speech. One of the longest running affectations was calling everyone "coach." In his defense, because he was an athletic director, many people in his world were coaches, but I remember one time he called my brother on the phone, and soon as Tom answered Dad said:

"Heeeeeey, Coach"

My brother snorted.

"Dad, this is Tom. Did you mean to call me? You know I'm the son that never even liked sports, right? I have to be the furthest person from a coach that you know."

To which my father replied, "How you doing?"

That was another one of my father's common phrases. "How you doing?" was said with a weird drawn out "dooooing" that made all my college roommates think he sounded like the comedian Louie Anderson. One of my college roommates, Bob, would always imitate him saying, "Haaaaaaay Bob, this is Matt O'Hare, Danny's Dad. How you dooooo-ing?" And even though Bob had met him a dozen times in South Bend, had been my roommate for years, and even lived with us in Ocean Pines one summer, he would still always say "Danny's Dad," which Bob found hilarious. Of course, once my father knew that Bob found it hilarious he did even more, because he never minded going for the cheap laugh.

Pretty much everyone who went to Worcester Country School (WCS)/Worcester Preparatory School (WPS) has either mimicked my father's voice or heard someone else do it. A commonly repeated catch phrase he used to say when someone was goofing off was, "No no no, if you want to do that you go to Stephen Decatur!" Stephen Decatur High School is the local public school in Berlin, where apparently you are allowed to do things like goof off.

He often trod the line between being sardonic and sarcastic. One of my brother's favorite moments is a good example of this. My brother and I were respectively in the same grades as Alan and Mark Decker, and both were very good friends of ours (Mark has been my best friend for years). When Mark was younger, he was a little heavier and pretty short. Alan, on the other hand was taller and thin. One day my brother and I were watching Star Wars; there was a scene in which R2D2 and C3PO were standing at a door and C3PO was knocking on it. My dad looked up and said, "Mark and Alan want to come in!" It was a stupid little comment, but my brother still laughs about it. That was a typical type of joke from my dad.

Mr. O'Hare, as he was known to his students, taught speech to every ninth grader at WCS/WPS for decades. He forced them to give speeches without reading them on paper, although he would allow three-by-five note cards, as long as they had only notes, not the whole speech. He was a desired keynote speaker, as he was so natural at a microphone. He was exceptional at engaging and reading the audience, and would test them with jokes or quips and was always able to adjust on the fly. He had a way of leaning on the podium, the way a farmer leans on the bed of a pickup truck, a stance that exudes familiarity. Since he passed away, I have been looking for videos of his speeches online and only found the last speech he made, given just a few months before his stroke, and where he read every single line off a legal pad. I was not at the event, but had I been there I would have known a little sooner that something was really wrong with him.

Matt O'Hare was a ham. He emceed the Maryland Athletic Directors conference almost every year, and even when he was not the emcee, he was always upstaging whoever was talking, especially if he felt the person was not up to snuff. And it's not as if he needed a podium to get in front of an audience. He would use any excuse to make an announcement at lunchtime in the school multipurpose room. He would referee the alumni basketball game, and then do a halftime skit with his friend and co-referee Malcolm Van Kirk that involved a bucket, a cup of water, and confetti. At one fundraiser an art auctioneer didn't show up, so my father stepped in and conducted the entire auction himself, and apparently the fundraiser broke all auction records that night (according to my dad, so...). The crazy part of that story is my dad wasn't connected to that fundraiser at all. He was on vacation drinking in a bar next to the fundraiser, overheard the auctioneer didn't show up, and just stepped in and took over.

Dad would perform in the yearly talent show, usually singing, something for which he had absolutely no talent. Dan Freed, the music director at WCS, once told me that being tone deaf was actually extraordinarily rare, but my father had the gift. Dad could not hit a correct note if his life depended on it, and even if he did hit the right note by mistake, he would not be on it long.

Naturally, every year my father would direct the WCS school musical. Apparently he directed a total of seventy high school musicals or plays in his career, but the yearly school musical was his big event. He always threw himself into this endeavor like a man possessed. For the month preceding the musical, my father lived at the school, working sixteen or seventeen hours a day. During that month, he was awful to be around; he was grumpy, irascible, or furious. We just avoided him as best we could, until we attended high school.

Once we were in high school and we were actually *in* the shows he directed we had the pleasure of being berated by him in front of all our friends at rehearsal, often for some ridiculous or nonsensical reason. Usually it was because he was mad at someone else, but he wanted to show everyone he was not playing favorites and was willing to take it out on his own kids. It might have been that he was concerned about the perception of nepotism, or maybe he was just nuts because it was that one month every year when he was being creative. Passion and creativity are bedfellows. Now that I have worked on well over one hundred film, theater, television, and commercial productions—and worked with many different directors—I understand how emotionally raw and fragile people can get while making art. I like to think that the reason I was a decent producer is because I was used to dealing with an egomaniacal director before I even entered high school.

One of his favorite *I'm-really-angry-but-I'm-pretending-I'm-not-by-making-a-bad-joke* phrases was, "You're making me Italian here!" He would scream it at people to convey his displeasure, often, during rehearsals of the musical. My mom's ancestry is Lithuanian and Italian, and while she, too, would yell at us at the drop of a hat, my dad was even more quick to yell and would do so more violently; yet he of Norwegian and Irish decent believed this trait was unique to Italians? There are layers to this that I am not too interested in exploring, but hearing it was always unsettling, and never funny.

It should be said: my dad was violent, though probably not any more violent than the average person of his generation. He hit us, but never with a belt, and for someone of my generation that always seems to be the litmus test. It's almost like you were not really hit if a parent didn't use a weapon. He used to grab me by the scruff of my neck and shove me towards things, like a wall or those swivel barstools we had in our kitchen. He also liked to pinch, he could pinch really hard; whenever he left a bruise, it was usually from pinching. His verbal violence was far worse on my brother. For about three years, my father yelled at Tom every single day, but then my mother would yell at me, and then my brother and his friends would beat me up, so I guess it all balanced out. Still, I've heard so many stories far worse, and remember, I'm a fairly smart cisgendered straight white male who was good at sports, so I am not looking for any sympathy.

My father called me an asshole more than he called me by my name. He called me asshole so much it was practically his nickname for me. But he also often told me how proud he was of me. My father could be affectionate and kind, and then just as easily be cruel and violent. The hardest part was I never knew which father I was going to get.

I only bring it up because my dad struggled with serious depression and anxiety, and I believe this was one of the ways it manifested. He tried to hide it from everyone. We saw it more than others, but he hid it from us with violence, as much as he hid it from others with humor. I can't blame him for that: he hid it from himself, too. Had my father read this chapter, he would have said, "Not bad...I guess, but I could have done without that last paragraph." And that would have been about as far as he could have gone with that thought. He would not have denied anything I wrote, but he would not have addressed it either. Because if he did, he would have to address his mental health issues, and he never seemed ready or able to do that.

Maybe it's because of that, despite being well-liked for being a character, that he was not necessarily close to many people. He had a few really good friends that will not be in the rest of this book, not because they are undeserving, but because I just did not know them well enough, or I had to cut the stories out for narrative purposes. One was his high school buddy Jim Betustak, who my dad spoke to at least once a month, pretty much his whole life. Another one was the dentist and fellow Notre Dame fan Jack Hughes who visited my dad in the nursing home all the time. The third was Megan Wallace who I believe was always my dad's favorite colleague at school. Also there was WCS/WPS Headmaster Barry Tull, who was standing next to me the second time my father got his Last Rites. There were others too, but not as many as you would think. He was a character, but he didn't have that many close friends. Even among his close friends, I'm not sure how well they knew him.

My father did not volunteer much, because he was almost always at school. One thing he did often, to feel like he was giving back, was speaking at events to raise money for Multiple Sclerosis research. Because my Aunt Peggy was afflicted with and bedridden by MS at a pretty young age, he always donated his services to any event in support of MS research. He also never accepted money for any speaking engagements, though if someone insisted on paying him he would ask that they donate the money to MS related charities. That was his pet cause, other than the school to which he devoted his entire life. He certainly could have made more money with his public speaking, but he never wanted to get paid for it; maybe he looked at it as his gift to the world, I honestly don't know.

Another incredibly important aspect to my father: he showed up. He went to games of former students, their plays, film premiers; he did anything he could to support them. He also always went to funerals. He got that from my grandfather, Ed O'Hare, who always said that someone from the O'Hare family needed to represent them at funerals so the family of the deceased knew we cared. After my grandfather passed away, my father took up his mantle. He zigzagged around the country attending funerals of distant relatives and friends he had not seen in forty years. His ability to show up, while occasionally annoying to his sons, was one of his better qualities.

My dad hated Catholic funerals where the priest insisted on doing the eulogy. Catholic priests get moved around all the time, and it is rare that a priest ever gets to know a parishioner who has died. My father sat through hundreds of funerals and memorials, but he disliked Catholic ones the most.

A couple of years before his stroke, I had a conversation about what he really believed:

"Dad, do you still believe in God?"

"Yeah, sure. I mean, I'm not crazy about it like Bonnie or anything. But I'm not sure Jesus believed in God as much as Bonnie does."[2]

"But do you still think of yourself as Catholic?"

"What else am I going to be? I don't really see myself as a Methodist. I have too much personality."

"Good one."

"I guess I could be Jewish, but I don't think I have the writers. I'm not funny enough."

"Correct. Not even close."

"I mean, I'm always going to be Catholic, I'm just not religious about it."

"Okay."

"You know I was going to be a priest, until I learned what nun meant," he said, ending the conversation about religion the way he ended all conversations about religion. With a joke about not having sex.

In the end, my dad was a big, weird, complicated man who, like all people, had good and bad qualities. He had lots of interests outside of sports, but I feel like sports is the best lens through which to examine him, so I'm going to focus on that for a bit. And the first sport he taught me is the first sport he loved:

Baseball.

---

2 My Aunt Bonnie is a born-again Christian.

THE BASEBALL FILM

Even if they are not a fan of the game, most Americans has a favorite baseball film. *The Sandlot, The Bad News Bears, 42, Moneyball, A League of Their Own, Major League, Pride of the Yankees, Damn Yankees, Sugar, Mr. 3000, Cobb, Bull Durham, Field of Dreams, Eight Men Out, Everybody Wants Some!!, The Rookie, For the Love of the Game, The Battered Bastards of Baseball*—this is far from an exhaustive list. There are countless great baseball films, including my personal favorite, *The Natural*. And just like in *The Natural*, they usually end with some great championship moment, some amazing crescendo of victory as the team finally comes together, to overcome all obstacles.

Not all baseball films do this, however. Some barely show any baseball at all. As is the case with my father's favorite baseball film, *Bang The Drum Slowly*, which is really just about how the different people on a baseball team dealt with someone who was dying. He saw it in the theater in 1973 and knew right away Robert De Niro was going to be a legendary actor, but this was told to me long after De Niro became a legendary actor, so take it with a necessary grain of salt.

If you aren't familiar with the film, it stars Michael Moriarty and De Niro, who respectively play a pitcher and catcher on a fictional New York major league baseball team. De Niro's character kind of stinks at baseball, but star pitcher Michael Moriarty finds out that De Niro is dying and thus he gets it written into his contract that De Niro has to be on the team; and if Moriarty is sold or traded, De Niro has to go with him—they are a package deal. There's an interesting side plot regarding how Moriarty's character also sells insurance, since baseball players in the 1970s didn't earn enough on baseball salaries alone to make a living. Vincent Gardenia plays the team's cranky manager and earned an Academy Award nomination, while Danny Aiello plays a wise-cracking troublemaker in what was his feature film debut.

If you haven't seen it, you should. I have not ruined anything for you by that description; in fact, all of what I have described happens before you see any real baseball action, not that there is much baseball action in the film. It's more about life and death, rather than baseball. Actually, it's more about labor than it is about baseball, but that is for another book.

I think it's telling that my father considered this his favorite baseball movie. Don't get me wrong, it's a great film and I can understand anyone liking it. While a little maudlin, *Bang the Drum Slowly* is pretty honest and rough around the edges. It's raw. All of its characters are flawed and no one really overcomes anything. It's just life. There is no joy in winning, no sorrow in losing. It's not what most people imagine when they sit down to watch a baseball movie. Yet, it was my father's favorite. We had a conversation about why when I was making my case for *The Natural* being the superior film. This is what he told me:

"Remember that time I let you stay up late to watch the end of Game 1 of the '88 World Series? The A's are up 4-3 on the Dodgers in the bottom of the 9th. Eckersley, best closer in baseball on the mound, hasn't given up a home run in months. There's a guy on first, two outs, and Tommy Lasorda calls on Kirk Gibson to pinch hit. Gibson has two bad legs and can barely walk to the batter's box. Vin Scully says, 'If Gibson hits it on the ground it's over, he can't even run to first.' Gibson fouls off a couple of pitches, lets a couple of close ones go by, the count goes full. Eckersley throws an outside fastball and Gibson takes an awkward step and muscles it, all arms, over the right field fence. Stadium goes nuts. Gibson is pumping his fist faster than his legs, 'cause he can barely even get around the bases. You and I were so excited that we were screaming at the TV, woke your mom up – she thought the house was on fire. We would have woken your brother up, too, if it were possible. We were jumping up and down, hugging and high fiving and we weren't even fans of the Dodgers. Now let me ask you, how are you going to make a film with a moment better than that? You can't. And if you did, no one would believe it anyway."

So that was my dad's answer to why his favorite baseball film was *Bang the Drum Slowly*. Maybe it isn't the most straightforward answer to the question, but that was my dad's way. When I was younger, I used to think you could solve the problem of what was the best *this* or what was the best *that* as if it was some sort of math equation. I used to keep lists of my favorite films, favorite songs, favorite books, etc. I would break them down further into genres, to really try to get at what was the best. I think part of this was that my competitive spirit was turned on a little too high, but it might also have been that I didn't understand that different perspectives lead to different tastes. I mean, sure, that's obvious *now*, but back then I was a cisgendered straight white guy who was good at sports, so I was pretty certain the world was either created by or for me, so it took me a little while to see past that.

When I finally did, I figured out that one shortcut to get to know people is getting to know what they love. I remember reading one of Gene Siskel's obituaries, and it mentioned how he used to always say to people, "Tell me the truest thing you know." That which we love, that which resonates in our hearts and reflects our spirit, those are the truest things we know. Sometimes it's just a movie about a bunch of grown men running around in their pajamas playing a game. Sometimes it's a father and son high fiving and hugging and screaming at a TV three thousand miles from where a guy with two bad legs just hit a ball with a bat. This got me thinking about the experience of films versus the experience of sports. Films are experienced by the viewer while quietly sitting down in a theater, or on a couch. Sports are often experienced standing up, screaming, cheering, or at least clapping. My dad loved *Bang the Drum Slowly* because it spoke to him about human nature and friendship, and because it had great performances. Films like *The Natural* that end with a big, exciting crescendo might be mimicking a story that takes place on a field, but lacked the human connection of the shared energy at a sporting event.

There's a passage in Cicero's *Tusculan Disputations* attributed to Pythagoras. When asked what it meant to be a philosopher, Pythagoras referred to sport—I think specifically the Olympic games—to explain what it means to be a philosopher.

He said:

That the life of man seemed to resemble those games which were celebrated with the greatest possible variety of sports in Greece. At those games three types of people could be found. The first, whose object was glory through bodily exercises and training, competed at the highest level. The second were those who exist wherever a crowd is gathered, who were drawn to the games to buy and sell wares in order to make profit. Lastly there was one class of persons, and they were by far the best, whose aim was neither applause nor profit, but who came merely as spectators through curiosity, to observe what was done, and to see in what manner things were carried on there. And thus, we come from another life and nature unto this one, just as men come out of some other city, to some much frequented mart; some being slaves to glory, others to money; and there are some few who, taking no account of anything else, earnestly look into the nature of things; and these men call themselves students of wisdom, that is, philosophers: and as there it is the most reputable occupation of all to be a looker-on without making any acquisition, so in life, the contemplating things, and acquainting one's self with them, greatly exceeds every other pursuit of life.

For me, this passage connected the sports fan to the philosopher. The curiosity inherent in attending an event—whether it be an athletic contest, concert, ballet, theater, or any shared moment of existence between the actors/competitors and spectators—creates a bond. What Pythagoras doesn't connect is the emotional component of that shared curiosity. It is more than just wanting to see what will happen. Philosophers are not robots collecting data, in the same way sports fan are not dispassionate about the outcome of games. Philosophers do not want to understand merely for the sake of understanding something, they want to understand because it adds to the richness of their existence. And the same is true for the spectator.

What's more, the spectator is not alone: it's a shared experience. Just as actors feed off an audience, players feed off the crowd. Watching a live sporting event, even on tv, has a different feeling than watching a sporting event that happened in the past. Whether we admit it or not, I think most of us have a subconscious sense that we are a part of that event, we are living together with the event itself, we are connected to it. In a stadium that is clear, as the crowd undoubtedly has an effect on the players as the players affect the crowd. But I believe that feeling, while mitigated some, still exists while watching on TV, especially if you are watching with someone else. I know it makes no scientific or logical sense, but investing our energy into a live event, we become a part of that event as it becomes part of us. We allow ourselves to be seduced into superstition and magic. Even in some convoluted and non-substantiated way, we can wonder if Kirk Gibson would actually have hit that home run if my father and I were not somehow pushing out into the universe that he could? If we are watching a sporting event that already happened, there's no way we could believe that. Watching a film, there is no way we could recreate that feeling of connectivity to a live sporting event. So, (and I'm just guessing here) for my father, the end of *The Natural*, while beautiful, paled in comparison to the Kirk Gibson moment. He had real life crescendos that were better.

Bang the Drum Slowly didn't try and recreate that big, exciting moment. It was just a really great film about dealing with death which also happened to be about baseball.

I still don't think I have figured out the truest thing I know, but weirdly, I'll probably never forget Kirk Gibson's home run, at least in part because of a film made fifteen years before he hit it.

LITTLE LEAGUE

Until I became a drunk, I was pretty good at sports. As a chubby kid, I couldn't run very fast, but I was pretty tough because I had an older brother with older brother friends who used to beat on me every day. Back in the 1980s, I think that was the closest to brotherly affection an adolescent boy could get, so I guess I will conclude it was done out of a perverse sort of love. However, one of my problems, like many a fat kid, was that I was really ticklish. So much so that when they used to hit me, it would sometimes make me laugh. Once the little kid they punched started laughing they would get embarrassed and angry and then hit me really hard, doing their best to get me to eventually cry. All said, this made me pretty tough.

So I was chubby and slow, but I was tough and not afraid of much. I was the ball boy for soccer and lacrosse, and played pickup basketball and football, but the first organized sport I played was baseball. I excelled at baseball. I mean, it was little league in Berlin, Maryland, but I could really mash it. I played first base, batted cleanup, hit well above .600, and literally never struck out all season long. The only time I was walked, it was intentional. I was up there to swing the bat.

My coach was named Ned Mumford, and even years after I stopped playing, he seemed so regretful that I gave up on baseball. When I would bump into him leaving The Style Guide or Farlow's Pharmacy, he would ask if I was still playing baseball, and when I said I wasn't he would just shake his head and say, "You were just a natural ballplayer." But he was wrong. I could hit, sure, but it wasn't because I was a natural. It was because of my dad.

My father had two sons. I was the younger brother, and I loved sports. My older brother Tom was far more interested in comic books and Dungeons & Dragons. He would read comic books at baseball games while I would learn the reason why lefty batters had a natural platoon advantage. He would read comic books at football games while I would learn the difference between a nickel defense and a dime defense. He would read comic books at hockey games until a fight broke out, then he would pay attention—he liked those. Tom played right field in Little League, and it wasn't because he had a good arm, it was because he could not care less about sports. The regular world bored Tom, and the world of sports was the most regular part of the regular world to him. In this way we could not be more different. Don't get me wrong, I love Dungeons & Dragons, and though I never cared much about the X-Men, I had at least a passing knowledge of The Fantastic Four, Thor, and Spider-Man. But I loved all things sports; I was constantly making a competition out of anything and everything, and I could not get enough of watching or playing sports.

My dad must have recognized this early on, and was only too happy to nurture my competitive nature. After watching the first practice for our Little League team and realizing that we each only saw about five total pitches all practice, my dad went to a toy store and bought fifty soft plastic and foam balls that were roughly the size of baseballs, and a floppy rubber mat that was the size of home plate. He took me out to the WCS lacrosse field, handed me a bat, filled a bucket with the balls, and started lobbing them at me. He made a deal with Tom that if Tom shagged the fly balls he would buy him Fritos, and Tom begrudgingly agreed.

Dad threw two hundred balls at me before every game and after every practice. The only rule was that I was not allowed to watch them go by. Since there was no catcher or backstop, it took too long to get the balls behind me, so I had to at least try to make contact. Not that he needed to make that rule, I wanted to swing. He taught me to go with the pitch, hit it where they were not, and worry more about good contact than trying to hit it hard. He'd pitch me inside and try and jam me up. He'd pitch me so far off the plate I would have to step over to get a piece. Eventually it clicked and I got it. I could hit anything. The pitcher could be throwing junk, it didn't matter, I could hit it on a bounce. Pitch me outside, it didn't matter, I would get there and get a piece. My dad's mantra was, "Wait for your pitch, until then just get enough to stay alive. Just keep making contact. Just stay alive."

By the third game I lined every hit into the gaps; by the end of the year I was clearing the wall. I became the toughest out in the Berlin Little League, possibly ever. My team cruised that year, but before every single game and after every single practice, Tom got his Fritos and I got my two hundred swings.

After the regular season ended, I was named the starting first baseman on the All-Star Team for Berlin. Our first All Star Game was scheduled to be played in the brand spanking new Northside Park in

Ocean City. It was the first game ever played there, as it was the park's grand opening weekend. Our old ball fields in Berlin had not changed at all since the 1950s, but Northside Park was shiny and new. They had four fields that were perfectly designed to back up to a "press box" with announcers and everything. To me it was like I'd hit the big time. In the first inning of the first game, we were fielding and I was manning first base. The OC All Stars had kids on first and second, no outs. The batter smacked the ball right over my head, and the runners, assuming the ball was well on its way to right field, took off. I leapt, snow-coned the ball, and came down with it in my mitt. The runner at first saw it all go down, but he slipped and fell. I tagged him out. The runner at second was now rounding third totally confused by his third base coach screaming at him to go back. Our shortstop was already heading towards the dug-out—he could never count. Our second baseman was standing over the runner from first, pointing at and teasing the kid that slipped. No one was anywhere near second base. Every parent and coach were scream-ing different instructions at different children who collectively had no idea what was happening, so I made a beeline for second base. Fat kid slugger versus Little League leadoff hitter. I beat him by a step. Triple play, unassisted.

As we headed back to the dugout, we heard the scratch of the PA system turning on. The announcer spoke in an almost incredulous tone:

"Folks, I believe we have the first official triple play of Northside Park."

Long pause

"Unassisted."

I looked up at the stands at my dad and brother. Tom was reading his comic book, had no idea what was going on, and did not care. What was so strange was my father wasn't looking at me. He was looking at the other fields. I shrugged and went to get my batting helmet which only sort of fit my enormous head. What I didn't know until later is that my father wanted to see everyone's faces when they heard that there was an unassisted triple play in the first inning of the first game at Northside Park. He knew how rare an unassisted triple play was, whereas I had no idea. I mean, it was the first time I had done it, but it was only my second year of playing baseball. I figured it couldn't have been that rare, right?

Later he told me everyone stopped what they were doing to look at our field. Fans from other stands came over to ask how it happened. Everyone in the stands was pointing at me. I had no idea. I was look-ing for some Big-League Chew and cheering on our leadoff hitter. That was my last organized baseball game, which we lost to the Ocean City All Stars, and after that I only played lacrosse in the spring. But it was quite a way to go out. In Major League Baseball there have only ever been fifteen unassisted triple plays. Thirteen of them have come from middle infielders. Only two have ever come from first basemen, with the last one coming in 1927. Things more common in baseball than an unassisted triple play from a first baseman: everything.

My dad loved telling this story. My father had never seen an unassisted triple play in person before—or after—and the fact his son had done it was pretty special to him. He used to say:

"I don't know how many unassisted triple plays there have been in Major League Baseball, but I know you can count them on two hands. And an unassisted triple play from a first baseman? I don't know if it's ever happened in the majors. But then again, Berlin Little League is not exactly Major League Baseball."

So yes, I was good at sports. But I was the best at Little League baseball, and I now realize, that was all because of my dad. Unassisted triple plays are pure luck, they require multiple flukes to happen at the same time. You don't have to be the best infielder to field an unassisted triple play, you just have to be in the right place at the right time. If not for all that extra practice, maybe I wouldn't have made The All Star Game. Then I wouldn't have made the unassisted triple play. And dad wouldn't have had that story.

I guess in the end, he earned that one.

Kevin McNulty, Lee Riley, Eddie Murray, and Our Baltimore Connection

Apparently there are places in the country where it is frowned upon to take children into bars. Wherever that is, it's certainly not Ocean City, Maryland. Growing up, my parents would take us to BJ's On the Water at least once a week to get seafood skins and steak sandwiches. I think my dad always liked going there because he could watch five different TVs and eat seventeen bowls of free popcorn. So I guess in a way, BJ's was my first "local" where I could be considered a regular. After BJ's, the bar I was in most as a kid was Charles Village Pub in Baltimore.

While Ocean City has the word "city" right there in its name, it only had about 5,000 permanent residents back then, so it was not much of an urban center. When we said "the city" what we meant was Baltimore, but because it was two-and-a-half hours away, we really only went there for the Baltimore Aquarium, the Inner Harbor shopping, and sporting events. Our family did not have much money when I was very young, so we weren't going on trips to Baltimore until the early 80s. And while I never went to a Colts game, we did go to their training camp a couple of times, and I still unconsciously flip off Mayflower trucks. Still, most of the time I was conscious of the world around me there was not football or any other major professional sport in Maryland; there was just Memorial Stadium and the Baltimore Orioles.

As I will expand upon later, my father was a New York Yankees fan, but he never once pushed that team on me. I didn't even know he was a Yankees fan until I was in my twenties. When we were growing up dad bought me Orioles gear and even managed on multiple occasions to get me my favorite player's autograph: Eddie Murray.

Now before any of you assholes criticize Eddie Murray[3], I want you to think about his facial hair alone. You will never be as cool as Eddie Murray's facial hair. No one will ever be as cool as Eddie Murray's facial hair, so shut up.

There are a few truly great hitters to wear a Baltimore Orioles

3 I'm looking at you Kyle.

uniform. Some of them were O's for a year at the end of their career, or a weird blip that only die-hard fans remember. Like Reggie Jackson, who led the league in slugging percentage as a thirty-year-old in 1976 playing right field. His only Baltimore season may have been statistically his best outside of an Oakland uniform. Long after helping revitalize baseball in the late 1990s, Sammy Sosa had a forgettable stint with the 2005 O's that none of us care to talk about. Vladimir Guerrero, one of the greatest free swingers to ever play the game, ended his career with the O's in 2011. While he went 0-4 in his last game, it was "Game 162," which might have been the spark that changed both how the MLB wildcard system works and the fortunes of Orioles baseball.

None of these guys are Baltimore legends. If you want to talk Baltimore legends, you have to start with Cal Ripken Jr, arguably the best shortstop of all time. He played his entire career in Baltimore, and changed the shortstop position forever. Combining some of the best defense from the position with a big bat, Cal—the wholesome hometown hero—has to be mentioned when speaking of great Orioles. In fact, it is actually against state law to talk about baseball in Maryland without first mentioning its patron saint, Cal Ripken Jr. More kids are named Cal or Calvin in Maryland than anywhere else in the world—probably.

Also, there are a disproportionate number of children and dogs in Maryland named "Brooks," after legendary third baseman Brooks Robinson. Widely considered the best defensive third baseman of all time, his bat was good enough to get him in the Hall of Fame, even if he was known for his glove first.

Then you have the other Robinson. Frank Robinson spent only six years playing for the Orioles, but his 1966 season at the plate might be one of the top five best of all time[4]. In six years, he helped get the O's to the World Series four times and win it twice. Without doubt a legend, but like Brooks he played his whole career before my time.

Eddie Murray, on the other hand, was named Rookie of the Year in 1977 when I was almost two years old. While I obviously don't remember that season, by the time I was conscious of baseball he was manning first base; he and Cal were the best players on the 1983 team, the first team in any sport I really remember. While that Orioles team went on to win the World Series and Cal won the American League (AL) MVP, Eddie was cleanup hitter, came in 2nd in the AL MVP vote, and was just the coolest man on the planet to seven-year-old me.

---

4 He hit 49 Home Runs, had 122 RBIs, went .316/.410/.637, and won the triple crown which has only happened twelve times in history. He won the MVP and the World Series MVP.

One of the greatest switch hitters of all time, "Steady Eddie" eventually became only the third player in MLB history to hit 500 home runs and have 3,000 hits. Hank Aaron, Willie Mays, Eddie Murray. On their own, either of those marks guaranteed a ticket into the Hall of Fame, but he did both for good measure. He is the career RBI leader for switch hitters and played the most games ever at first base. But what he was really known for was being a clutch hitter. Teammate and longtime baseball announcer Ken Singleton once said Murray was, the best clutch hitter he had ever seen. Mike Boddicker, (the last Oriole pitcher to win 20 games) added: "If my life depended on a run being driven in, Eddie Murray would be the only guy I would want up at the plate."

Murray was also known as a student of the game back before people were students of the game. Today, of course, baseball is a game for nerds, but back in the day baseball players were not exactly known as thinkers. Murray did not have analytics or stat departments helping him be a better hitter, or understand the pitcher's tendencies—he did that all himself. When Cal Ripken Jr. broke Lou Gehrig's record for consecutive games played, which was widely considered the most unbreakable record in sports—he gave a post-game speech and thanked four people: his dad, his mom, his wife, and Eddie Murray. Ripken credited Eddie Murray for showing him "how to play the game day in and day out." But in those days, I didn't know any of that. I was just a kid that wanted to play first base, and the only first baseman I had ever known was Eddie Murray. Let's just say, I got spoiled real quick.

And so would you if you had grown up in the 1980s and had been sitting in Memorial Stadium as this man among men with a throwback moustache strode up to whatever side of the plate the pitcher feared most, while every single man, woman, and child in attendance chanted in unison, "Edd-ie! Edd-ie! Edd-ie! Edd-ie!" You, too, would recognize you were witnessing a living legend.

Now the reason some people don't like Eddie Murray is because a right-wing nutjob sportswriter named Dick Young wrote a column about Eddie's family that contained flat-out lies, and made them look terrible. Eddie decided not to talk to the media after that. Some in the media had thin skin and took it personally. But again, I was just a kid. I didn't know any of this. To me, Eddie was the best. My father knew that I loved Eddie, and for my birthday he managed to get me an autographed baseball.

My father was able to get Eddie's autograph because one half of our Baltimore connection was Lee Riley. Because my parents had moved from the Indiana to Ocean Pines, and Baltimore was two-and-a-half hours away from Ocean Pines, they didn't know many people that lived in Baltimore. Lee Riley and Kevin McNulty, who were lacrosse coaches and teachers at Worcester Country School that both came from Baltimore and still had family living there were about as close as we got. In the case of Kevin, I think one-fifth of the Irish Catholic population of Baltimore were somehow his cousins. I have actually met more of his cousins than my own. I will get back to Kevin.

Lee Riley's parents didn't just live in Baltimore; they literally lived right next door to *Eddie Murray*. When you hear stuff like that as a kid, it does weird things to your brain. I only knew a few people that lived in Baltimore: these were Clan McNulty, the Riley's, and the Orioles. So even to this day, whenever I meet someone from Baltimore, for a second I wonder what Oriole lives next door to them.

Anyway, one summer day just before the school year started, my father and I were walking through WCS and we bumped into Lee in the hall outside his English classroom. I asked if his parents had seen Eddie Murray lately because I was always thinking about baseball.

"Actually, you'll love this," Lee replied. "My mom just told me that Eddie had a terrible game the other day, went 0 for 5 with two strikeouts, so she baked him an apple pie and brought it over to him. She always carves '33' into the crust, that's Eddies number. He likes that."

First of all, I knew what Eddie's number was, I had a giant poster of him on my wall, but let's move on. I was talking to someone who not only knew, but was related to someone that baked a pie for *Eddie Murray*. Plus, I liked apple pie, and obviously Eddie liked apple pie, another thing we had in common. I was pretty young and did not fully make the connection as to why you would get a pie for doing badly, but whatever—I knew someone who knew someone who baked a pie for the best baseball player to ever live[5].

Years later, I found out just how close the Rileys and Eddie had become. When Eddie was inducted into the Hall of Fame, he invited them to attend the ceremony. When they couldn't find a hotel room, Eddie's family let the Rileys stay with them in their lodgings. Lee says it was one of the highlights of their lives.

Dad used to take us to Baltimore by himself a couple of times each summer. My mom rarely made the trip with us, as the summer was her busy season selling real estate at the beach, so it was usually just Dad and his two boys. Our typical trip to Baltimore consisted of waking at dawn, and driving to the Baltimore Aquarium, where we would walk

5 WRITE YOUR OWN BOOK, KYLE!

around looking at fish for two hours. Then we walked over to the Inner Harbor to buy comic books and sandwiches, afterwards driving to park somewhere between Charles Village Pub and Memorial Stadium. Next we'd head over to Charles Village Pub for clam strips and mozzarella sticks before walking to the O's game. At the pub we would often meet up with Kevin and/or Lee. When my dad had one of them for an audience, he would perform. He always had a joke or a funny story prepared for them. He also would try and get people in the pub to start singing the Notre Dame fight song. This eventually became such a thing with him that when the bartender saw him coming he'd tell my dad he'd be eighty-sixed if he tried to get people to sing the song more than once.

If Kevin or Lee did not end up meeting us there my father would usually strike up a conversation with other patrons. He really enjoyed talking to strangers, and since it was likely that the people in the pub were there to watch the game, either on person or on TV, they would always start by talking about baseball until my dad would get them talking about something else.

I know I've already said it, but my dad had the gift of gab, being a master at conversation. His preferred technique was getting people to talk about themselves. He often started by asking where they were from and where they went to school, and in Baltimore, that means "What high school did you go to?" Baltimore is a big high school town, and unlike most other cities, high schools are really culturally identifying for its residents. Since my dad knew all the athletic directors from all over the state, he always knew a little something about whichever school the person attended, and that would get them talking.

You might think my dad would only be able to do this trick in Baltimore, since Baltimore had just three dozen or so high schools. At least that is what I thought until I went to college with kids from all over the country. He could do it with kids from California to Texas to Minnesota. I remember he met an upperclassman from down the hall that I barely knew and asked him where he went to school. The kid said St. Xavier in Cincinnati, and dad replied, "Oh yeah, Xavier? Your big rival is Archbishop Moeller, right?" The guy kind of nodded like, *How do you know that?* but then kept talking. People usually just keep talking if you show them you are paying attention, and my dad loved getting people to talk.

Even when we walked over to the stadium, my dad would talk to people along the way. While my memory of these early days is a little spotty, I clearly remember walking down the street in the middle of the day talking to strangers about some high school football game that happened a decade before. I am not sure why we were in the middle of the street, but there were a bunch of us there and everyone was talking about some football game that they all remembered that somehow my dad had brought up.

Here's a neat fact about Memorial Stadium: it was smack-dab in the middle of a regular old neighborhood in Baltimore. When walking those streets, it was house, house, house, house, stadium, house, house, house...it was like going to the neighborhood playground, but a really *big* playground. Don't get me wrong, I love Camden Yards, and think it is the best stadium on the planet. But Camden Yards is a cathedral, while Memorial Stadium was your neighborhood church.

Memorial Stadium was a unique place that was so very Maryland. Not only was it in a neighborhood, but in those days it was the only place in the MLB where you could get a crab cake at a concession stand. Earl Weaver used to grow tomatoes in a patch of dirt down the foul line. I swear I remember that you were allowed to bring in crab nets to scoop up foul balls. Imagine walking into a baseball stadium with a five-foot wooden pole. Those were the days.

Once we arrived at the stadium, Dad allowed us to choose one luxury food item. Tom always picked the crab cake, I always went for the sundae that was served in a batting helmet. Tom would get peanuts in the shell and I would get Cracker Jacks, and we probably ate hot dogs too because, hey, we were only human. Plus there was no way my dad was going to get himself a hot dog and not get us one.

On the way home, my brother usually liked to sit in the back and read the remainder of his comics if he had any light, and I would sit in the front so Dad and I could listen to the last few innings on the radio. We almost always left before the end of the game so we could "beat the traffic." Other than sports and theater, my father's favorite thing to do in life was to beat the traffic. I realize now that my father had a few triggers that caused anxiety, which we understood even if we did not have the vocabulary for it in those days. Traffic was one of them. As the traffic increased, so did his rage, it made him absolutely nuts. He loved cities but hated driving in them, and the closer we came to a city the more tense things were. So beating the traffic became a really important thing in his life.

Once we got over the Chesapeake Bay Bridge and were finally on the good side of the bay, we knew we'd beaten the traffic. My father could finally relax, as the passing headlights would become fewer and fewer, and even the air became cooler. This is the time when I learned to love to listen to baseball on the radio. In fact, I still prefer to listen to baseball on the radio as opposed to watching it on TV. That might be because in those days, the Orioles radio baseball announcers were Jon Miller and Joe Angel, two of the greatest voices in baseball radio history. I was spoiled with Eddie and I was spoiled with Jon and Joe. Listening to them call the last inning or two as we crossed the bridge and sped home was a pretty great way to end our adventure to Baltimore. By the time we hit Cambridge, the game would be over, so my father would switch to listening to showtunes or old-time radio plays, and most likely my brother and I would be asleep.

Now that I have a child, I realize how well-designed these trips were. Let's be honest, my dad just wanted to go see a baseball game. My brother couldn't care less about baseball but was enthused about the aquarium, so he would eagerly get out of bed before dawn. Going to the Inner Harbor and letting Tom stock up on comic books before the game ensured he would not complain about being bored while my dad and I kept score and talked about the game. We went to four distinct locations and yet he only had to move the car once, a total dad victory there. And we got to beat the traffic.

My dad loved taking me to different stadiums, over the years we went to Veterans Stadium, Three Rivers Stadium, Busch Stadium, Comiskey Park, Wrigley Field, Shea Stadium, Yankees Stadium, Royals Stadium (now known as Kauffman Stadium), Safeco Field, and Camden Yards, but Memorial Stadium always felt like our home stadium, as that's where I saw the most games with my father.

It was in Memorial Stadium that my dad taught me to keep score, which is such a baseball thing. No other sport has something like fans keeping score like baseball does. For those that don't know, baseball stadiums sell scorecards and pencils and you can fill in the scorecard as the game unfolds. It is sort of a complicated way to teach kids about stats, and while it can be fun, it is totally unnecessary for enjoying the game. Still, Dad was adamant that I learn how to do it and always paid the extra dollar to get the scorecard.

He also used to point out to me how fielders would reposition themselves based on who was up to bat, long before anyone employed the defensive shifts that are so common today. Because baseball moves slower than other sports, I began to understand the ideas behind why things were the way they were. I know that sounds like a big concept to come from a silly game, but causality is real in sports. Everything happens because of other things happening. Newtonian physics is on full display in sports. Even though baseball is unique and not easily translatable to other team sports, I started to understand the theory behind all sports by watching games at Memorial Stadium. I learned that strategy and intelligence mattered, and there was more than just speed, hand-eye coordination, and strength to being great.

Dad would often tell a story about a particular day game at the stadium when I was keeping score. It was one of those rare games we actually stayed all the way until the end. If you stayed to the end of an event, you had to let everyone else clear out before you leave, which is another way to beat the traffic. We were sitting at our seats as the stadium emptied and he was showing me how to total all of the players' stats on the scorecard. On this day, Eddie Murray had gone something like 3-5 with a double and a homerun and five RBIs. Dad said to me, "That's a pretty good day!"

Apparently I looked at him with my eyes wide and said, "I wonder how many pies he's gonna get for that!"

Kevin and Lee were the only people I knew from Baltimore when I was a kid. Both coached lacrosse at Worcester Country School, and both returned to Baltimore after their time at WCS. Lee left for Baltimore after leading the WCS Mallards varsity men's lacrosse team to their first undefeated season. Kevin took over coaching the varsity team the following year, and only coached for that one year before also leaving for Baltimore. Kevin had a one-loss season, which I'm sure Lee has never let him forget.

Even though they moved off the Eastern Shore, my father was always good about keeping in touch with them, especially after my parents divorced. After I left Maryland and football returned to Baltimore in the form of the Ravens, Lee and Kevin would host a huge tailgate party for every Ravens home game. Dad would be at most of the tailgates, even though he rarely had tickets to the games. He just wanted to go to the party to see his friends, and then, I guess, beat the traffic.

A few words about Kevin, one of two people to whom this book is dedicated:

I have known some funny people in my life. Adam Wade, Alex Howarth, and Colin Quinn would all be in the top five, but I am going to go on record[6] and say that Kevin McNulty is the funniest of all of them. He is just relentless in his ability to look at things from an absurd angle, and he never misses an opportunity for a joke. He is the archetypical fool from those Shakespeare plays, and Dad loved being around him.

Kevin has a big personality. My dad had a big personality too, but there are a few big differences between the two. The first is that while my dad told jokes, Kevin is funny. Huge difference. The second is that

6 For all seven people reading this book.

Kevin has impeccable timing. My dad had comically bad timing, which could be funny, but in a "laugh at" not "laugh with" kind of way. The third difference is that Kevin has a golden heart. Now, that is not to say my dad was a monster, but not many people in this planet have a golden heart. Sure, you can look at Kevin on paper and see he checks all the boxes of being a good person. I'm a good person too. It's not hard to be a good person, but that is not what I am talking about.

Kevin owns a condo in Ocean City, about a three-hour drive from his home. After my father's stroke, every time Kevin would go to his condo, he would drive over an hour out of his way to visit my father at his nursing home in Snow Hill. He would bring Dad fried chicken and diet soda, a new hat, a new t-shirt or jacket—just something, every single time. He would take a picture with Dad and send it to us. He always let us know he was there for him, and he was there for him until the very end.

There are plenty of people that will line up to tell me how much they loved my dad, but even though most of them were fifteen to thirty minutes away from his nursing home, they never visited, some of them not even once. A few visited him once or twice, but that was all they could manage. Some said they couldn't bear to see him that way. Others said they would try and go, they were just so busy. I am not trying to disparage the people that didn't go, I understand completely, and I certainly can relate to them—I didn't want to go either. It was hard for me, but I do not have a golden heart like Kevin.

I don't aspire to be like Kevin. I only went to see my dad in the nursing home out of self-imposed duty. I told myself it was my job as a son. I never looked at it as a choice of something I could or could not do. I *dreaded* going to see my father. I don't know how many times I called my brother or my mom after leaving the nursing home to say I couldn't do it anymore, but it was often. I know Kevin didn't like seeing my dad that way either, but he never once said, "I just can't do it anymore." After every visit, he would call me and say if it was a good day or a bad day, or relay some of the crazy stuff Dad said. Then he would say, "I'll be back down in two weeks and I'll bring him an orange soda then. He said he wants to drink orange soda now."

My dad had two brothers, but he never spoke to Mike and he barely ever spoke to Harry. Kevin was the little brother my dad wanted. It sounds awful to say, but we were much closer to Kevin than anyone in my father's family. Every year my family has a reunion in the Midwest, but we never went. Instead, we went with Kevin to his family reunion in Ireland.

Kevin is a funny guy, and he was a pretty good lacrosse coach[7]. He was a great friend to my father, and has been a great friend to me and my brother. Lee was one of the speakers at my father's funeral, and I know my dad would have been proud of his speech. I asked Kevin to speak as well, but he said couldn't do it. He was there, of course—he was always there—but it was too hard for him. In their own ways, Lee and Kevin have come to represent Baltimore for me. Their unquestionable love for the Orioles, even through all the rough years, makes rooting for the O's that much easier. And somehow, just being who they are makes Baltimore that much better of a town.

---

7 Though, I guess, not as good as Lee.

Taking the Next Step

If you thought exercise and completely overhauling your diet is tough, have I got a challenge for you: sit still for twenty minutes.

Anyone who thinks meditating is not doing anything has never meditated. Anyone that thinks meditating is easy has not meditated. I had no idea how to meditate, but I viewed it with amusement and occasional derision. After reading about anxiety, and finding out meditation is one way to treat anxiety, I became curious and read some articles about it online. Then I happened to mention to my friend and former upstairs neighbor Carl Hansen that I wanted to start meditating. It was in February of 2020, and Carl did a five-minute guided meditation for me over the phone. Over the next week, we did three more phone sessions and Carl sent me some resources that really encouraged me.

The harsh truth of your existence is that everything in your life is demanding your attention all of the time, and you have most likely trained your body and mind to believe that if you are not always doing *something* then you are acting incorrectly. For instance, you are reading a book right now. That's awesome, and I thank you. But if you were not reading a book, would you be sitting still, not looking at a TV or your phone? Just sitting still, perhaps in the darkness, with your own thoughts? Of course you wouldn't, only a crazy person would do that, right?

Well, at this point I am a well-established crazy person, so sign me up. Carl sent me a book by Shunryu Suzuki called *Zen Mind, Beginner's Mind: Informal Talks on Zen Meditation and Practice*. There are so many great quotes from this book that I am just going to recommend that you read the whole thing, but if you aren't going to read it, I'll tell you the simplest idea from it is probably the one I most needed: just meditate. There is no wrong way, just sit and do it. Can't sit because of bad knees or back? Then lie down and meditate.

Once when I was really anxious and felt like I couldn't meditate, I had a glass of whiskey first and then meditated. I didn't make a habit out of this, but on that day, it got me there. Like most things in life, you just need to find a way to begin. Whatever route you need to get to medita-tion, I suggest you try. I started with five minutes, and it took me two months to get to twelve minutes. I can sometimes do twenty, but usually my knees start getting loud around fifteen.

Meditation is very similar to exercise, as it is something that you need to do regularly. If you wait until a crisis, the meditation is not as helpful. But if you do it every day, or four or five times a week, you will likely maintain emotional health. That being said, there is a shortcut if you feel anxiety building up: take off your shoes, stand on dirt, and breathe. You need a skin-to-dirt connection. I know it sounds crazy, but there is this thing called the Schumann resonances which are basi-cally the extreme low frequency of the Earth's magnetic field. Appar-ently some studies were done where EEGs of meditating people showed their brain waves exactly matched the Schumann resonances. I'm not sure about all that, and I have not read any of these studies, but for me breathing barefoot on dirt worked to stave off a couple of panic attacks, so it might be worth a try.

The other thing that helped was learning *how* to breathe. There are a few different breathing exercises you can do if you don't have the time or space for meditation. The easiest to remember and learn is the 4-7-8 breathing technique. You just breathe in for four seconds, hold your breath for seven seconds, and breathe out for eight seconds. Do this for a minute or two and you will calm down long enough to get to where you need to go—hopefully to a doctor.

Once the COVID-19 lockdown happened in 2020, Carl and I started meditating together over the phone every single day. Having him reach out to remind me—or to keep me honest—was a little like having a workout partner; his expertise was like that of a personal trainer. On this journey, I don't know if I would have been able to take this next step without Carl. While that is a testament to Carl's friendship, it is also a condemnation of our society. I now believe meditation should be a regu-lar practice of a healthy life; for everyone, not just those struggling with anxiety.

A little over a year after my father's death I was visiting Tom West-cott, my former soccer coach and biology teacher. I mentioned to Coach Westcott that I had started meditating for anxiety, and explained that one of my symptoms was a fast heart rate. He told me about a time he found my father, crouched down in the school's library, holding his knees to his chest with his forearms and breathing very deliberately. Westcott was immediately concerned, but my dad explained that he had tachycardia, and his doctor taught him this practice of calming down his heart rate. He said his doctor told him to "hunker down" until the tachycardia passed. Westcott and I worked to figure out that Dad would have been in his forties when this happened, roughly the same age I was when I started experiencing anxiety.

The conversation I had with Coach Westcott that evening was one of the primary motivators for me to write this book. I always assumed my father had depression, but I never considered that he had anxiety. Looking back, I can now see plenty of examples of my father struggling with anxiety (for instance, his rage at being stuck in traffic). I wonder how bad my first panic attacks would have been if I had known what a panic attack was before experiencing it. My hope is that sharing these experiences might help mitigate the loneliness others feel as they deal with their own anxiety. I also wonder how much meditation would have helped my father, even if I can't fathom someone with that much rage meditating. It reminds me of Amanda Palmer's song "Ukulele Anthem," where she sings about Sid Vicious playing a four string fender bass as opposed to a ukulele. She postulates that if only Sid had played a ukulele, maybe he wouldn't have killed his girlfriend:

> If only Sid had had a ukulele, maybe he could have been happy
> Maybe he would not have suffered such a sad end
> He maybe would have not done all that heroin instead
> He maybe would've sat around just singing nice songs to his girlfriend

I think it's natural for children to regret what their parents might have missed out on, especially if it is a technological advance or new medication that would have helped them. But meditation is so simple, is completely free, and has been around for thousands of years. My father lived in a culture where meditation was not accepted, so I understand him not having a clear path to learn how to practice it. However, my father wasn't someone who was afraid of new things. After all, he grew up in and moved to areas that did not have lacrosse. He knew nothing about that game. And yet, as you will see, he was one of the big reasons lacrosse is so prevalent on the Eastern Shore of Maryland today.

IMPY, DARKY, AND MEETING KEVIN GATES

Lacrosse was the only thing I was ever legitimately good at. The reason I was good was because of some influential coaches whom I'll discuss in a moment. But for those that don't know anything about the sport of lacrosse, it is unique. It's one of the hardest sports to play. You need to be fast, strong, tough, and dexterous to be able to play it. It's also probably the only truly American game. It existed here long before the Europeans ever set foot in America. Native Americans called it "racket" or "ball" or "stickball". In those days, it was played by anywhere from a dozen to thousands of people on the field at the same time. That must have been such a spectacular sight, to see one thousand athletes faceoff against another thousand athletes. These matches were used to toughen up youth, but they were also religious events. The sport became a game of healing, and a game that promoted peace between nations. It became such a major part of many of the cultures of indigenous people of North America that it was used to settle disputes between different factions. Lacrosse provided conflict resolution in a humane yet still competitive way, while Europe was in the midst of the Thirty Years War.

A French Jesuit missionary in the 1600s gave the sport the name lacrosse. Lacrosse players today are a tight-knit fraternity, unlike in any other sport I have ever seen. If you played the sport, you can almost always tell a former lacrosse player on sight, in a way you can't with football, soccer, or basketball. There's something about lacrosse players that's just different, and it's hard to put into words. Those that have played "lax" will understand what I mean, and those that haven't played it won't. While it's growing in popularity, it's still a small community, though nowhere near as small as it was in the 1990s when I played.

At that time being really good at a sport meant going to a summer camp which focused on it. Kids got the benefit of learning the game from different coaches and – as long as the coaches were good – the more coaches a kid had, the better player they became. Kids would also get to go against different competition than they were used to, so they had a real opportunity to grow as a player. Even though my favorite sport was basketball, I never attended basketball camp. But I did attend soccer and lacrosse camps almost every year from twelve to seventeen years old. Day camps, sleepaway camps—it didn't matter. For at least a few weeks every summer I immersed myself in lacrosse and it was probably a big reason why I was recruited by so many schools.

At sleepaway camps, I got to live on a bunch of different college campuses, which gave me a sense of what that school would be like. One summer, Alex Howarth and I went to soccer camp at Duke and lacrosse camp at Notre Dame. We lived in the dorms, ate in the dining halls, and spent all of our free time hanging out in the student unions. Since most college athletes live on campus through the summer, you get a chance to see how those student athletes live, and even interact with them. In fact, as a thirteen-year-old I was dicking around with Alex in the LaFortune Student Union at Notre Dame when I hit future Chicago Bears linebacker Chris Zorich square in the back with a lacrosse ball. He stood up and looked right at me. He was a large specimen of humanity, and I had yet to hit my last growth spurt, so I was pretty sure I was about to die. But he just gave me the ball back and said, "Here you go little dude." Now that I think about it, I probably could have thrown the ball as hard as I could at his face and it would not have hurt him, but it was still nice of him not to kill me.

We also went to local day camps at Salisbury State College (now Salisbury University) and Worcester Country School (now Worcester Preparatory School). My father initially resisted holding camps at WCS, but Jim "Impy" Townsend convinced him that Big Macs were not going to buy themselves, and if he wasn't going to pay a living wage to coaches, he might as well allow them a chance to make some cheddar in the summer. Besides, I was getting older and it seemed like I might actually be good at sports, so Dad probably saw this as a chance for me to get a little extra instruction close to home. Coincidentally, my father started allowing summer camps just before I started 6th grade.

"Impy" is one of the all-time great lacrosse nicknames. Not a single person I have ever met who knows Jim Townsend calls him anything other than Impy. Apparently it started when his little brother was a baby and couldn't say the name Jimmy—he just said something that sounded like "Impy," and it stuck with coach his whole life. In fact, he is so "Impy" to me that if someone told me that they met a former coach of mine named "Jim," I would guess people whose name isn't even Jim first before I would think of Impy.

I met Kevin Gates at Impy's lacrosse camp. At the time, Kevin was a senior at Salisbury State College and was helping out Impy at the WCS lacrosse camp. Kevin Gates is going to come up later, so remember him. At lacrosse camp, my only impression of him was as a hungover college lax player who drove a crappy car that coaches called the Batmobile.[8] That was literally all I remembered about him from those days. Kevin never coached me at that camp or ever; I was in a different group and never had any interaction with him, but he will be a character later, so like I said, don't forget him.

Impy was quite a character in his own right. I first saw Impy when he was a sophomore or junior attackman at Salisbury State, when I was maybe in fourth or fifth grade. The Salisbury offense largely revolved around him getting the ball behind the goal and driving his defense-man into the ground, therefore causing the defense to slide and chaos to ensue. For those that don't know, lacrosse allows players to go behind the goal, like ice hockey. If a team has really strong attackmen they will get them the ball behind the goal in order to get the entire defense to "turn around," thus making it easier for the rest of the offense to get open for a shot. Impy was the ideal strong attackman. Physically powerful, tough as they come, and absolutely fearless. I can still picture him wet, muddy, and bloody. I have a feeling he scored lots of goals, but I don't remember much else about his play. I had not played lacrosse yet and I was just learning what each of the positions were. I didn't know I was going to be an attackman, but my dad would always point out Impy, probably because he was the one making the offense happen. It's likely I gravitated towards attack because of Impy.

Impy took over as the head varsity coach of Worcester Country School lacrosse when Kevin McNulty moved back to Baltimore. Impy was in many ways the archetypical "gruff" coach: the last time he shaved always seemed to be four days ago, and he was strong and tough, but I wouldn't describe him as svelte. Impy was maybe the most frightening growler I ever met. Sure, he would yell like most coaches, but athletes get used to that pretty quick, and I don't think any student athlete would ever say a coach who merely yelled was scary. It was not the yelling; it was when he got quiet and then would smile maniacally and start growl-ing... holy shit, terrifying. If you told seventh-grade me he had killed before and would do so again, I would have believed you. Hell, I might believe it today.

While Impy was my PE teacher, he was never technically my coach

---

8 It was a 1967 Chevy Impala with a 357 engine that was his grandmother's car before he went to college. When he pulled it out of the garage, two dead mice fell out of the sun visor, so maybe it should have been called the Ratmobile? This is the kind of joke Kevin Gates would tell.

outside of camp, as just before my 9th grade year he left our program for Washington College, and eventually the head coaching position at Rensselaer Polytech Institute (RPI). Though I never actually played for him, he gave me a ton of personal instruction. From the end of soccer season to the beginning of lacrosse season, he would pull me out of gym glass and have Shelia Rose, the girls PE teacher, run the whole class while he took me outside to run drills. Keep in mind that the gym class would only be indoors because it was cold. So while the rest of my class was inside the nice, warm gym playing warball or floor hockey, I was out in the freezing rain learning how to drive the goal from behind the cage. In those days, I was still fat and slow, but so was Impy, and he knew I had the potential to be great, and Impy really understood greatness.

Impy was my first connection to a lacrosse legacy, for lack of a better word. He was from Corning, NY and went to Corning East High. There was another person from Corning who was a generation ahead of Impy, Jim "Darky" Darcangelo, who in the late 80s and early 90s was a living legend in lacrosse. In the era before Gary and Paul Gait dominated at Syracuse, Darky was possibly the best-known lacrosse personality in the world, and certainly was in Maryland. As a midfielder at Towson, he won handfuls of awards and a national championship in 1974, went on to dominate for the Maryland Lacrosse Club for years, and was a key member of the Team USA that won the World Championships in 1978, 1982, and 1986. He was also the founder of Lax World, a lacrosse store that eventually expanded to have 16 locations nationwide. Just invoking his name was like a Catholic invoking the name of a family saint. Every single time Impy would take me outside and I would unconsciously shiver or drop a sarcastic remark about how I was pleased it was only sleeting, Impy would launch into a Darky story.

"You know, when I was a kid, each storm in Corning would bring like a foot of snow, easy. We'd all be bundled up inside watching cartoons or drinking hot chocolate with those little baby marshmallows or something, and my mom would look out the window and say, 'there goes Jimmy Darcangelo, off to the wall with a snow shovel and his lacrosse stick.' Because he would walk two miles to school in a foot a snow to shovel enough space by the wall that he could get four hours of 'wall ball' in even on a snow day. That's what makes a great lacrosse player."

Then I would usually say something like, "Well it never snows a foot here."

That was when he would lean in and get his face really close to mine with that scary smile and growl, "So what's your excuse?"

Best growler I ever met.

Jim Darcangelo had spoken at our athletic convocation at least once, and he seemed like a legitimately nice guy, although I only met him a couple of times when I was pretty young. What little I remember of him was that he seemed self-deprecating, humble, and funny. He spoke to everyone, from the youngest of kids to the grandparents, about the importance of repetition in sports, and especially lacrosse. "Repetition builds skills. Hit the wall, early and often," he would say. For those that don't know, "wall ball" or "hitting the wall" in lacrosse means throwing a lacrosse ball against a wall and catching it when it bounces back, and doing it over and over and over again. I still remember him telling the story about when he got the call that he had been added to the US National Team in 1986. He was already a legend in the sport, but what did he do? He hung up the phone, picked up his stick, and went out to hit the wall until it got dark. He really emphasized that the wall is the key to being great.

Like other sports, lacrosse requires footwork and fundamentals. Unlike other sports, lacrosse is not a natural game. In that way it's not like soccer or basketball—it is actually more like baseball. Now you have probably heard the old adage that the hardest thing to do in sports is to hit a round ball with a round bat. I would argue that the hardest thing to do in sports is to save a 95 mph off-hand hip-high shot from ten yards away while being screened by a fat crease attackman, but let's not nitpick here. The point is, lacrosse does not often come naturally to people, and without hours of practice against a wall you just will not be good at it.

I didn't have a wall, but I did have a piece of plywood that I leaned against a tree. It made a deep, hollow thud, which echoed through woods of our Ocean Pines neighborhood every time I hit it with the ball. On average, I probably spent three hours a day practicing. I practiced like Darky did. Three hours a day of that incessant thud, every single day. I found out years later that the neighbors literally sold their house because of me—or, I guess technically, because of Darky.

Here's the thing you need to understand about lacrosse in the 1990s and before: it was a small world. Most Americans in those days did not play lacrosse or even know how it was played. Many had never even heard the word before. We had no traditional media whatsoever. If you played lacrosse, or loved the game, you belonged to a very small community, a community that told stories. There were never lacrosse highlights on TV and there was no internet, so there was no such thing as a casual fan of lacrosse. Lacrosse legends grew through oral stories, and, in a way, the closer you could connect yourself to a legend, the more authority you had. That is why any good urban legend happened to your cousin's best friend who you actually met once.

For instance, most Americans alive in the '60s and '70s knew who Jim Brown was because of football and his films, but only those in the lacrosse community knew he was one of the best lacrosse players ever to play at Syracuse University. When I was growing up in the 90s, I heard that Jim Brown could run around or through anyone and had a shot so fast no one would see the ball until it hit the back of the net. Everyone in the lacrosse community knew a story about Jim Brown, or at least that he was a dominant player at Syracuse.

Now I want to be clear, there is no question Jim Brown was one of the greatest athletes of his generation and a fantastic lacrosse player. But one day when I was just out of high school I met a gentleman and former lacrosse player (who will remain nameless) who was vacationing in Ocean Pines. He found out I had played lacrosse and right away we started swapping stories. When I learned he played at Syracuse, I brought up Gary and Paul Gait, and then Jim Brown.

"...and Jim Brown too. He was the best lacrosse player ever! They say his shot was so fast you wouldn't see it until it hit the back of the net."

The old man snorted.

"I played with Jim Brown. His shot was one of the slowest on the team."

My jaw dropped. How was this possible?

The man went on, "He was a great midfielder for sure, faster and stronger than maybe anyone alive at that point, but he had a pretty bad shot. The reason no one saw it until it hit the back of the net was he used to shoot wormburners."

Wormburners are underhand shots where you skip the ball along the ground. They are not fast, but sometimes they are very hard for the goalie to see because of so many people being in the way. It's almost a trick shot.

"But I thought..."

"Jim is a great guy, and a one of kind athlete. He took to lacrosse like a fish to water, he was a natural. But he wasn't the best lacrosse player ever. He was just the most famous lacrosse player ever. There's a difference."

That day I learned how those telling the stories made and transformed the legend. There was no footage of Jim Brown playing lacrosse, so it was up to storytellers to establish and maintain the truth. In this era of everything being recorded, it's hard to remember that not so long ago the concept of truth was still fungible. While reading *Orality and Literacy* by Walter Ong, I realized that lacrosse was my spiritual connection to an ancient oral pre-literate culture whose amorphous beauty was not completely stomped out by facts that came with the whole world being recorded. Unlike other sports, lacrosse stories required humans to keep them, and pass them on. The stories were alive. They changed the more I thought about them, they evolved with me. Now we have video of everything. Sure, there are great things about the camera (I have made films and I love technology), but when I was growing up the lacrosse player was only as good as the bard telling the tale. And—for those who know him, prepare to do a spit take—Impy was my bard.

My dad truly loved sports. It did not matter what kind of sport it was, he would watch it, study it, and try to understand it. He was no athlete himself, but he knew sports better than anyone I have ever known. Even though he was not a kickboxing fan he could watch a kickboxing match and in a minute predict who was going to win based on how the two kickboxers moved. I remember the first time he saw jai alai, and he quickly understood the rules and what would make a better jai alai athlete. He was like the Bobby Fisher of watching sports. My dad did not grow up with lacrosse; he was from the Midwest and had never seen a lacrosse game until he moved to Maryland. He never played lacrosse, but he more than loved the game, he immersed himself in it. People that met him considered him a lacrosse guy, and my father helped bring lacrosse to the Eastern Shore. In fact, in 2012, thirty years after he got rid of baseball at WCS for lacrosse, my father was named the Lacrosse Man of the Year for the Eastern Shore by US Lacrosse. Andy Jones, the first Salisbury State College lacrosse coach, asked my dad to start a lacrosse team back in 1982, before any other school on the lower shore had a team. Now almost every school on the lower shore has a lacrosse team. He built the WCS program up from nothing, it was a gutsy move, and it changed the culture of sports on the lower shore. Even so, he had never lived lacrosse. He never played it, and he never coached it. He never spent thousands of hours hitting the wall. He never got hacked on that one spot just above the pad that left a consistent bruise for a whole season. He never ate a shot off his shin.

Impy, on the other hand, grew up in the game. He ate, drank and breathed lacrosse. He bled for lacrosse, the game made him who he was. His childhood heroes played lacrosse, and it's likely he wouldn't be able to conceive of life without the sport. I knew the difference between Impy and my dad: hearing lacrosse stories from my dad was like reading about a war in the newspaper, whereas hearing lacrosse stories from Impy was like speaking to a combat veteran. In those days Impy told me Jim Darcangelo was the best lacrosse player ever, and I believed him because he had lived the life.

Now sure, Impy was probably biased because he was a Corning East guy and Jim Darcangelo was too, and as a kid he always looked up to Darky. But I believed everything Impy told me. Maybe it was because my father had taken me to see Impy play; he had pointed him out to me, and explained he was the one that made the whole offense work. Impy played my position, and he played it well. He was the lacrosse authority in my life. I absorbed everything Impy was willing to impart to me.

I won't sugar coat it: coaches lie all the time. Impy would say crazy stuff that, to this day, I'm not sure was true. He said Darky used to sleep with his lacrosse stick in his hand so he never lost the feel of it. That one sounds a little farfetched. He told me that he used to tape his stick in his off hand for full practices until he was confident going both ways. That is a little more believable, but still a little suspect. Impy also told me that Darky was like the Barry Sanders of lacrosse before Barry Sanders. When he would score he would not celebrate but just run back up to midfield to wait for the next faceoff. That I believed.

One of the few things my father ever wrote was something I asked for one Christmas when I was in my early 30s. I asked for my family members to write a story about someone else in the family, so I could learn about them. No one did this besides my dad, and he did not write about someone else. He wrote about me.

Since he died I have been looking for it, but can't find it. I remember what he wrote about, though. He wrote how he had never scored a goal before. He did not know what it was like, but saw his son score dozens of goals. Every time I scored, apparently I didn't celebrate. I just went back to the line and pointed at my father, and he pointed back at me. Every time.

It sparked a memory from after the Cambridge game my senior year: Alex's dad was talking about why our coach did not give me the ball more.

"No one can stop you Danny, you should just get the ball every time and go to the goal. That should be our whole offense. Just give you the ball and get out of your way. Not that you want to score. It's like you apologize after you score."

First off, Alex's dad did not take losses well. So he was just kinda venting and mad at the time. Second, I was a weird kid, and I just didn't do things the way other kids did stuff. So it probably made sense to him that I somehow felt bad about scoring, since I didn't pump my fist or do a stupid dance. But I never apologized for scoring. I was just used to it; it was not a surprise. That might sound arrogant to someone who did not practice a sport for over 2,000 hours, but when you have logged that much time, it should not be a shock when you're successful. When I had the ball and drove the goal I was supposed to score. Impy taught me that. That was my job. That, or beat my guy, draw the slide, and hit the open man.

When you practice alone for thousands of hours you create a million narratives in your mind. You have won thousands of championships, you have mimicked the greats fifty thousand times. Because of Impy, even though I had never seen Jim Darcangelo play, it was Darky who I was imitating. I practiced scoring and not celebrating. Looking back, almost thirty years later, I think that was pretty weird. Like I said, I was a weird kid.

I'm lucky to have been coached by Impy, and for him to have told me Jim Darcangelo stories. I'm glad that I learned the game had nothing to do with celebration. It was hard work that made me a great lacrosse player, and it was love that made me respect the game. My father probably had no idea what he was doing when he brought lacrosse to our school. As it turns out, in a small way I brought my father into that world, and for a while—at least in those moments after a goal—he must have felt that he had done something right.

THE OTHER COACHES

O cean Pines, like most home owner associations formed in the 1960s, was racist by design. In the original HOA covenants and declarations, two neighbors on either side of them had to approve the people buying lots in the Pines. This was a way of being racist without being overtly racist. I lived in Ocean Pines because it was a place my parents could afford and it had parks near the water. My parents did not make Ocean Pines racist, or want it to be racist, or want to live in Ocean Pines because it was racist by design. Even so it was racist, and it was where I grew up.

Similarly, my dad worked at, and my brother and I attended, a "white flight" school. My dad did not set out to work at a white flight school. Such schools started after the "1954 Brown v. Board of Education" ruling by the US Supreme Court, and because integration took some time, most white flight schools were created in the late sixties and early seventies. My dad came from a school called Wawasee Prep in Syracuse, Indiana. He went to high school at Wawasee Prep, then after college taught and became a school administrator there, it was pretty much all he knew. It was a Catholic school, not a white flight school, founded six years before "Brown v. Board of Education" in 1948. I don't think my father would have ever left Wawasee Prep if it hadn't closed its doors in 1975. He was without a job and since all he knew was prep schools, he looked for another such opportunity. That's when Franklin Lynch, then Headmaster of Worcester Country School in Berlin, Maryland, hired him.

Even though my parents grew up in the 1950s and 1960s and lived through the Civil Rights movement, and even though their first date was literally at the 1968 Democratic Convention, they were shocked at the racism they saw on the Eastern Shore. The Eastern Shore is often compared to the Deep South when it comes to race relations. In fact, Somerset County (the county boarding Worcester) was one of the last counties in the nation to integrate its schools. My parents worked very hard to teach us that racism was wrong, but keep in mind we lived in a racist HOA and went to a white flight school, so obviously the village required to raise children might not have been cooperating too well with them.

However, I do believe my parents provided the best a foundation they could, given the situation we found ourselves in.

When I was five years old, my parents bought a house on Crows Nest Lane, which backed up to White Horse Park and the glorious Ocean Pines basketball courts. The Ocean Pines basketball courts were some of the best-maintained outdoor courts I've ever played on, and they even had lights allowing you to play at night. When I was about ten years old I started spending more and more time on those basketball court, and by the time I was twelve I spent almost every night there, once it got too dark to play lacrosse.

The basketball courts were right behind the police station, and while a sign clearly marked that the courts were only for residents and guests, no one ever complained—unless Black people came to play on the courts. Then some kid's parent would usually go to the police station and the police would come to the courts, ask everyone where they lived, and ask everyone for their identification. Being twelve years old I did not have an ID, but the police told me that was fine, that I could stay. They trusted me because I was white, which bothered the hell out of me. If people did not produce an ID, they would kick them out except for me, or the other white kids.

After this happened a couple of times and games were broken up, I got pretty annoyed. I'm not saying there wasn't a selfish motivation behind this, but I decided that when guys showed up who did not live in Ocean Pines, I would ask them their names, and then if the police came I would say they were all my guests. Yes, it was probably more because I wanted to play good games as opposed to my deep-seated sense of justice... but still, this happened more than a few times. When I claimed that all of these grown men were my guests and I rattled off their names, the police officer always got mad at me and demand that I produce an ID, to which thirteen-year-old me replied something to the effect of, "Do you want my driver's license or college ID?" This just pissed them off even more. But in the end they left us alone to continue playing our games.

This was an important foundational point for me and something that I feel needs mentioning. I loved sports, and competition. Any system that was designed to take sports or competition away from me seemed like a bunch of bullshit, and I was going to fight it. I know, I am a hero. White savior. I am surprised someone has not made a movie, yet. The point is, even though I was in the right, I was being selfish. Or maybe it's the other way around, but does it matter? That's what great about sports: justice is a foundational aspect.

Sports have a way of teaching us life lessons by just existing in the space of our unjust society. I don't want to get too deep into how our culture works, but the mere existence of sports and the intrinsic idea of *fairness* or *justice* built into the concept of *sportsmanship* or *rules applying equally to everyone* puts pressure on societal structures of injustice. This wasn't exactly the lesson one would expect to learn in a racist cocoon of a white-flight-educated HOA-living upbringing, but such is the magic of sports.

The whole time I lived on Crows Nest Lane, only two college students lived on that street, and both of them were hired by my father to coach. One was Shane Brey, brother of long time University of Notre Dame head basketball coach Mike Brey. Shane was my assistant basketball coach for a couple of years; he taught me the chop step and how to do a post move with a drop step, but he also taught me how to lift weights, and how to drive stick shift. He occasionally got me to pick him and his friends up from the Green Turtle at 2AM when I was only fifteen. He's an awesome dude. He was our next-door neighbor for just a couple of years, and his parents were only able to buy the place because I drove the previous owners crazy by throwing a lacrosse ball against the plywood "wall" for three hours a day. Shane had the relentless positivity of someone that worked out, and there is no way I would have been a decent athlete without his influence. The only reason I was recruited to any colleges was because of the time he spent with me in the weight room, and he did it because it made me better. He got nothing out of it, other than me occasionally picking him up from the Turtle, at 2AM.

The other college student was Ava Hartman, whose parents lived at the end of the cul-de-sac a couple doors down from Shane. I believe she was in the last semester of her senior year when she moved in with them full-time. Before that she was Impy's roommate, and she relished telling me (most likely very sanitized) stories of Impy in college. Impy got her a job at WCS as a long-term sub for the girls PE teacher, and later she became a fifth-grade teacher there. For roughly three years, she drove Tom and I to school instead of our father. I'm not sure how this was worked out, but it was a boon for Tom and I because she arrived at school fifteen minutes later than my father so we got fifteen more minutes of sleep, she let us listen to cool music, and we had a morning reprieve from any possible paternal bad moods. All she asked in return was for us to run into the donut shop and get her a large coffee with "extra extra cream" and "extra extra sugar," which I am pretty sure we teased her about even before either of us drank coffee.

Coffee choice aside, Ava was very cool, and seemed more like an older sister than an adult to us. She coached girl's lacrosse and field hockey and was really well-liked by her players. We would joke around with her, but she always got the upper hand because we were dumb kids and she was a grown-up. One morning she told us it was her twenty-fifth birthday, and my brother said, "Twenty-five? You're twenty-five? Jeeze, how's it feel to be half a century old?" She responded, "I don't know, I guess it feels like I'm better at math than some moron teenager?"

What made Ava so cool was how unabashedly honest she was with us. Adults were not really like that—in fact, most kids were not like that, either. I remember one time I was probably twelve and she had just started working at WCS, I was walking past her house on the way to the boat ramp. Her parent's house was tucked way back in the woods, and there were only a few spots where the sun came through for any real length of time. It happened to be a sunny day and Ava was in a beach chair in her parent's driveway in one of those sunny spots trying to get a tan. She was reading a book and wearing a bikini, but I was twelve and it was just before I was interested in girls, plus she was a decade older than me, so I didn't really think anything of it. When I came up, I probably talked about frogs or something, while she was doing her best to cover up and kind of nod along. Then she said, "Danny, I'm not really comfortable with you being here while I'm in a bikini. Can you leave?" To which I apologized, and spent the rest of the day wondering why someone would wear an outfit they weren't comfortable in, and what that had to do with me? Now I get it.

Ava is one of those people you meet in your formative years who has an oversized influence on your life that you probably don't grasp, unless you spend too much time looking back at your life. For instance, last year an ex-girlfriend sent me a poem she had recently written about me. It was a nostalgic poem about our time together in New York City and it was titled, "Thank You Black Shirt." It was about how I always wore a black t-shirt.[9] I laughed, because I didn't realize how often I wear black t-shirts; when I looked in my drawer, over half of my shirts were black. I can now remember as clear as day Ava telling me that she loved a man in jeans and a black t-shirt, but I never put the two things together until writing this book. She might have only loved a man in jeans and a black t-shirt for one day when she was twenty-four, but apparently this statement has been driving my fashion choices for the last thirty years.

A couple of summers after I first met her, my parents asked Ava to watch Tom and I while they went away on vacation. I think I was fourteen and Tom was sixteen, and Ava was working as a bartender in Ocean City to supplement her tiny income from teaching and coaching, so she was not around in the evenings. One night, while she was working, Shane was throwing a party, and Tom and I snuck over to his place. Tom had a few beers, and though I'm not saying Shane knew, he and his

---

9 To be clear, I am not now and never was a fan of Mussolini.

fellow college buddies got Tom home right before my brother threw up all over his room. Ava found out and was, of course, not pleased with us. The next night—after going next door to yell at Shane—she did not go to work and instead stayed home with us to make sure we didn't get into any more trouble. Tom went to bed relatively early, but I stayed up talking to Ava for a long time, and she said something that has stuck with me for years: "Everyone makes mistakes, but some mistakes are bigger than others." I asked her if she'd ever made a big mistake and she told me she had, and she told me about it. I'm not going to repeat it—it's not her book—but her telling me about that mistake might have been a trigger for me becoming more honest in my own life. Many years later, now that I myself have become a coach, I've always been honest with my players about my failings. I tell them about dropping out of school, my drug addiction, being homeless, and living in my car. I do that because, up until that point with Ava, I don't think I ever had an adult be so honest with me. It really meant so much. While she was never my coach, she was massively influential on *how* I coach.

The two other coaches that had an oversized influence on me were Tom Westcott and George Zaiser. Zaiser coached my 6th through 8th grade soccer and lacrosse teams, and he was my art teacher starting in 5th grade. He was also our class sponsor. I don't know how much I learned about the various games from him, but he was a great middle school coach because he got his players excited. He taught passion, though his infectious energy sometimes made us think that he probably had a few screws loose. Now that I know him as an adult, I can confirm that he does.

He was also a great art teacher. He taught me things that stuck with me. Even though I have absolutely no talent for the fine arts, one of the reasons I love losing myself at museums is because of George Zaiser.

Tom Westcott taught biology and coached varsity soccer. His influence as a biology teacher certainly pushed me further towards environmentalism. More importantly, his friendship through the years has helped me through some difficult times. After dropping out of school, I coached soccer for a few seasons with Coach Westcott. It was coaching with him that I came to understand how his relationship with his players was unique compared to all the other coaches I had known. Most of his players became his lifelong friends after he coached them, and they continued to support the team and the school because of him. I can't stress enough how rare something like this is. While I am happy to be friends with the kids I have coached, I don't know if I will have the ability Coach Westcott had to maintain those friendships for lifetimes. It is something truly special. He always looked at coaching as having nothing to do with winning or losing, but molding boys into men. Lots of coaches say the same thing—Coach Westcott meant it.

Since we're on the subject of racism and Coach Westcott, he recently told me a story about my dad. This all came up because long after my father retired, apparently some racial incident happened at WPS. Maybe it was bubbling under the surface for a while, I don't know, but in 2020 after George Floyd was murdered on video by a police officer, there was no official response from the school, and that did not sit well with many students. Those students bravely wrote a letter condemning the lack of response about racial inequality from the administration, condemning the school curriculum for ignoring education on race relations, and demanding it adopt a zero tolerance policy for racist behavior among students and faculty.

The students got ahold of me and asked me to sign it, which I did. I then passed it on to many of my classmates and fellow alumni, requesting that they sign it as well. About a dozen did. I passed those names on to the student leaders and received a very interesting email in return. I won't share the whole letter, but this part is important:

> As we said, we are grateful for your support, but not surprised by it given your family's reputation. We recently spoke with a Worcester graduate who felt that your father was an exceptional and powerful advocate for him when he experienced discrimination at the school. We hope that with your continued support and the support of other alumni, students, parents, and board members we can help make our school a place where fierce advocacy is not an exception, but a norm.

And I was all, say what now? I never saw my father as an advocate for anyone. Just a few days after receiving this email, I happened to be at Mr. Westcott's farm and we were talking about the letter[10] and the situation at the school. I brought up the email and the mention of my father being an advocate, and Mr. Westcott lit right up.

"You don't know the story about Lamont and ____[11]?"

"I know Lamont but I don't know the other guy."

Lamont was one of the first Black students to go to Worcester Country School. He was two years behind my class in school and we played sports together. I knew him fairly well, but I didn't know the story. I'm not going to name the other guy because I don't know him at all.

---

10 Mr. Westcott was one of the few former or current teachers to sign the letter.
11 I'm not going to name the racist kid because I honestly I forgot his name and who knows, maybe he learned his lesson and shouldn't be punished for being a shit head in high school.

"You don't know _____? He was a real shithead. Anyway, it was Lamont's first week of school and _____ walked up to him at lunch time and threw two pieces of fried chicken at Lamont and said, 'I figure you will like this more than me, why don't you have it.' Lamont got very upset and told a teacher, and they sent both Lamont and _____ to your dad's office[12]. Your father asked Lamont what had happened, and then he had Lamont wait outside while he shut the door to his office with _____ inside. Lamont said he could feel the walls of the office shake with how loud your dad was screaming at _____.

Westcott was grinning ear to ear as he went on with the story. "According to Lamont, your dad thundered, 'Who the hell do you think you are you worthless piece of shit? What do you think you have earned in this life? Nothing, that's what!' Just going on and on berating this child. Then your dad threw the door open and had Lamont come inside the office. Lamont looked at _____ and he saw _____ was terrified. Lamont said, 'I knew white people could turn red, but not until I looked at _____ in Mr. O'Hare's office did I know that white people could turn purple.'"

"So your dad then calmly asked Lamont to take a seat. He turned to Lamont and ignored _____. He said, 'Lamont, I'm so sorry this has happened to you. This isn't right. So you tell me what you want me to do. Do you want me to suspend him, do you want me to expel him, or do you want me to beat the shit out of him? Because I'll do whatever you want, just say the word.'"

"So Lamont said, 'Mr. O'Hare, I think _____ has been punished enough.' And your father looked at _____ and said, 'You better be thankful to Lamont for saving your ass today. Now get the hell out of here.' And Lamont said he never got shit at Worcester again."

I was silent taking this all in. I could see my father saying these things, I just didn't know he actually had. It was almost as if he was saying lines from a script written long after the incident to make him seem like something greater than he was. My father had died a year before I heard this story, but this moment I may have been more proud of him than I ever had before.[13]

"I'm stunned," I told Mr. Westcott, "it's almost hard to believe that happened and I never heard about it. I wonder how much of that story is true?"

Mr. Westcott smiled.

"Knowing Lamont and your dad, I would bet most of it. Besides, who cares? It's a good story and it's how Lamont remembers it."

---

12 At that time my father was in charge of discipline at WCS.
13 Yes he was an adult threating a child with physical violence, but the kid was an asshole.

Jerry Schmidt Was on the Cover of *Sports Illustrated*

Jerry Schmidt was the first and only lacrosse player to ever have his picture on the cover of *Sports Illustrated*. This was true until Jerry Schmidt passed away in 2004, and it was true until Paul Rabil's 2018 cover. But for the entire time I was coached by Jerry Schmidt, he was the only lacrosse player to ever be featured on the cover of *Sports Illustrated*, and the accompanying article was titled "The Tough Game." Needless to say, he was one coach that did not really care what your excuse was.

Jerry Schmidt was not my best coach, and he was not that influential on me as a human being. I learned to look at lacrosse as a job while playing for him, and the love of the game kind of faded away. I don't think he is to blame for this; he coached me from ages fourteen to seventeen when I was just starting my journey into depression.

That being said, I learned more about the technical aspect of lacrosse from Coach Schmidt than from everyone else combined. First, he gave me a jump rope and told me I had to jump rope every single day. By the end of freshman year, I was jumping rope religiously, and by my sophomore year I wasn't slow anymore. Adding quickness changed every aspect of my game, in all of the sports I played, but especially lacrosse. In order to be great in lacrosse you have to be fast, there is no other way. I elevated my game and that really came from jumping rope every single day. I can't understand why more coaches don't recommend this to their kids.

Here are some other things he told me to do in the first few weeks of coaching me:

Shoot sidearm. That's right, he told a freshman attackman to shoot sidearm, and I broke every scoring record at the school.

Roll the wrist over on bounce shots to create a spin. It makes the ball kind of weirdly skip and stay low. Goalies hate it because almost no one does it.

Shoot at a defenseman's legs. They are almost always moving, so by the time the ball gets there, they will have moved out of the way, and thus will have created a perfect screen. The goalie might expect a screen from the crease attackman, but won't expect the ball to come under the defenseman.

Bull "dodge" the first time I get the ball. This isn't really a dodge, you actually run over the defender. He was okay with me losing the ball that first time as long as I knocked the defender on his ass. This is only something you tell big attackmen.

Poke check when riding. Again, I don't know why more coaches do not teach this one either, but they really don't. Good poke checks are a lost art in lacrosse. You can cause plenty of chaos with a poke check and never get a penalty for it like you do a slap check.

"Eef" the ball. I think he made up the word. It was his term for getting the ball to a teammate or into space. Kick it, poke it, slap it, whatever it took to move it. While the word "eef" wasn't that important, the idea behind it always stuck with me. All coaches teach this, I just like his word.

Jerry Schmidt was a client of my mom's, having just bought a retirement home in Ocean Pines when he mentioned he used to coach lacrosse and might be interested in coaching in his retirement. Mom quickly introduced him to my dad. Coincidentally, this was mere days after Impy had put in his resignation, and my dad could not believe his luck. Jerry Schmidt was not just a great former lacrosse player, he was a legendary coach. He started the run of Hobart College's dominance, winning three Division III National Championships there. In eleven seasons, he never had a losing season. He was Lacrosse Coach of the Year in 1977, coached the 1978 US National Lacrosse Team (which Jim Darcangelo played on), and was inducted into the National Lacrosse Hall of Fame in 1983. He had forgotten more about lacrosse than most people would ever know, and he just wandered into my dad's life.

Coach Schmidt only lasted four years at our school, the four years I was in high school. He was grumpy and mean, but he was funny and sarcastic, too. Mostly, I think he was just over it all. He was coaching because that is what he did, but I don't think he loved it anymore. If he did, he had a weird way of showing it.

He was also a bit of a prankster. Not only was he the lacrosse coach, he was also the boys PE teacher. The girls PE teacher, Shelia Rose, could be a little much to deal with. One day my dad brought a new scissor lift into the gym, which was going to be used to change out light bulbs and hang banners. He told both Jerry and Shelia not to touch the lift under any circumstances, and then he left as the third grade PE class was arriving. For some reason, Shelia wasted no time getting in the scissor lift, leaving the kids to Jerry. Jerry waited until she was all the way up before kicking out the power cord. Since third grade gym was pretty loud, he pretended to not be able to hear Shelia's calls for help during the whole period.

Honestly, that was Coach Schmidt at his best, at least when he was at WCS. Like teachers, some coaches are better for certain kids than others. I had teachers that were great for me but were horrible for my brother. When he coached at Worcester, Jerry Schmidt was probably only a great coach for me. He taught me strategy early on, and because I worked hard to develop my skills on my own, I could apply the things he was teaching us to the game when most other players on our team were still working on their skills. He rubbed a lot of the players the wrong way, whereas I didn't care who was a jerk to me. I just wanted to play lacrosse.

When I played basketball, I fouled out of every game but one, from freshman through junior year. It was usually in the last minute, but I played aggressive defense and I got every bit of those five fouls. In fact, the one time I did not foul out, Coach Joe Mulford got mad at me and told me I wasn't giving *him*[14] my all. He was right, something was just off, and I didn't have my usual intensity. I modeled my playing style after then—Detroit Piston Dennis Rodman, focusing on defense and rebounds only. I played with fury. Coach Mulford got me to listen to Cat Stevens before games to try and calm me down so I would not get fouls too early. I'm not sure why, but I played basketball with a fire I didn't have in any other sport. In lacrosse, however, I played with a coldness, almost detached from emotion. I believe part of that was due to Coach Schmidt's influence.

Coach Schmidt came from areas where lacrosse was played at a higher level than it was on the Eastern Shore in the early 90s. He was often frustrated by our lack of knowledge and was constantly criticizing us for it. Even if he was right, for most players his coaching did not come across as making sense. For instance, he didn't impart the wisdom that transitions and ground balls are more important than offenses or defenses, but rather drilled us ad nauseam on rides and clears, fast breaks, and ground balls. We did not do a good job in these drills because we hated them, so he kept making us do them because were bad at them—but we just didn't understand why. It was a negative feedback loop. Perhaps he was simply used to dealing with more sophisticated players, or perhaps he was a little checked out. Most likely it was a little of both. The end result was that most of the players felt like they could never do anything right.

---

14 I love Coach Mumford but he was a demanding coach that always kinda made it personal. I specifically remember him saying to me, "Three ticky-tack, bull shit fouls? You didn't give me your all tonight." And then he just walked away.

The years he coached me, I only ever came out of the game for penalties or to get yelled at. I never once asked to come out, no matter how hurt I was or how tired I was. As soon as the penalty was over, or he was done yelling, I went back in, so I never watched the game with him. I wish now that I had. He never even pulled me aside in practice to watch my position played by someone else. It's hard to learn about what you're doing while you're doing it, especially when there are twelve other people moving in a relatively small space. I think I would have learned more if he had taken me aside and showed me what was actually happening.

But in the process of passing all his other wisdom to me, I somehow lost the love of the game. The night before our first game of my senior year, Coach Schmidt resigned. I believe my father once thought that Schmidt was his greatest coaching hire ever—after all, Coach Schmidt was already in the National Lacrosse Hall of Fame. However, the results did not match the resume. No players other than me were ever recruited to play in college, and I was most likely already put on that path by Zaiser, Impy, and Shane. After Schmidt resigned, Coach Mulford took over as head coach, and while I loved Mulford, by senior year I was just going through the motions. Although I broke all the scoring records at the school[15], I couldn't care less. Lacrosse now meant nothing to me. While I was supposed play at University of Notre Dame the following year, I was not looking forward to ever picking up my stick again.

Instead, I picked up a gun, and headed to Frontier Town, for the summer that would put the last nail in the coffin of the golden boy asshole I was once destined to become. From that point on, I was just going to be an asshole.

---

15 Keep in mind these records were only twelve years old at the time, and my records were later smashed.

POSTMODERN, NARCISSISTIC BLATANIST

I was in Pittsburgh on an October night in 1994 at 3 AM, lying in bed with a dancer, holding her close. Posters and homemade art adorned the walls of the small room. A senior at Point Park University, she had a disarming smile and long blonde hair that smelled like Outrageous shampoo. We looked out the window while talking about what had happened the last few months, and what would happen the next few months. I had just finished the first half of the first semester of my freshman year, and was heading home for the midterm break. I stopped in Pittsburgh for one night, what would be our last night together. There was a huge full moon, and the shadows of cumulous clouds slowly and steadily crawled across our faces, one after another.

My dancer and I had literally slept together almost every night that previous summer—holding each other while we slept, but never once so much as kissing. We lived and worked at a Western theme park called Frontier Town in West Ocean City. She had one of the best rooms in the park, above the Golden Nugget Saloon overlooking the whole street. We would meet after leaving our respective significant others and listen to Indigo Girls or Tori Amos and talk until she fell asleep.

But on this October night she was not tired. We had been apart since August, and we had both changed so much in that time. There was too much to say and that night she couldn't sleep until she had said it all. She talked about the future as most young people do at three in the morning. Me, I was already nostalgic for the past.

At that moment, sometime between three and four in the morning we saw a flash of light in the sky. And then another, and another. Then we heard the boom. The sky was full of fireworks. This isn't a metaphor. Someone was setting off an entire firework show in the middle of the night.

"Oh my god, it's actually fireworks," she said. She turned to face me, still in my arms, our eyes only inches apart. "This can't be real life," she went on, searching for the correct eye to focus on, "this has got to be a movie."

At some point, anyone who is in love feels like their life is a movie. The dancer and I did not have sex that night, or ever for that matter. I never wanted to have sex with her—and I am sure she never wanted to have sex with me, but I was in love with her. Even though I have not spoken to her in years, I still love her and am still in love with her. I wanted her to be in love with me, which I think is a little wrong. Why should we want others to feel the same way about us as we feel about them? Shouldn't we want them just to be who they are and feel how they feel? Especially those we love—if we do love them, then why would we want them to be something else? While I could never imagine having sex with her, I felt a real romantic love. It is the strangest relationship I have ever had. I honestly don't know if a movie like this has ever been made, but if it has, I can't think of it.

I probably told her that our lives were not a movie—but they were a *story*, and since we most commonly think of and experience stories through the lens of film or television, most people start to think of their lives this way. In a way they are correct, since we are living in a story, but it is more than a film could ever be. I like to think we live in a play, or at least are audience members in the play of our life: watching the play of our life, participating the way a live audience does. However, I'm sure I didn't think all of that in those days. Maybe I was halfway there.

A week later my dancer discovered the reason fireworks were going off at three in the morning. They were filming a movie at Three Rivers Stadium. We were in a movie after all.

We referred to Frontier Town as "Frowntown." This name came from three Frontier Town bumper stickers spliced together to spell out Frowntown and stuck on the wall inside the "Pan for Gold" storage cabinet. Frontier Town was the kind of magical place that ruined the people that worked there. It was a Western theme park staffed by teens and early twenty-somethings that had almost no rules; the employees lived in the park in bunk houses above the General Store and Saloon. Each day I could be assigned a different part: stagecoach outlaw, train outlaw, drunk outlaws, the announcer, the piano player, the goofy deputy, the marshal, and the train engineer. The Can-Can girls danced three shows a day and worked the "Pan for Gold" area and by far had the hardest jobs. The hardest role for the stage cowboys was that of Casey, the train engineer. Playing Casey was fun, but it was complicated work and brutally hot. You drove a real steam train, had to build the fire and keep it burning at just the right temperature, watch the steam pressure, and try not to start a forest fire—it was a whole ordeal. You also got robbed seventeen times, which in this case is actually way more fun than it sounds, and you always got the "gold" back by then end of the ride, anyway. For the gunfights, we used replica Ruger 22s and a super-illegal sawed-off 12-gauge shotgun. I also had a replica 1851 Colt Navy black powder .44 revolver that sounded like a goddamn cannon when I fired it.

Living where I worked, pretending to be someone I wasn't, and spending most of my waking hours existing in a different century really messed with my mind. I loved playing cowboy. I loved goofing off with children, riding horses to a gunfight, and getting shot off roofs. I got lost in the existence of the unreal.

Once you settled into your place at Frowntown, the outside world disappeared. I know that sounds cliché, so let me give you an example: during the Can-Can show, the outlaw drunk comes in hooting and hollering, so the marshal and deputy chase him all over the stage, disturbing the dancers, stopping the music, and breaking up the dance. One of the Can-Can girls pretends to quit, then walks into the audience and asks to sit on a gentleman's lap. Then, about a minute later, she screams and runs back onstage claiming that the man pinched her butt. The announcer brings the man up and has a trial on stage with all the characters participating.

It was a fun thing for the audience, and sometimes we heard some mildly inappropriate things from the "volunteer", but nothing too bawdy. One of the first things they would ask the man was his name and were he came from, and sometimes people tried to make up funny names, which usually got a polite laugh.

But one day in July of 1994, a guy came up on stage with a big shit eating grin on his face. Toby, who was the announcer that day, asked him his name. He thought for a second and said, "O.J. Simpson!" The crowd erupted in laughter and jeers as if it was the funniest thing ever said at the Golden Nugget Saloon. Toby looked at me dumbfounded, completely bewildered as to why that was funny. I was playing the marshal and just shrugged.

What we didn't know was it had been four days since the slow-speed white Bronco police chase that had been one of the most watched events at that point in American television history. It was a historic event that practically everyone in the US was talking about. Four days later, the only people in the US that didn't know about it were people in a coma, and those of us at Frontier Town.

So when I say the outside world disappeared, I meant it. I would wake up at dawn after maybe an hour or two of sleep, feed and water the goats for the petting zoo, and then clean out the horse stalls and brush the horses and get them ready for the day. I was in costume all summer long, so I never wore shorts or a t-shirt. I only had two pairs of jeans: my marshal jeans and my outlaw jeans; and I had five shirts—three for marshal and two for outlaw. The streets were sand, and some of the gunfights got to be pretty painful, especially when you got shot off the roof—that one always hurt the worst. But we were young, and the hardest part of the day was just avoiding dehydration.

The park gates opened at 10 AM and the sandy streets streamed with curious and amazed children. I always said it was the greatest job I ever had, because I got to play with guns and kids all day long, but doesn't sound right anymore. I think about this time whenever people use the term, "halcyon." It was a transformative experience for everyone that worked there. For that blip of time we lived in an unreal world, where there even was a constant soundtrack playing. We existed fully in character for a majority of the day, and experienced a world separate from the reality that everyone else lived in. Our temporary reality created by this false world of imagination would disappear with the autumn, but for those few months it was liberating—although sometimes all of that freedom can break you.

It broke me. I remember the moment it happened, remember exactly what I was doing, remember the light, remember the song that was playing, and even remember the smell of the hay.

The park had just closed for the day and I was hauling a couple of bales of hay to feed the goats. I was pushing a wheelbarrow through the thick sand of the back street, in between the ice cream shop and the train depot. "The Weight" by The Band was playing on the loudspeakers, and the front street was completely empty except for one beautiful woman. She was walking slowly up the street into a gentle afternoon breeze; her boho maxi dress and her long blonde hair were chaos, juxtaposed with her perfect posture and precise dancer steps. The sun was getting low and placed just to the front and left of her, pushing its amber late afternoon shards between the leaves and branches of an old tree, illuminating her face with every other step. I recognized her right away, even though I had met her only once, during my first summer there. I didn't know her name then, and I still don't. I just knew she was the reason for a whole mess of drama at the end of the season the year before I had first arrived.

Now, almost two years later, she was back and walking down the middle of the street, in perfect time with the song, looking straight up at the Blockhouse, where her old lover was. You couldn't see into those windows, but she knew he was there. Her smile was wicked and alluring. She called out to her former lover, stopped and waited. The song stopped. The whole world stopped, only the sounds of the goats chewing and a peal of distant laughter were heard. She just waited, and never let the smile slip from her face. A full minute passed and nothing else happened. Then we heard footsteps on the stairs, and the door to the Blockhouse squeaked open.

This might have been one of the most beautiful moments I have ever seen. It had nothing to do with me, I was just an observer. I don't even know if what I was witnessing was love or not. It was just a snapshot, just a scene from other stories, from other lives. I was background at best, but more likely I was off screen entirely. Still, that is the moment that broke me for good. I think it's because, at that moment in time, I was nothing, I was free, and life was beautiful.

Frowntown was liberating destruction because it knocked me off my path. It was probably the healthiest thing for me in the long run, because I wasn't being honest about my depression, even to myself. After the love of my dancer, I realized the fairy-tale myth about "finding our one true love" is most likely a social construct, and wildly damaging to our psyches, although not right away. In those days, I thought I was still in love the person that I considered the love of my life, but I also loved this dancer, and that I must be a terrible person for betraying both of them. This "one true love" nonsense had me so twisted that I hated myself for loving at all.

Love was not the only thing I learned about in that fake world of the Old West. Other than me, everyone that worked there was creative and brilliant. They were all skilled musicians, dancers, or artists. These yahoos I met at Frowntown introduced me to so much art, music, and philosophy that in the short two summers I spent there, my education far surpassed the twenty-some months I'd spent in a university classroom.

But this is what really happened to me: one character died, and another began. The character that was going to be a healthy member of society, a stalwart sports-loving lawyer (or banker or business owner) who was on seven different boards and who coached his kid's Little League team, got shot dead daily in those summer gunfights. Or, more realistically, he was killed by a perfectly-placed tree that sprouted one hundred years before the former dancer stepped into its dappled light.

There's just no way to say this without sounding pretentious, so fuck it, here goes: I became overwhelmed by an abundance of beauty. By living in a fictitious world, absolutely free of the ridiculous cares of the mundane world, something just snapped in my brain. I could no longer stay on the path that seemed so clearly laid out for me from an early age.

This might have been my first prolonged experience with mania, or this might have just been a rejection of societal structures. Maybe it was a little of both. But either way, the character in the play of my life that I was going to be perished somewhere at Frowntown.

That's not to mean who I was as a person was completely obliterated. When people talk about soul, this is maybe what they are referring to—the aspect of a person that exists no matter how much their personality and plot changes. A few threads of the cloth that cover my life certainly cross both pre-Frowntown and post-Frowntown characters' timelines. These few threads seem to be constants of me. The most obvious thread is love. I know, it's corny and stupid, but it is true. Try as I might, once I love someone I love them for life. No matter what they do to me, no matter who I become. My love is forever.

Another one of those threads is postmodernism, which I know sounds pretentious to say, too. I guess that's just the theme of this chapter. But I'm not pretending, I have always gravitated towards postmodernism. It's probably because I spent my youth in the 80s and 90s consuming postmodern art, which was the prevalent zeitgeist of the age. I've examined my life over and over again since adolescence, and when I create art, I spend as much time thinking about the art's context, as I do its content. While postmodernism might not create narcissism, it certainly doesn't oppose it in any real way. Since I spend so many hours in reflection and have not yet obliterated the self through the Noble Eightfold Path, I have been accused of being a narcissist. I don't deny that, but I would like to clarify that I don't think I am pretty like the Greek figure Narcissus did, I just think I'm pretty cool. Blatanist is a term I invented (as a narcissist would) to describe my art style that shuns subtlety—I don't do subtlety, that's bougie shit.

It was almost a decade ago when I first started using the descriptor Postmodern Narcissistic Blatanist to describe my art style, but what I have since realized is that it has little to do with art and more to do with how I see the world. That being said, I have always been hyper-self-aware. Now there is a big difference between being hyper-self-aware and having Somatic System Disorder[16]. While SSD might seem similar

16 The Mayo Clinic defines Somatic System Disorder (SSD) as "characterized by an extreme focus on physical symptoms — such as pain or fatigue — that causes major emotional distress and problems functioning. You may or may not have another diagnosed medical condition associated with these symptoms, but your reaction to the symptoms is not normal. You often think the worst about your symptoms and frequently seek medical care, continuing to search for an explanation even when other serious conditions have been excluded. Health concerns may become such a central focus of your life that it's hard to function, sometimes leading to disability."

to hyper-self-awareness, they are very different. SSD did not manifest itself in me until after my father passed away, and I only first noticed the symptoms abound the time I had the anxiety dream (which I will get to in the Chapter titled *Dreams*[17]). I had never heard of SSD, and it wasn't until almost a year into therapy that my therapist explained it to me. But because I am hyper-self-aware I quickly figured out that it came from watching my dad slowly die over three-and-a-half years. I know there is a long way to go to make this connection, but I think it's important.

As I've detailed, my dad had a massive hemorrhagic stroke in 2015. He then had brain surgery about a week later, and somewhere between those two events his brain suffered significant damage. He may have had some pretty serious unrelated issues before the stroke—or maybe they were related. Either way, after the surgery he did all the therapy meant to get him back to his normal self. Tom even moved down from New York to Maryland for a month to make sure Dad did physical therapy every day, so he could get into a better rehab facility, and things were starting to improve. In the months after the stroke, a dozen different doctors saw my dad, each prescribing different medications, and he was in and out of three different facilities and the hospital.

I understand that this is common, and it's the patient's or the family's decision on how to navigate the healthcare process. My father was incapable of making such decisions, so my brother, my mother, and I stepped up and did so as best we could. We could not prescribe drugs or dictate what he was or was not given, however. I saw firsthand the brutality of the American medical industrial complex and, holy shit, it is *terrifying*. Again, I think everyone involved in this process was acting in what they believed was my father's best interest. They were just wrong.

My father was in his own room in at Mallard Landing (an assisted living facility) when his psychiatrist—who had only seen him three times over a six-month period, and for less than twenty minutes each time—suddenly switched all four of his psychotropic medications on the same day. Four off, four on, on the same day. I questioned the doctor if it was wise to do this and he said my father should be fine. Yet the next afternoon, my dad had an episode of extreme confusion at dinner and was kicked out of his room and placed into the facility's "Memory Care" unit. (Do not assume they care for your memory here. It means the door is locked with a code, and people without short-term memory can't remember codes.)

Now, I'm not a doctor. I'm not going to be a Monday morning quarterback regarding my father's care. I love doctors, I listen to everything

17 Again, proof I'm a Blatanist.

they tell me, and I almost always try to follow their advice. But man, once someone hits that nursing home, they just medicate the hell out of them and no one seems to be able to stop it.

Eventually, while in "memory care," my dad was on seventeen fucking medications at the same time. I still remember where I was when I got the phone call from a doctor who hadn't seen my dad until that day, saying Dad was having a bad reaction to his Parkinson's medication that a different doctor had prescribed. I was at the Delmar and Route 13 stoplight, and I think about this interaction every time I am at that light.

"Yes Mr. O'Hare, this is Dr. _____. It seems Matthew is having a bad reaction to the Parkinson's medication, so we would like to put him on anti-anxiety medication."

"But my father doesn't have Parkinson's," I replied. "He just has a tremor. Why not take him off the Parkinson's medication?"

"It's not our recommendation to take Matthew off the Parkinson's medication at this time."

"Okay, but, why is he on Parkinson's medication at all?"

I heard some papers shuffle.

"Matthew was put on Parkinson's medication because he has developed D.I.P."

"And what is D.I.P.?"

"Um...It's Drug Induced Parkinsonism."

A long pause.

"Right, so, he doesn't have Parkinson's, he has a tremor because he's already on too many drugs, and your solution to this is to give him more drugs, and when he has a bad reaction to that drug, your solution will be—correct me if I am wrong—to give him more drugs. Right?"

"It's our recommendation that Matthew gets the anti-anxiety medication because that should help with his bad reaction to the Parkinson's medication."

"And it you believe it is safe to give him this?"

"Yes."

A longer pause.

"Mr. O'Hare?"

"Yup, I'm here. Look, I'm sorry, I have a deep respect for science and I really don't want to be an asshole here, but how can you know it's safe to give him this? My father is on seventeen different medications. Tell me, has there ever been a study done when this medication was given for D.I.P. to patients who were on all of the other seventeen different medications my father is on? Of course there hasn't. There's no way we know this is safe."

"Mr. O'Hare, we use this medication all the time."

"I swear I'm not trying to make your day worse. I'm not trying to be a jerk. But how can this be the right answer? How can giving him *more* drugs be the solution for his being over-medicated?"

"Mr. O'Hare, we're just trying to give Matthew the best treatment possible."

"Mr. O'Hare is my father."

"I'm sorry?"

"No, it's not you. How about this? You can give my father the medication if you study the effect on him and report your findings to...science, I don't know. Something. Just record it somehow. I mean, at this point I would let you do whatever you feel is necessary to my father, as long as you learn something from it and humanity learns something from it and it gives some fucking meaning to all of this. Here's an opportunity, right? Now we'll know what will happen if someone is on seventeen different medications and then we add one more to the mix. Can you do that? Can you promise me that?"

"Mr. O'Hare, we don't have those resources."

"Well then, why not take him off the Parkinson's drug instead?"

"Mr. O'Hare, it's not our recommendation to take him off the Parkinson's medication."

"So, you won't take him off that?"

"That's not our recommendation."

"So what am I supposed to say?"

"We'd like to put Matth—your father—on anti-anxiety medication. We believe it will help your father."

The longest pause.

"Mr. O'Hare?"

"Fine."

Less than one week later, my father was in the hospital receiving last rites from a priest. The medication was too much for him. He had become unresponsive and was just twitching and spasming. They took him off all of his medications so he could die in peace.

He didn't die, though. He wasn't that lucky. He was also not allowed back to Mallard Landing. I believe my dad's downturn was caused by this last medication that the Mallard Landing doctor put him on, but that's just conjecture. I never spoke with that doctor again, and as far as I know, he never even saw my father's file again. My guess is he had no idea that the drug he prescribed didn't work. My guess is that doctor would do the same thing again, and have the same conversation with another helpless family member.

So somehow, by being completely helpless, by making one bad decision after another, and allowing my dad to be drugged long enough to be kept alive while being tortured until he ran out of funds, I got broken again. Unlike the first time I was broken back at Frowntown—when I was broken and freed and my mind sprung open—this time I was broken and placed in a cage by that same stupid mind.

I'm not blaming the American healthcare system for my anxiety. It's not the system's fault I was designed this way. The culture, the zeitgeist of my youth, my education, the people I met along the way, and of course my genetics, they all contributed to this state of madness I experienced. Like I said before, I most likely inherited plenty of this, but I know the trigger. The trigger was that fucking stoplight in Delmar, and the helplessness I felt at that moment and in every moment since.

SOUTH BEND THE FIRST TIME – QUITTING LACROSSE

I attended college at the University of Notre Dame. I don't like to talk about it, and it's not like I even graduated from there. I went there to play lacrosse. My playing career lasted negative-two minutes of the first lacrosse team meeting.

Why did this happen? I never told my father the whole story, but here it is: I went early to the first team meeting with some other players. A few of them were talking about a party they attended the night before, and how they had sex with a drunk girl. I am not exactly sure, but it sounded like multiple people had sex with the same drunk girl, and she was pretty wasted. That was it. That was enough for me. I got up and walked out, and I passed the coach on my way. He asked me where I was going and I mumbled something like, "This isn't for me." But what I meant was, "These guys can never be my friends, and I certainly can't go to war with them."

I regretted it immediately, but I told no one. Don't get me wrong, I don't regret never associating with those guys ever again. Nothing is worth that. After years of looking back, I wonder if maybe I misinterpreted what they were discussing. But even if I did, I just couldn't find a way to play lacrosse anymore. I regretted no longer playing lacrosse, and I regretted coming to Notre Dame. It was my first week on campus, and rather than working out and battling for a position on the lacrosse team, I entered the first really deep depression of my life. I slept roughly fifteen hours a day, I didn't go to class, and when I wasn't sleeping, I was listening to depressing music and writing even more depressing poetry. First semester freshman year was off to a capital start.

We are now going to talk about mental illness. First off, I am not trained at anything, really. Certainly I am not qualified to talk about the brain or mental illness. I am not offering medical advice, nor am I suggesting you try and gather understanding from what I am going to write. That being said, I am going to tell you what I wish someone had told me back then.

As you know by now, in high school I played three sports. Whenever

I finished practice, I went home and to the OP basketball courts, or worked on the wall (plywood board) for a few hours. I had PE three to four days a week. I exercised a minimum of three hours a day, but often it was more like five hours a day.

During the summer before my freshman year of college I started at Frontier Town, which was very physically demanding. From the time of adolescence, my almost non-stop physical activity caused my brain to release endorphins regularly that made me feel good. Plus, I was literally dating the person I thought was the love of my life, whom I had loved since I was in second or third grade. I was with her every day until I went to college 1,000 miles away from where she did. Remove the endorphins and remove the girl, and what's left but depression?

Of course, there were several reasons for this depression, and the first and foremost was that I hated myself. I mean, I did then and I do now. I don't know why. I also love myself far too much. That doesn't really make much sense, but our brains are not simple little Lincoln Logs all neat and tidy. It's more like M.C. Escher on steroids and mushrooms all day long in there.

Endorphins trigger a positive response in the body that is similar to that of morphine. I don't know much, but I know that if you turn off the spigot of endorphins you better replace it with some drug,[18] or things will go downhill quick, as they did for me. I spiraled for a while, got into super-depressing music, and then pulled myself out of it and joined an intramural lacrosse team. I played in two games, was ejected from the first one for fighting, and threw my back out in the second. When I went to the doctor,[19] he did an MRI and diagnosed me with a herniated disc. I quit the intramural team—they all hated me anyway—and started playing basketball every day, because that was the sport I really loved.

I stayed relatively funk-free during my second semester, acted in a play, and kept playing basketball. I went from academic probation in the fall to Dean's List in the spring, but no one told me why. I didn't know anything about how my body and brain worked. I didn't understand that without that daily self-made drug cocktail of endorphins, I was in for a terrible, crushing reality that I was fully unprepared to handle.

I begged my parents to let me leave Notre Dame, but they said no. I should have just left, but I wasn't a real person yet, I was still working on getting there. So I went back for sophomore year, and I did well. I was involved in the Sophomore Literary Festival, directed my first play, and played lots of basketball. I also started smoking cigarettes and hanging

18 Again, not medical advice.
19 His name was Dr. Moriarty, I shit you not.

out with a guy named Prof, who is now a cop, but he was pretty far from being a cop in those days. I also spent too much time in coffee houses reading poetry, and hanging around open mics. Once I actually caught a guy plagiarizing Maggie Estep, and even had a copy of *Aloud: Voices from the Nuyorican Poets Café* with me as proof, showing him the poem he claimed to have written. At first he swore he wrote it, then admitted he heard a woman read it at another open mic, but he said she claimed to have written it. That was awkward.

I was having a great year, but the best thing I did that year was coach lacrosse. I was the offensive coach for the first-ever lacrosse team at Saint Joseph High School in South Bend. Personality-wise we probably had the best team ever. It was mostly guys that had been cut from the football team for smoking weed, rejects from other sports, and some guys who had never played organized sports. Only a couple of them had even heard of lacrosse before the season. I'm not joking, it was a cast of characters too unbelievable for fiction. One time a fifteen-year-old sophomore was smoking a cigarette on the sideline. We huddled up and he was hiding it in his glove. His glove was steaming, and we all looked at him like, *What the hell?* He just said, "Sorry coach, you want me to put it out?" Then he took a drag and stomped it under his cleat. He was a first-string middie. I'll never forget him taking that last drag.

Still, by some magic we all came together and went undefeated in the regular season. We would win games by 15-20 goals. By the end of that season I had not lost a single game as a coach. It was pretty awesome. We ran a simple triangle motion offense that was hectic to say the least, but had a great attackman that would be recruited by Impy at Rensselaer Polytechnic Institute (RPI). This kid had the ability to take over the game and dominate, just like I had a few years before. He was easy to coach, and he got better every day he played. It was a great experience.

We had a ton of good players besides that attackman, including another good attackman and an incredibly fast and strong midfielder (not the smoker from before, though I think he was kicked off the football team for weed, so I guess he was kind of a smoker). We probably had a good defense too, but who cares about defense?

Our first game was in Naperville, IL, and my father flew out for the game. He told me years later that he would never forget how when my all-star attackman scored the first goal, he high-fived all of his teammates and went back up to the line, and then looked at me and pointed, just like I used to point to my dad. I didn't remember that, but my dad did.

I think we won that game 22-2. Lacrosse was still a new sport for the Midwest in the spring of 1996, and I'm pretty sure many of the guys on the other team didn't understand the rules. I know some of the refs sure didn't. Still, my dad attended the first game I ever coached, and that was pretty cool of him. That was the kind of thing he did: he showed up and he supported me. I know he was disappointed when I stopped playing lacrosse, but I don't think he ever knew how disappointed I was that I stopped playing, too. I had to stop sometime. That's the thing with sports: someday the sport ends and your other life needs to begin.

Still, I didn't know what was going on in my brain behind all the endorphins and exercise. Things seemed good, I was healthy. I went back home for the summer. Our beloved family cocker spaniel, Candy, had just died, which was really hard on my mom. I got a job working on a rough framing crew, building townhouses by the Yacht Club in Ocean Pines; these became Mumford's Woods. After work, I cooked dinner and played basketball practically every night. The trees had started to sing to me for the first time, but I noticed no one else heard them. My parents no longer fought, because they no longer spoke. My mom left my father for my boss. I know I said it before, but come on, that bears repeating.

My father lost it. It was only three weeks before I was supposed to return to South Bend, but I offered him my support. I told him I would stay behind and help him through this. We had dinner together and I drove him back to his car at the school. He was sitting in his car, while I stood outside of it, his window down and I was making my case for why I should drop out of school and stay with him until he got through everything. He just got angrier and angrier at me the more we talked. Finally he screamed that I was ruining his life, and he sped off. I will never know why—maybe it was just because my mom was gone and I wasn't—my father somehow blamed me for what was happening to him.

I went back to South Bend and lived off-campus at the Campus View Apartments, and I got a job at Colorado Steakhouse. The love of my life stopped talking to me, probably because I was letting myself descend into madness. For my whole life my father had called me an asshole, but now I really became one. I stopped playing basketball, I started smoking, and stopped going to class again. I went into the woods between my apartment building and campus, built little campfires, and read Nietzsche until I fell asleep. I dropped out of school. I told the St. Joe head coach I was not going to coach lacrosse again. I eventually started dating someone that really hated me. I flirted with self-destruction.

I was super depressed, but I was also starting to face the reality from which I previously had been hiding. It was a dark hole I had to go down. When I dropped out of school I became scared of falling behind intellectually, so I asked my neighbor who was an English major to rec-ommend books to me. She gave me dozens of books and got me read-ing again. I met Gary, Clint, and Jean at Colorado Steakhouse and they started to become my adopted family. Gary taught me to fly fish, Jean taught me to tend bar, and Clint introduced me to a ton of music, includ-ing (but not limited to) David Bowie, T-Rex, Pulp, Gene, and Suede[20].

This happened to be when things started to get really bad between my dad and I. He started saying some terrible things about my mom and her family, really terrible things I don't know are true, but that haunt me to this day. I stopped taking calls from him. He had somehow conflated my dropping out of college with his life falling apart. I ended up not speaking more than five words to my dad for a full year. I also stopped taking calls from my mother, because she started telling me terrible things about my father's family, too. I couldn't handle all the slander. If you are getting divorced from your spouse, do not say terrible things about your spouse's family to your children. Remember: you are talking about your child's family. Those words are not easily forgotten. If your child is like me, they will *never* be forgotten.

I retreated into books, cigarettes, a self-destructive relationship, and depression.

Let me be clear about this person that hated and dated me. She is beautiful and I love her to this day. I haven't spoken to her in twenty-five years, but I think about her almost every day. It's probably because she has so many songs. I was just at that age when you discover so much great music, and she is associated with a bunch of the best.

There is one important lesson I learned from all of this, but it took years to have the hindsight to understand it: I was most likely always depressed, even if I did not show it. I was able to hide it, to balance my emotions somewhat through all the exercise I was doing. But every time I stopped exercising, depression rushed in. Eventually I replaced exer-cise with smoking cigarettes, and then drinking. This self-medication, while unhealthy, likely allowed me to be a functioning member of soci-ety and deal with my depression. When I finally quit smoking and cut way back on my drinking, the depression was right there waiting for me, and even brought along its friend, anxiety. When reading about panic attacks and anxiety, I saw they were common in people who had a his-tory of alcohol abuse. I mentioned this to my therapist, who said people most likely abuse alcohol because they already have anxiety and depres-sion. Going back over my life, it's obvious that is what I did.

20 Clint hates when people list bands, songs, or books in books.

Remember, I'm not suggesting people should turn to alcohol, tobacco, or drugs to deal with mental illness. Just don't be surprised when they do. But I *am* suggesting that our extreme demonization of alcohol, tobacco, and other drugs might contribute to people not reaching for those crutches in a time of crisis. I know this isn't going to be a popular notion with doctors or scientists, but I think smoking cigarettes is better than jumping off a bridge. If you chose to smoke cigarettes to get through a tough time, I'm not going to judge you.

When we were traveling Europe together, my brother asked me why I smoked so much. I thought about it for a second and gave him an honest answer: "I smoke to feel something inside."

I know now that I wasn't capable of being more honest at the time. However, I should have said, "I smoke to feel something inside *that I don't hate.*"

Quitting lacrosse, dropping out of school, my parents divorcing, losing the love of my life, my dog dying—none of those things caused depression. It was always there, it was always a part of me. Those events just let it come to the surface to be recognized by others, and eventually myself.

ART

This one is really easy.

I was making a documentary about racism in Salisbury, Maryland in 2018 and was able to interview Mayor Jake Day. The interview went on for a few hours, and while it began with us discussing military history and race, we eventually got on the topic of architecture. Jake had studied architecture at Carnegie Melon, and while most of his points were too tangential to make it into the film, there was something that resonated deeply within me. Without getting too far into it, highway systems in the U.S. were largely used to destroy thriving minority neighborhoods. This happened in Salisbury with Route 50, and it happened in most small cities across the U.S. Most highways were built right through minority neighborhoods, dividing the people of those communities from their collective history. It's not something that is often considered but the labor that builds a community represents the lives of its people's ancestors, and not being able to look back at the labor of our ancestors is another way we are severed from a stable foundation. Combining this severing with redlining and a bunch of other abhorrent practices caused the American ghettos to be formed.

These ghettos were unnatural places created by displacement, and often contained hastily built utilitarian housing. These communities were not grown organically, they were thrown together as a byproduct of systemic racism. One of the many issues with this is the architecture in those ghettos, as these were not homes built by ancestors there was no thought put into the aesthetic design of these homes. These were not communities built by the community itself, and this was massively detrimental to the mental health of the inhabitants.

Jake explained how there have been many studies done on the effects of where we live, what we witness in a day, and how that effects our brain. For humans, spatial relationships form the psychology of place. The psychology of space affects how people perceive themselves in relationship to the physical world. Everything matters even the proportion of the building to the street. For instance, when the street is wide and the building is short, it creates a feeling of placelessness. Other things, like attachments on the buildings, or the material palettes used, affect people's perception of themselves. All of that will shape perceptions of value—not just of the buildings where they live, but that person's perception of the value of themselves. This is perceived without needing or being able to verbalize it. Jake brought up Dr Margaret Tarampi, a friend of his who has written extensively on this subject, that architecture affects our mental health. Not just the architecture of our homes, but the architecture we are exposed to and see every day. Our homes, our schools, our offices, our streets, our green space... they all affect our mental health, and the more aesthetically pleasing they are, the healthier we are.

This got me thinking about all the inputs into our mind from external stimuli. Think about television, my old nemesis. Is there anything less aesthetically pleasing than one of those newsfotainment channels, the ones with banners and words scrolling, and smash graphics, and people literally yelling over one another? Imagine a person inviting these images into their brains every day. Of course such a person will not be healthy!

The same is true with social media. Social media companies have literally hired experts on addiction to figure out how to make their sites more addicting. That's horrifying, but it has also been very successful. While I resisted social media for years, I became convinced that I needed it for my business. After spending a few years on it, I picked up a book called *The Shallows: What the Internet is Doing to Our Brains* by Nicholas Carr. After I finished reading it, I deleted my social media for good. I believed my anxiety was only getting worse with the constant input of unsolicited information.

Then I became conscious of the art I was ingesting. Sometimes it would be great novels. Sometimes it was just binge watching *Schitt's Creek* or *30 Rock* on Netflix. Sometimes it was Amanda Palmer's "Ukulele Anthem" on repeat for hours. Sometimes it was books on history. Sometimes it was Agatha Christie. Sometimes it was comedy albums. Sometimes I just listened to *Les Mis* for the 5,000th time. Whatever it was, I controlled it. Shunning the worst elements—social media and newsfotainment—really helped me with this process.

A couple works of art I want to mention are Langhorne Slim's *Strawberry Mansion* album, and Adam Wade's *You Ought to Know Adam Wade* audio book. Both of these guys are my friends, and those two works were extremely comforting to me in the time when I was most in crisis, though for two very different reasons. One line in particular from

Langhorne Slim's *Strawberry Mansion* still rattles around my brain all the time. It's from the song "Panic Attack" and the "she" mentioned is a healthcare professional. "She said, do you ever think about dying, I said, no but sometimes I lie." Langhorne has always gotten me. It comforted me to hear that he was going through the same things I was. That is a weird thing about humans, that hearing a song where someone sings the thoughts we are afraid to say somehow comforts us. Now that I think about it, I guess it's not that weird, as art is communication between the artist and the audience. We consume art to feel something. Hearing a song where the singer vocalizes thoughts we are afraid to speak out loud shines a much-needed light on the dark hollows of the mind.

For Adam Wade's *You Ought to Know Adam Wade,* it was totally different. I was able to just get lost in his stories. They were funny, universal, and incredibly personal. The funny stories about his father, right when I was dealing with grief for my own father, pulled me out of the moment I was experiencing and allowed me to take a longer view of life, which was exactly what I needed.

After I had consumed the work of both artists, I reached out to them to thank them. It was good to connect. Adam and I spoke for a couple of hours about anxiety. Other than my therapist, I would say he and Len Foxwell[21] were the two that helped me understand anxiety the most, and were really there for me in those early days. I am really thankful that Adam and Langhorne keep putting themselves out there, and I'm sure they have helped many people. I know they have helped me.

Writing this book helped me realize how influential art has been in my life. More than a few times art has changed my direction in life, spurred epiphanies, and even pulled me out of deepest despair. I doubt I am alone in this. Art, in whatever form we consume it, might be the single most important force for understanding our world. Just like eating junk food, consuming junk media is unhealthy. Sure, we might be able to do it sometimes, but when we make a habit out of it, we're going to have issues.

Part of taking control of our mental health is to literally control our mental nutrition. It sounds so elementary, but we have more and more been willing to give up control to others. Becoming conscious of this is a necessary step towards mindfulness and good mental health.

---

21 Len Foxwell's section was mostly cut out of this book, but he really helped me in the early days of my anxiety. He'll be mentioned briefly in about 100 pages. Editing a book is hard.

RETURNING TO IRELAND, THE FIRST TIME

The best place for a homeless poet to be lost was Ireland in the late 1990s. I had no desire to go to Ireland before I went. By 1997 I had dropped out of college and was working as a bartender in South Bend, and had no intention of traveling anywhere. Meanwhile, my brother Tom and his best friend, Kirk, planned a two-month European backpacking trip for that autumn. However, Kirk got a great job and backed out of the trip last minute, and after some gentle prodding from my mother, I ended up going with my brother instead.

Before my brother and I got to Ireland, we had visited Iceland, Luxembourg, Amsterdam, and Paris. Tom wanted to go to Ireland because he said we had a place to stay with friends he had met that summer while working at Phillip's Crab House in Ocean City, but Tom says lots of things. I was not entirely sure we had a place to stay. I didn't want to spend the extra money for a flight to Ireland, as I had no desire to go, but Tom convinced me that staying at his friends' home would save me money in the long run. The flights in those days were dirt cheap, and arguing with one of my brother's rare moments of logic and frugality was difficult.

We flew to Dublin and then hopped on the DART (Dublin Area Rapid Transit) to Blackrock. Technically we went to the Seapoint station on the DART, also known as the least-used DART station. There, we were met by Méabh[22].

This is a hard story to tell, because I can get way off track. I went to Europe for two months and ended up staying close to a year. There is a book in that story alone, but that is not this book. Let's just say I fell in love with Méabh that week and I fell in love with Ireland.

Okay, we'll get back to Ireland in a moment, but I am going to talk about what I mean by the word "love," because this is important. As I have said before, I fall in love and I never stop being in love. That's just how I'm wired. As far as I remember, I fell in love for the first time in second or

---

22 It's pronounced Maive.

third grade, and I am still in love with that person. I still think about her every day, and perhaps once a month I still dream about her at night. We don't talk, she is no longer in my life in any way. I don't know how to write about her in this book, I was hoping to not mention her at all, but that turned out to be an unachievable goal. I'm certain she doesn't feel the same way about me that I feel about her, and it actually makes my heart glad to know that. I don't need or even want reciprocity when it comes to love.

Why exactly I don't want reciprocity with someone I'm in love with is complicated, but I'll talk about that in a second. What we need to address first is the, "how can you be in love with multiple people at once?" question that's probably sitting out there for some readers.

Remember that as a child I used to believe in the "one true love" nonsense with which we incessantly indoctrinate our children. We probably invented this "one true love" story because it's easier than having complex conversations about relationships with kids. I think that's dangerous, as I will discuss in later chapters. But what's missing from the conversation when we use the "one true love" copout is that people love differently. There are not quantifiable coefficients of love, and love is not a measurable external force with rules that we can understand. It's a construct, and we use a word "love" and the phase "in love" to encompass many different feelings, and the meanings are different from one person to the next. In a relationship, two people might both profess that they are in love with each other, but they might feel two very different things. Just because they use the same word doesn't mean that they feel the same emotion. Love is not a universal constant, even if we desperately want it to be.

Which brings me to what I mean when I say "love." This word is so tired from overuse that no one blinks an eye when we use the same verb to describe our emotions towards both our grandmother and a basket of chicken wings. What a fool's errand it is to try to qualify and quantify love. We can, at best, talk around the idea of love with analogy or metaphor. One of my favorite lines written about love is from a Japanese folk song that translates roughly "more than the cicada that sings his love, the silent firefly burns." It's such a perfect line, considering it is being sung. Another favorite lyric is from the Iron and Wine song "Fever Dream." "I want your flowers like babies want God's love, or maybe as sure as tomorrow will come." That idea of innocent desire for unconditional acceptance and trust just wrecks me, but you might not like these lines or attach any meaning to them at all. Because love, just like our taste, is unique for each of us.

So what do I mean when I use the phrase "in love" as opposed the word "love?" The best way for me to make the distinction is this: when I love someone, I am comfortable around them. I feel I can be honest and can relax, unlike how I am around strangers, or those I know but don't necessarily love. I can learn to love someone, and once that bond is built, it seems unbreakable. While I can come to love someone over time, that hasn't been my experience with those with whom I am in love. When I meet someone with whom I am in love, I feel as if I already know them. I'm instantly energized.

You might be thinking that I believe in love at first sight. Maybe I do, but at the same time, that sounds trite to me. There's just something old about the connection. Something unknowable that I feel existed before I existed. When I met my wife Caroline, the first words I said to her were "marry me," but that was almost more of a joke. Still, there was something more in that moment. I felt I knew her somehow.

One cold and rainy night in New York, many years after our trip to Europe, my brother and I went into one of our haunts, St. Andrew's Bar. The bartender there told me about a new scotch whiskey he had just gotten in called Talisker Storm, and he poured me a glass. I smelled it, letting the alcohol climb up my nose. I sipped it; it was perfect for that night. Tom swirled it in the snifter, took a swig, and gave his thoughts:

"It tastes like a wooden boat on fire in the sea."

The bartender laughed and concurred.

"Right?" He gestured to me. "What do you think?"

I closed my eyes and tilted the snifter so my nose was deep in the glass. I kept smelling it and smiling.

"It tastes like going home to a place I have never been."

Tom rolled his eyes. The bartender backed away. I took another sip, lost in a moment of nostalgia for a time and place that hadn't yet existed.

Talisker Storm is not my favorite whiskey of all time, but it is my favorite whiskey to drink around a fire while it rains. Or maybe it's my favorite whiskey to sip while telling stories about fire or rain. It's just a scotch, and yet the olfactory and gustatory delight of this particular whiskey contains a familiar spirit that I have always known. It's not that I am in love with the whiskey, it just reminds me of a place that I know is special to me that I just haven't found yet. And yes, I know how crazy this sounds. But this is how I understand the feeling of being in love.

I'm still in love with everyone and everywhere I have ever been in love with. Of course, I'm not constantly thinking of those people or places. Being in love is not what I would describe as comfortable. When I am in love with someone, there's a part of me that wants to be better than I am. I'm inspired to read, write, create, or just move. I become charged. I connect with their energy, which can dictate my being—the energy will influence me. This is why I can be in love with places, with a certain light, with a tree, as well as with people. Of course, I can be comfortable around those I am in love with, I'm not saying this passion causes discomfort. I just wouldn't describe it as comfortable.

I've been in love with Caroline for twenty-three years, and I have lived with Caroline for twenty of those years. I'm not creative every moment of every day, but there has never been an extended period of time when I haven't been working on some creative project in those twenty-three years. I've written books, plays, stories, made movies, and even dived deep into complex D&D campaigns that I created. One of the reasons why my therapist suggested I read *The Soul's Code* was because he noticed that if I wasn't being creative, my depression level would increase. I think this is connected. The love I feel for Caroline is easy and comfortable, it's like falling asleep watching British murder mysteries, but *being in love* with Caroline is why I have sleepless nights editing a film no one will watch, or writing a novel no one will read.

In my young adulthood I moved constantly. I was always leaving those I loved. I needed to leave, there was some emotion beneath my logical level of understanding that pushed me to run away. Just that feeling of being in love made me want to go. Townes Van Zandt in "I'll Be Here in the Morning" sings, "there's no prettier sight that looking back on a town you left behind." Whatever that emotion is that he is capturing with that lyric—and I truly don't think there is a word for it—is what was always pushing me. I wasn't comfortable until I felt that emotion while looking back on the town I had left behind. Or, more correctly, looking back on the people I had left behind.

Because of my inclination to constantly move and my innate curiosity of others, I have come to know many people extraordinarily well in a very small measure of time. Some of those people I have been in love with, and some have said they were in love with me. Very few of them are still in my life in any way. I'm guessing that's because of my personality being, I don't know... challenging? As a reader of a book I have written, you are seeing by far the best version of me. The reality is that I'm not easy to be around. It sounds like a cliché, but I don't know how Caroline has put up with me for as long as she has. Most people, even those that say they love me, can't stand me for long periods of time. For instance, my own brother in the middle of an argument once growled, without a hint of irony, "why do you always have to be you?" In what I thought was an otherwise pleasant conversation, my father once said, "at best, you're pretty difficult." *At best!* My mother once paused, sighed, thought about what she was going to say and then told me, "I love you, I just don't like you very much."

One of my exes once referred to me as the nicest bad boy she ever dated, which for a second I thought was rather cool. She then said that it wasn't that I was bad in a dangerous sense, it was just that something was really off about me. I asked if she meant that I was like when something tastes bad, and she just hesitated for a really long time before changing the subject. She said this while we were dating, mind you. Another ex said I was "like a cross between *Untamed Heart*[23] and *Say Anything*.[24] Interesting for an hour-and-half, but after a while really exhausting." Again, this was said while we were dating. Probably the nicest thing any ex ever said about me was when Ericka, decades after we dated, said I was a "human rainy day."

But no matter what someone says to me, or how their feelings might change for me, once I love, I love forever. No matter if someone cheated on me and then gleefully told me about it with the hopes of hurting me, or told me they hated me and I was ruining their life, or told me I was a waste of their time, or told me I smelled bad, or whatever—I still love them to this day. I don't enjoy testing this hypothesis, but it seems no matter what someone does to me, I still love them eternally. With respect to love, something in me breaks permanently and I can't put whatever that is back together. And that's not always bad.

For instance, during the summer of 1997 when I was twenty-one years old and living in South Bend, I met a girl who was sitting under a tree reading poetry. I stopped to talk to her, and I remember telling her I just wanted to know someone who would sit under a tree and read poetry. We talked about poetry for hours under that tree, and that night she came over to my house. We sat on the couch, which was my only furniture in this huge two-story house in which I lived alone at the time while my roommates were all home for the summer. She and I read poetry to each other by candlelight, I gave her a massage, we smoked weed, and we kissed. I talked about how I had dropped out of school, and how I had no plans other than to work as a bartender and read. In those days, I had no dreams, I just wanted to read poetry and to know others who did. I wanted to get rid of the idea of becoming something, and just exist in the moment. She slept that night in my arms, on the

23 1993 Christian Slater, Marisa Tomei film where Christian Slater's character is a dishwasher who believes he has had a heart transplant from baboon. This is because of the "plant growing out of my arm story.
24 1989 John Cusack, Ione Skye film about a guy who is incapable of shutting up.

couch. I don't think I slept. I could rarely sleep that summer.

I saw her twice more that week before she left town. I forget her name. She made me a hemp necklace I wore for years, until it finally became so threadbare and worn it fell apart, not unlike my memory. I am still in love with her. I dreamt about her just the other night, not long after I started writing this book, and twenty-three years after I had last seen her. I bet it has been twenty years since I could remember her name. But I will never forget her sitting under that tree in her hippie skirt, reading poetry. I will never forget how the moonlight streaming through those huge windows paled her freckled skin in that big, empty house. I will never forget her accepting me as what I was in that moment, not what I was going to be. We did not have sex, though we certainly could have. Our moment was about a connection, the connection is what mattered. She was the present, the urgency of a summer evening, but at the same time the emptiness of any specific need or desire. Maybe she was my first real taste of oblivion, as we existed without any ties to our past or, as it turns out, our future. She was a poem. I wonder if I was something like that to her, if she even remembers me, or if she is even still alive. I know it doesn't matter. We never love equally, and it is very easy to love those that don't love us at all.

So, getting back to Ireland: when I say I fell in love with Ireland, I mean that in one week it became more of a home to me than any place I have ever been. To this day there is no place where I am more comfortable and more inspired.

There are places that exist that resonate deep in our being, that match the rhythm of our spirits. Maybe for most people, it's where they grew up. The word home has so many layers of meaning, I can't say for sure I fully understand it. There are people that match our rhythms too, those who we are instantly attracted to, or who provide us a comfort others never will. These are people and places that inexplicably complement our lives, imbue our stories with meaning, or free that kernel of who we are that we had buried deep inside. We belong to these people and these places, they do not belong to us. They are our mirrors, allowing us to see ourselves anew.

My brother and I traveled to Ireland on October 29th, 1997. On November 2nd Méabh's mother made a big Sunday meal for us, my first of many Sunday dinners cooked at her home. On November 3rd I wrote these words:

Dinner last night was so beautiful I can't even begin to explain it. I love this country, and I love Méabh, and I love her whole family.

Enough said, I can't say enough about this place. Words best left for poets. Words best left for the heart to digest.

The day we arrived, Méabh had ridden her bicycle to the Seaport station to pick us up. It was raining, she was wearing a light raincoat with a hood covering her head. She walked her bike beside us and spoke quickly, every word sounding like an intentional note of a familiar song. She said something inconsequential. Later she referred to it, and Tom made it clear he hadn't been listening. But I had, and I let her know. She smiled at me for the first time.

I don't know if my experience in Ireland was unique, but the people I casually met there were so different than people I met in America. People in Ireland were sincere, but at the same time they didn't take themselves too seriously. There was kindness mixed with self-deprecating humor. There was a genuine curiosity that existed in everyone I encountered there—I found it hard to go to a pub in Ireland and not strike up a conversation with a complete stranger. In fact, the only way I was able to go to a pub and not get into such a conversation was to bring a book. Everyone I met there had a deep respect for reading books. The Irish barista was better read than the American English teacher. They were all dreamers who read books. They were my people.

The land of my youth, the Delmarva Peninsula, is old. Buildings are decrepit and anything new is generic and without soul. This society was built on injustice and the deep wounds of slavery still festered, having not yet scarred over. There was so much beauty in this crumbling world, but that was almost all due to Nature, who was far more energetic and prepared for this time. She sped to reclaim her dominion. I loved the land of my youth, or better put, I loved the earth, the sea, and the rivers. But I felt no kinship with the people. The young with inspiration left, and indeed from an early age every adult that knew me for more than a minute was sure I was going to leave. I knew I didn't belong, even if I couldn't identify why. The conflict I felt was largely unspoken by genteel society, and I was pushed out the door the same way they pushed conflict under the rug. America had a problem with its past that it refused to address, and the end result was that the old places fell over and the old people were forgotten. The place of my youth, the only home I had known, was a collection of too many bad memories and too few remembered dreams.

When I went to Ireland, I drank in a pub that had been there for five hundred years. And it wasn't considered that old. The building itself had actually stood for nine hundred years. Nothing in America exists that is close to being as old as that. I was welcome in that pub. I told stories in that pub, and stories were told to me there. I felt connected, necessary, and ephemeral all at once. The people of Ireland are not just the inheritors of an ancient culture, they are the creators of that culture, its stewards, its champions. The landscape reflects this. It's impossible to go to Ireland and not be struck silent by the deep shades of green of their pastoral farms. Certainly climate has much to do with this beauty, but it's also culture. Irish agriculture is grass-based, which is what the earth wants. Animals eat the grass, give it poop, move on, and the grass regrows. This is what the bison did in America for thousands of years, eventually creating some of the most fertile soil on the planet. Irish farmers learned from nature and worked in conjunction with nature. America chose another way: instead of respecting the dirt and learning from it, we got rid of the bison, grew corn, turned it into ethanol, and burned it in our cars.

I think I felt at home in Ireland because ancient places don't push you away. American ghosts haunt, Irish spirits guide. The Irish have learned from the mistakes of the past, and they know they need the dreams of the young to have any future. I felt at home in Ireland because I was welcomed.

Who I am and how I am wired means that I will always love Ireland and Méabh. I don't know if I would have loved one without the other, and I will never know. In life we don't get second chances.

After that first fateful week, I decided to move to Ireland. My brother and I continued our tour of Europe, and when he returned to New York, I returned to Ireland for the first time. Now the reason I am telling you about Ireland at all, is that it is relevant to the story of my father and I.

There I was, an unwashed drifter landing in Ireland in mid-December 1997 with about $300 in my pocket and no place to stay. I spent the first couple of nights in a hostel, found a job, and about a week or two later rented a flat in Ranelagh. I loved my little flat in Ranelagh. I lived at 7 Edenvale Rd, in one room heated just by a fireplace, and had less than a minute of hot water per day. I usually used peat moss for heat, unless I was really flush and then would splurge on actual wood. I had a wooden table, a wooden chair, and two candlesticks which provided all the light I would use to read and write.

During in my time in Ireland I worked at seven different places; because I was an illegal immigrant I did pretty much anything I could for pay. This was in the midst of the Celtic Tiger, the late 90s Irish economic boom, so there was plenty of work to be had. I was a cocktail waitress (that was what the barman called me), a bouncer, a waiter, a barman, a laborer, a barista, and finally a cook. The early weeks were especially hard, as at first I was so broke I had insufficient money for food. I would usually get a shift meal in most places, which was the only food I ate that day. I walked to and from work in order to save money on bus fare. When I worked in pubs I worked late at night, and on the walks home I would keep looking down for dropped coins. This was before the Euro was launched, and Ireland was still on the Irish Pound, or "punt." There were one punt coins that late night revelers easily dropped, and I scoured the gutters and sidewalks on the long walk home looking for them. Usually I picked up enough for a pack of cigarettes. I did the same thing on the way into work, when I worked as an early morning barista.

For my first two months in Ireland I almost always held two jobs, working roughly sixty hours a week. When not working, I wrote and read voraciously. Throughout my time in Ireland, I read on average four books a week, I also discovered Nick Drake and Kila (still two of my favorites), and had my first taste of whiskey[25].

Ireland spoke to me in a way no other place ever has. It has always been hard for me to write about, because any words I use will sound trite or come out wanting. My life was perfect when I was there because I had a clean slate. There were no expectations, no one wanted anything from me. It was true freedom.

At the same time, I was lucky to have surrogate parents. Méabh and I dated occasionally but were always friends, and Méabh's parents were very kind to me. I think Méabh's mother unconditionally loved me. She was a grade school teacher and, according to Méabh, always seemed to have an affinity for boys. Once her oldest moved out of the house to become a doctor, I was the only boy around. At least that was how Méabh explained her mother's love for me. I tried to explain to Méabh that moms always liked me because I was polite and liked to eat what was put in front of me—for most moms that was enough.

It was not the same with Méabh's father. I think he had a hard time figuring out what to make of me. He certainly didn't want his brilliant daughter, a future doctor, to end up with a bum, which I was, for the most part. But at the same time I was a curiosity in his house because I was from America, and he had lots of questions about America. He knew I loved to read, and gave me books. I read everything he gave me, and then I discussed it with him with confidence. As much as he probably didn't want me around Méabh, he did like having me around. We

---

25 I believe Méabh literally means "one who intoxicates" which if true is truer for her in more ways than one.

talked books, but we also talked about Irish politics, American politics, and pretty much anything embarrassing that had to do with America.

For instance, in a rare moment that he had the television on, he was flipping channels and landed on the Jerry Springer Show, which had just started to be shown on Irish TV. On screen was some argument between a mother and a daughter who were both trying to date the same guy. He asked me if this represented most Americans. I laughed.

"Honestly, I have no idea where they find these people. They really must scour the worst corners of America for them."

At that moment the mother on TV said, "Look, we're from slower lower Delaware."

Méabh's father, surprised at our luck, quickly looked at me and pointed. "And where is that?"

I shook my head.

"That would be about five miles from where I grew up."

My father wrote to me, saying he wanted to come visit on his Christmas break. I told him not to come. He came anyway; he literally showed up one day at Méabh's parents' house completely unannounced, as he had their address but not mine. Méabh's father told him to get lost. I love that man. He literally would not even let my dad in for a cup of tea.

Now, Méabh's father had his reasons. By this time I had told Méabh's father that my dad blamed me for his failures. I told him about my father driving away from me while screaming that I was ruining his life. I told him how my father was violent, but how he stopped when I got bigger than him. I told him my father was a bully and he treated me like shit, because my father did all of those things, and I was mad at him. Méabh's father didn't want anything to do with my dad, and I guess in his own way wanted to protect me from my father. It was pretty nice of him.

Méabh's father told my dad to leave the address of where he was staying and said he would get word to me. I came home from work with plans to spend the next day and night alone with Méabh, a rare thing since I worked sixty hours a week and Méabh was in medical school. Instead, I saw a note from Méabh that my father was in town.

I met my dad for coffee at a little café called Café Mocha on South Anne's Street, just off of Grafton's street. We talked for thirty minutes and then I left.

Yes, he had traveled all the way to Ireland and I only had a cup of coffee with him. That was still the longest we had spoken in almost a year. It was an awkward, painful conversation, and he was clearly still angry at me. The last thing I said to him was something to the effect of,

"I love you, Dad, but leave me alone." Honestly, I might not have said "I love you." I don't know.

Here's the thing about growing up: sometimes it's not easy. Sometimes you leave stuff behind. My dad was cruel to me and my brother. Then my mom broke him by cheating on him, and he blamed me for some reason I will never understand. I had to break from the cycle of emotional abuse, and the way I did that was by going to another country. For the longest time, I thought the reason he came to Ireland was just to keep up appearances. Maybe he was thinking something to the effect of: *Yes, the good son dropped out of college and moved to Ireland, but I visit him for the holidays.* But now I think something else was going on in my dad's brain those days.

At that point, my father had not spoken to his brother Mike in thirty years. If my grandfather was Willie Loman (and he basically was), my dad was Happy Loman and Mike was Biff Loman. I often heard how similar I was to Uncle Mike from both of my parents. I wonder if my dad started to believe the same thing that happened to him and Mike was happening between him and his son. He might have come to Ireland because he wanted to bury the hatchet and be on speaking terms with me, but when he saw me, all the anger he still had made it impossible for him to come close to any kind of apology or anything other than superficial conversation. Still, I think he feared I was going to become another Mike in his life.

Mike killed himself sometime between when my father had his stroke and when he died. I remember getting the phone call very clearly. It was 2018, and at the time I was running for state delegate in Maryland, and had just left an event in Caroline County where I had spoken at length about mental illness. It was dark out; Bill Duck was driving when I got the call from my mother. Mike had been living in a car and shot himself. Bill asked me how I was, and I answered honestly that I didn't know. I thought about the time I lived in a car, which I'll discuss later. I thought about how everyone in the family said I was so much like this person that I didn't know. I had a strong connection to Mike, but I also didn't have any relationship with him.

Many people said he was the smartest person in our family. I only really spoke to Mike once: he drove me from O'Hare Airport to South Bend when I had just turned nineteen. I didn't know he was picking me up from the airport—it was supposed to have been my grandfather—but he didn't get back from a trip in time so Mike had to come get me. I knew right away that it was Mike. He looked like a thin version of my dad. I don't think I had seen him in over a decade, and even then it was only in passing; he never wanted anything to do with Tom or me.

Mike and I actually had a great conversation the whole way to South Bend. He was a polymath, and he was challenging in his dialogue, which I liked. At that point he had read everything I had read, or at least he had enough of a working knowledge to guide a discussion to what he wanted to talk about, except for poetry. He didn't know shit about poetry.

After that car ride I thought I might have a relationship with Mike, but I never saw him again. I wrote him a few letters but he never responded. Apparently he still wanted nothing to do with me.

Anyway, I'm not Mike and I'm not my father. However, a part of both of them lives in me. I think I understand why my uncle killed himself, and also understand why my father stopped speaking to him. They were both wrong, but I understand being wrong. Being wrong is human.

Was I wrong to only have a cup of coffee with my father when he came to Ireland? Was I wrong to not properly introduce him to Méabh's parents and sisters? Was I wrong to not let him know where I worked? I still don't know. Sometimes I think so. Sometimes I think I did exactly what I needed to do to become the person I am today.

A few days after my dad left Ireland, I got a job at the same café where I had met him. I worked there as a barista and a waiter. Every time I passed the table where we'd had our coffee I thought about him. I loved working at Café Mocha, perhaps because part of me loves being haunted.

That Sunday night at dinner, Méabh's mother let her husband have it for not letting my father into the house, if only for a minute. Méabh's sisters, Aoife and Fionnuala peppered in their opinions while Méabh and I stole glances at one another.

"Surely you could have let him in for a moment?"

"I didn't know where you all were or when you were coming back, much less if Dan was with you. I don't know the man."

"But surely you could have given him a cup of tea?"

Méabh's father smiled.

"Dan told him not to come. He has his reasons. I trust Dan's judgment."

God, I love that man. Not many adults had ever said they trust me. No fathers of the girls I dated had ever said that about me before. As long as I lived in Ireland, I was invited to their Sunday dinners, and Méabh's parents treated me with a respect I have rarely seen to this day. Those dinners were some of the best I have ever had.

After about two months living in Ireland, I became a cook at Café Mocha. For the first time since being there I had a steady income and could quit my second job. I was able to spend more time reading and writing, and more time with Méabh. She introduced me to some great music, including her classmate Damian Rice's band *Juniper*, and my favorite live show at the time, *Kila*. We went to the Irish Film Center and saw some wonderful films including *The Tango Lesson*, which is still one of my favorites. Maybe more importantly, when I walked to work and when I walked home, I made it a point to never look at the ground. I could find my way from Ranelagh to South Anne Street just by looking at the chimneys, antennas, and rooftops I got to know so well.

I eventually came back to the United States because I started to believe that I was hiding in Ireland. It felt like a permanent vacation. I was also legitimately concerned about being exposed as an illegal immigrant and being deported. It's hard to feel like you belong somewhere when you know you can be kicked out at any moment, so I left Ireland because I felt like I didn't belong there, but almost from the moment I left I believed I didn't belong anywhere else.

ROBERT ALTMAN PICKED ME UP FOR COKE, AND THOMAS MERTON AT A URINAL

Yes, that's a weird chapter heading, but as any good storyteller will tell you, the easiest way to hook someone is to tell a story about someone they know. Since most people know of famous people, stories about famous people are easy. They are cheap, but they can hook you. That was something my dad understood.

You know when someone says you are "drinking the Kool-Aid?" They usually mean someone is so extreme that they are willing to believe anything, or have some manner of extraordinarily misplaced devotion. The reference is to the Jonestown massacre, masterminded by the cult leader Jim Jones. My dad worked with that very Jim Jones. It was at a summer camp or something similar, in Indiana or Ohio, I don't remember the details... but still. My dad was full of stories like that, and I never understood how someone could have so many weird brushes with fame. While everyone's probably met a famous person or two, my father was just an athletic director in a small town on Maryland's Eastern Shore, and yet he had dozens of stories like this.

My dad had this knack for meeting famous people, slipping into their world for just for a moment. I can't explain it, but somehow he passed this on to me. It might have been that my dad was very aware of celebrity, so when he encountered someone famous he was more likely to recognize them. But I'm usually clueless about celebrities, yet I have the same tendency, I don't know if such a propensity for famous-adjacent run-ins can be genetic, but it makes for some weird stories. Some of *my stories* were technically my dad's stories that somehow involved me—like the Robert Altman story.

I worked in the film and television industry for two decades, so naturally conversations at work would often be about films. From time to time, someone would bring up legendary filmmaker Robert Altman. They would usually mention *M*A*S*H*, *The Player*, *Gosford Park*, or *Short Cuts*, and then I would casually say:

"I actually met Robert Altman once. He picked me up for Coke."

Then I would pause, as I wanted that to register. The last sentence didn't really make sense, but most people were half listening anyway, so filled in the details themselves. Eventually they demanded I tell the story, which—like all stories that originated from my father—was wholly unsatisfying. I'd continue:

"When I was a kid, we would stay in lots of hotels. And when we would get to a new hotel, my dad would take my brother and I 'exploring.' Usually he would give us seventy-five cents each and let us get whatever we wanted from the vending machines, or play video games. One day we were exploring a hotel in northern Chicago and we ran ahead of my dad. As he came around the corner he saw a man holding me up so I could put money in the soda machine. My dad looked at him and said, 'you're Robert Altman.' Robert Altman put me down and shook my dad's hand and they spoke briefly. Apparently he was there making a film called *A Wedding*. I've never seen it."

Okay, so I have told this is a story for roughly thirty years, but when finally looking it up I found that *A Wedding* was made in 1978, and I was two years old then. Why would a two-year-old be running so far ahead of his father that he lost sight of him long enough for an acclaimed director to physically pick him up, and why was a two-year-old drinking Coke? I know it was the '70s, but come on! Still, don't ever let facts ruin a good story.

As I said before, my parents' first date was at the 1968 Democratic Convention in Chicago. That fact is undeniable and confirmed by multiple sources. However, depending on the era you knew my father, he claimed to either be in the middle of Lincoln Park with his Weatherman pals standing six feet away from Allen Ginsberg and Jerry Rubin, and fortuitously escaping right before the violence; or he was in the International Amphitheater visiting a friend who was a delegate. Either way, it really was my parents' first date and while this may have been a ominous sign for their marriage that went ignored, I'm glad they did because otherwise I wouldn't be here.

Another story my dad frequently told was about getting a last-minute front-row seat to see Peter O'Toole in *Macbeth*. After delivering the extraordinary soliloquy from Act V ("Tomorrow and tomorrow and tomorrow"), O'Toole paused for thunderous applause, calmly walked off stage opposite my father and vomited into a trashcan. Because my dad's seat was so far over to the side of the theater, he could see backstage. He always said it was the best performance he had ever seen, and he was amazed that anyone could perform at that level while being completely drunk.

It's a good story, sure, but depending on when and to whom he was telling it, it could also have been Richard Burton in Camelot, right after the song "How to Handle a Woman." Or, if you ask my best friend Mark Decker, it was Richard Kiley in *Man of La Mancha,* during the quick change in the first act's opening number, "I, Don Quixote." Mark swears this is the version that is most likely to be true, and backs up his claim by pointing out that the Macbeth soliloquy is in Act V and the Camelot solo is in Act II, and it's improbable that anyone that drunk could get that far into a show before puking. Anyway, Mark told the Kiley version of this story at my father's memorial and sang a beautiful version of "The Impossible Dream" for all those in attendance.

My father did tell another story about Peter O'Toole that Mark and I both agree upon. Dad had gone to see O'Toole in a play in Chicago, but a huge blizzard blew in and the performance was cancelled. My dad and a handful of other theatergoers were stuck in the lobby trying to figure out what to do when O'Toole himself entered and saw them all standing around. When he realized their plight, he invited them all into the theater, sat them down in the front row and then disappeared backstage. A few moments later, he reappeared with a book of Shakespeare's sonnets and proceeded to read them to the enraptured, tiny audience for two hours. I can't imagine what was going through my father's mind on that snowy night, sharing with just a dozen strangers the words of the greatest poet, read by perhaps the greatest actor.

We will never know if one or all of these things did really happen, or if they just happened in my dad's head. But I'm inclined to believe at least one of them happened, given my own penchant for experiencing such strange events.

For instance, Robert Duvall absolutely hates me, which is odd because we've never met. I was filming a commercial with *Teen Wolf* star Tyler Posey on the Paramount backlot in Los Angeles, the one that is made to look like New York City. Our director of photography was Barry Markowitz, who apparently can't go fifteen minutes without getting a phone call from Robert Duvall. When we were on the tech scout and his phone rang for the eleventh time I nicely asked Barry to ask Mr. Duvall if they could speak in an hour or so. Unprovoked, Duvall called me a Gucci communist and said I would never work in this town again even though he was saying that from New York and we were in LA (though it looked like New York at the time).[26]

Bear in mind that I worked as a waiter at five restaurants, a barista at two cafes, and a bartender in four bars. I waited on Muhammad Ali

---

26 So, what I actually said was probably closer to, "Tell that fascist that you can gossip and braid each other's hair in like an hour, but we need to do a real day's work now, something an actor like him wouldn't understand." As I said, totally unprovoked.

and Billy Jean King, both of whom I consider icons, and a shit-ton of other celebrities. I never treated them different than any other people, and when I was a waiter, I never even acknowledged who they were, which was a good habit for me since sometimes I had no idea who they were. While it was awesome and special for me to meet and serve Ali and King, when you work in service in NYC such is expected. That's not what I am talking about here—it's the random encounters that make fun stories.

For instance, when Caroline and I were planning our wedding we wanted to incorporate all family traditions into the ceremony, and the piece of Catholic tradition I chose was a reading from Thomas Merton's *No Man is an Island* ("Love not only prefers the good of another to my own, but it does not even compare the two."). I was talking to my father and going through all the various readings and poems we had selected and he knew every single one of them except for Merton's.

"Oh, you don't know who Thomas Merton is?" I asked arrogantly. I had probably read Merton for the first time three months before this call.

"No, I know Thomas Merton, I just don't know that selection. I actually met Thomas Merton once, at a urinal."

My dad was so weird.

I don't want to give the impression that my dad was some kind of star fucker because he wasn't. Yes, he used to hang out with Kelly McGillis at her bar in Key West in the early 2000s, when he drank pretty heavily after the divorce. Kelly liked him (so he said) because he directed high school theater, and she said her high school theater director was one of the greatest influences on her life. So yeah, he drank at Kelly's bar a lot, but overall I would not say he sought out famous people, but he respected them. Sometimes.

There was a time he was in Baltimore at a wedding or a bar or something and a band was playing. He drunkenly walked up to the band and said something like, "You guys are pretty good, is this what you do, or do you have a day job?" One of them laughed and said:

"Well, I'm the Mayor of Baltimore."

My dad laughed and very loudly yelled to Kevin McNulty across the room:

"Hey Kevin, this guy says he's the Mayor? I thought I was the Mayor?"

Kevin rushed over and said hello to Martin O'Malley[27] and quickly moved my inebriated father away.

Still, my dad was weirdly inspired by celebrity, probably because he loved sports and theater. Maybe he loved sports and theater because of

---

27 Who soon after became Governor O'Malley.

how they lifted up the spirit. Both are celebrations of achievement, and of the exceptional.

I think my father believed he was exceptional, even if he was never necessarily celebrated for being such. I remember after the stroke, he told a doctor he was a great athlete in college. Dan Crotty, who had flown across the country to see him, was sitting at my father's bedside when he said it, and Dan let out a little laugh and said, "Oh no." I'm sure Dan didn't know what to do at that moment, but it must have been a little funny (and a little heartbreaking) to hear my father profess athletic prowess he certainly never had. Maybe my dad believed that he was always going to be great, but didn't know how. Creating a fantasy that he was great in the distant past solved the problem. That, or perhaps he had so many memories of greatness—even if it was the greatness of others—that it made sense to his damaged brain that it was his life he was remembering.

When I was being scouted by Notre Dame they brought me to a football game for my official recruiting trip, the 1993 Florida State game.[28] Before the game, we were on the field and I got to meet O.J. Simpson. My dad had a picture from the stands of me meeting him, but you couldn't even tell what was happening, as it was taken from so far away. Still, he blew it up and put it on his wall... after the O.J. Simpson trial[29].

When I was at Notre Dame and working for the Sophomore Literary Festival I suggested we invite my favorite poet of all time, Gwendolyn Brooks. She lived in Chicago and agreed to come, and because I suggested her, I got to go to dinner with her and a few other students before her talk. At dinner, someone asked her if she preferred the term "Black" or "African American." She said she not only preferred Black, but she made us promise then and there to only use the term Black and always capitalize it. Brooks explained that "African American" popped up conveniently during the Black Power and Black is Beautiful movements, and it was a way to separate Black people from America by implying that they don't really belong here. Someone then asked her if we needed to capitalize "white" too and she said, "What do I care?"

Unfortunately, whenever anyone today mentions Gwendolyn Brooks, they often state how in 1950 she was the first "African American" to have won the Pulitzer Prize. Every time I read that, it bothers me. I was pleased when both the AP and the MLA finally adopted the guidelines of capitalizing "Black," even if it didn't happen until

28 Known as the Game of the Century. One of two dozen games known as the Game of the Century.
29 The Trial of the Century.

twenty years after Brooks' death.

I was enraptured by Gwendolyn Brooks. She was a force of nature, and I hung on her every word. As far as I know, her talk had the greatest turnout for any Sophomore Literary Festival writer, ever. The auditorium was standing-room only, and the crowd overflowed out into the hallway of Hesburgh Library, with people straining to hear her words. It was a snowy night in February 1996 in South Bend, and some people had driven three hours one way just to hear her speak.

After her talk, Brooks sat down at a table and signed books for two hours without taking a break. I stood by her side like an impromptu bodyguard the entire time and I couldn't tell you how many stories she listened to about how she had changed someone's life. She listened and never rushed anyone, signing everything they brought. I fetched her new pens and glasses of water, but otherwise just stood at attention by her side. At the end of the event, Brooks called the head of the Sophomore Literary Festival over and talked to her for a minute. I didn't hear what they spoke about, but apparently it was me. Finally the line was gone and she began packing. I offered to carry her bag for her. She looked at me curiously, without a smile.

"I hear you were the one that suggested I come here. Why?"

"Because you wrote *The Crazy Woman*."

She paused.

"I'm sorry, what?"

"Because you wrote *The Crazy Woman*," I said louder.

"I heard you the first time. That little poem? Why?" Brooks pulled out a copy of *Blacks* and flipped right to the page. I replied:

"When I was in fifth grade, it was in my American Literature text book. It was the first thing I ever read that spoke to me, and told me it was okay to be different. You were the first person that told me it was okay to not be what everyone else wanted me to be. It changed my life."

Brooks looked silently at me for what felt like a full minute. I knew how many stories she had just heard, and realized that every day for the last forty years, she had probably heard some version of the same story. But on this night, she made me think that maybe she was hearing something unexpected. She probably knew I needed to believe I was an original, maybe because she knew what that felt like. That *is* what the poem is about, after all. Or maybe she was just being nice. Either way, she signed the page and handed me my most precious possession. I helped her up and walked her through the library to her waiting car as she held my arm. After the driver opened the door, she gripped my forearm tight and looked me right in the eyes, but said nothing else to me; she just smiled and got into the waiting Lincoln Town Car, looking ahead as it drove away.

There are not many nights from 1996 I can remember like they happened yesterday, but this night was an exception.

My father taught me to hang out at the stage door. After every play or musical we saw, we would go around back to congratulate the artists for their labor. It became second nature to me. When Billy Joel came to Notre Dame, I went to the concert with my good friend Kyle, who is the biggest Joel fan I know. After the show I said, "Let's go around back and say hello."

"What are you talking about?" responded Kyle.

"Well, he's got to leave. Let's go say hi."

"I don't think we're allowed to."

"Eh," I said with a dismissive wave. We walked behind the Stepan Center and waited with three other people. After about thirty minutes, Joel came out and Kyle was completely dumfounded.

Now, like all white kids that grew up in the 80s, I liked Billy Joel enough, but I wasn't that big of a fan. I was at the concert because I liked live music and Kyle wanted to go with someone. I looked at Kyle and saw he wasn't going to say anything. A couple of people asked Joel for autographs, which he kindly obliged, and he took a picture with someone. He was about to get in his car when I called after him.

"Hey, Mr. Joel. Thank you for writing 'And So it Goes.'"

Billy Joel looked me in the eye and nodded.

"Alright," he said, and got in the car and left. Kyle was staring daggers at me.

"Of course *you* talked to him."

I was, in fact, at the same venue just a couple of months later watching a debate between P.J. O'Rourke and Michael Moore. My buddy John—the one we all called "Prof"—and I were there, and we were cheering on Moore and thumbs downing O'Rourke (I don't boo, unless it's sarcastic, but I will give someone a thumbs down). O'Rourke kept calling Moore a Marxist, and Moore was ignoring it for a while, until he finally protested.

"Look," Moore said, "you can't call me a Marxist because I have never read Karl Marx. I mean, he sounds like a good guy and, according to you, he agrees with me on everything. But still you can't call me a Marxist until I've read him."

Afterwards, there was a reception with the speakers that anyone could have attended, but there were only forty students present. Thirty-eight of them flocked around O'Rourke, so Prof and I got a chance to talk to Moore by ourselves for a few minutes. I offered him my copy of

The Communist Manifesto, which I happened to have on hand, of course.

"I know you say that you aren't a Marxist because you haven't read Karl Marx," I said, "but I thought maybe you would want to read him and see what he's about."

Michael Moore took the book.

"Are you serious? This is the guy?"

"This is the guy. I think you will like him."

Michael Moore laughed.

"Thanks, man. I think I will, too."

Alright, of course Michael Moore read Marx before 1996. Of course Billy Joel had heard a thousand people thank him for writing this song or that song. I would be surprised if Moore hadn't already been given thirty-five *Manifestos* and seven *Das Kapitals* by this point. But you know what? I still think giving someone a book is better than asking for an autograph, or posing for a picture with them. I believe my father taught me that.

It was Christmas Night in 2003 and my dad, Tom, Caroline, and I were by the fireplace of the bar at One If By Land, the fabulous New York restaurant in the former home of Aaron Burr. I was grabbing drinks for everyone, and heard my dad mention David Bowie. He would always pronounce it like Bowie, Maryland ("boo-ee") instead of the right way. I had given up correcting him, plus I was pretty drunk already. But it sparked a memory from when I'd worked as a freelance production assistant, when another PA had told me that he was dating David Bowie's goddaughter or niece or something.

There's something you should probably know about me: when I drink, I believe I become smarter, or at least I become more correct about things. Also, I have been told I become louder when I drink. I don't know if this is true or not, but people say it is.

Anyway, I loudly recounted this anecdote while holding three drinks and stumbling around the room when I bumped into someone. I looked, saw David Bowie, and apologized. He was there with his stunning wife Iman and their three-year-old, daughter.

He smiled and said, "No problem."

He was kind and gentle as he walked past this drunk asshole. While I was stiff, entirely frozen. I wished I had said something other than my hastily mumbled "Sorry." Yes, I was the least cool person around the coolest person to possibly ever live, but it wasn't that: David Bowie had saved my life. He had no idea, and while I had a chance to tell him, I didn't.

DAVID BOWIE SAVED MY LIFE
or
South Bend, A Second Time

I don't believe in free will. I'm not going to get into it too much, but I want to put it out there, because I think it's bullshit when people blame individuals for killing themselves. Yes, it's fucked up and sad when people kill themselves, but let's not act like they are making some kind of choice to make someone else's life worse. It has nothing to do with you.

Also, this needs to be said: if you are remotely considering suicide and not seeking help, put down this book now and reach out to someone for help. In the U.S. the National Suicide Hotline is 800.273.8255. I have many thoughts about suicide, and they are not going to help anyone struggling. Please seek professional help. I did, and it was the right thing to do. I wish I'd sought it out long ago. I would probably be much healthier right now.

Okay, so all that being said, I still think about suicide every day; or at least, I think about suddenly dying everyday, usually when I am driving. I don't think it's a big deal. Now, I don't fantasize about suicide, and I don't want to kill myself—in fact I don't want to die at all. I just think about it. I think about everyone I have ever loved every day, too. Thoughts move quickly and the day is long.

There was a time in my life that sits between the person I was and the person I became, between my first and second act. That time was really hard. At this point, you have no chance of following any semblance of a timeline so I'll try and make it easy for you.

Birth (1976)
Childhood (super good at crabbing)
Baseball (Little League 2 years)
Lacrosse (7 years)
College (South Bend '94 – '96)
Coaching Lacrosse (Spring '96)
Dropped out of college, started working at Colorado Steakhouse

in SB (Autumn '96)
Coaching Soccer (Autumn '97)
Europe Trip (2 Months, Autumn '97)
Ireland (6 Months Dec '97 – May '98)
Ocean City with Alex and seven sorority girls (summer '98)—
    WE ARE HERE
Coaching Soccer again (Autumn '98)
Homeless (September '98 – December '98)
South Bend Second Time (Octoberish '98 – May '99)

After returning from Ireland, I lived with my high school buddy Alex Howarth and seven sorority girls at the beach for the summer. Our three-story townhouse was a place of nightly parties that usually smelled of a mixture of sand, salt, stale beer, old pizza, and dried urine. It wasn't the right place for me at that time, but I had no sense of what I was supposed to be doing, so I just lived there because it was fun and Alex is a great guy. But in the autumn he left for graduate school, and one by one the girls went back to school, too. I was the last person to leave the beach house that year. The second-to-last-tenant—I think her name was Heather—left me her old Abnormal Psychology textbook with a Post-It Note on it that said "Maybe you can use this to figure yourself out." So yeah, I was in a pretty dark place.

After the lease was up, I had nowhere to go. I moved into my car, worked construction in the morning, and coached soccer in the afternoon. Each day I would shower at WCS, and park in the Meatland grocery store parking lot in Ocean Pines to read and smoke cigarettes until I was tired. Then I would find a quiet, dark place to park and sleep. I would read *The Brothers Karamazov* at night. Rainy days when there was no construction work, I would drive up to the Salisbury State College library and compare various translations of Gogol's *The Overcoat*. Clearly, I was not in a good place. Being homeless is bad enough, but obsessively reading *The Overcoat* should have been a clear sign to everyone that I needed help. Then again, I wasn't speaking to anyone about literature or being homeless, so no one actually knew.

I wasn't welcome in my parents' homes at that point, as it was a rough time for me with my family. My mother couldn't have a conversation with me without saying terrible things about my dad's family, and she was dating my former boss, who didn't like me (and the feeling was mutual). My father wasn't speaking to me at all, not a single word. Even though I was an assistant soccer coach at the school where he directed athletics, he would walk up, talk to Coach Westcott, and then walk away without acknowledging my presence. My father had decided to shun me since that time he visited Ireland and I only met him for coffee. Or perhaps he was upset that I stayed with my mom for two days after I returned from Ireland, and I didn't ask to stay with him. It's also possible he heard about my mom's visit to Ireland and perhaps that upset him?[30] I don't know for sure, but what I do know is he that was so angry at me that he refused to even look at me. I loved coaching soccer with Coach Westcott, but being shunned by my father was extremely hard on me.

One grey morning in early October, having slept in my car in a parking spot under some low hanging pine trees, I woke up early with about fifty small bites on my legs that itched like crazy. I knew I couldn't shower until after soccer practice, so I drove out to the beach. It was a warm morning, but the beach was empty. Lazy two-foot waves were breaking along the shoreline, and beyond them the ocean was like glass. I didn't have a bathing suit, but did have a ratty pair of cargo shorts, clad in which I jumped into the cold water until my legs stopped burning and itching. Eventually I got used to the cold and swam out past where my feet could touch the bottom. I treaded water for a few minutes, and then simply relaxed. I closed my eyes and sank to the bottom, sitting cross-legged with my palms down, caressing the sand on the ocean floor. I felt the heaviness of the water, each unseen wave pushing and pulling me. After about a minute, my calm was broken by the need to breathe, so I came back up to the surface. The morning haze was giving way to a sunny day, and I crawled out of the ocean feeling the October sun on my skin. I felt clean for the first time in a long time, and I collapsed on the sand to let the sun warm me. I fell asleep and missed work.

I drove to the construction office and walked in to talk to the construction manager. He was always nice to me, but I don't remember his name. I said I was done for good. He asked what he should do with my last paycheck. I said not to worry about it, they could keep it.

I was leaving, and I had no idea where I was going to go. Something about autumn makes me hunger for an open road and a new horizon, and I have no idea what it is. I felt it every autumn, and still do when the weather turns. The difference this time was that I knew I was done with Maryland forever, I was certain of it. Of course I was wrong, but I am wrong all the time.

I met my mom for coffee and told her I was leaving. She looked concerned, but I told her I was going to see a little bit of America, and I would probably go visit her parents in Rockford, Illinois, which made her happy. She gave me $100.

I drove to school and tried to talk to my dad, but he still refused to

---

30 This will be explained later.

speak to me. He just walked away, went into his office, and closed his door. So I went to talk to Tom Westcott, and told him I had to leave. It was about an hour before practice.

"There's only a week of the season left," he said, trying to get me to stay.

I shook my head, trying my best to hold back tears. I knew my childhood was over. My parents were now just people I knew, not family I could rely on. Even if they loved me, neither of them ever liked me much, and my father flat-out hated me now. I was uncomfortable even at my school, the place I had spent over thirteen years of my life and had always felt more like home to me than my own house. My dad had taken that from me, because it was more his school than mine. He took my home from me, too.

"I gotta go now."

"Stay for practice. Say goodbye to the guys."

I nodded.

After practice, I just got into my car and drove. I drove north without any plans, landing in Tunkhannock, PA at the home of John Burke, one of my roommates from Notre Dame. Burke was a year older than the rest of us, but because he got his MBA while simultaneously earning his bachelors in engineering, he ended up staying the extra year. Even though he was from Pennsylvania, he was a White Sox fan, so we usually ended up going to Comiskey for opening day (those were some cold opening days). Since I hadn't called to inform Burke I was coming, you would expect him to be surprised, but he registered no shock that I was knocking on his door at 10:30 PM on a Tuesday while smelling of a mixture of salt, sand, dirt, grass, sweat, coffee, and cigarettes. After suggesting I shower he offered me his couch and a blanket, telling me to stay as long as I wanted. He was working at Proctor & Gamble in those days and had to get up pretty early, so we didn't talk much that night. But I stayed there for a week, and every night we spent hours talking about what I was going to do.

John Burke might be my friend who is the most different from me. He's organized, focused, smart, and always looking for an angle or inefficiency that can be improved. He is goal-oriented, good with money, takes care of his health, and generally conservative in practice and thought. I was none of these things, but even so he always liked having me around. I think he liked hearing my perspective, even if he would never agree with it. I saw the world differently than he did, and he always recognized the value in that. At the time, I didn't realize how rare that quality is in people. For the next few days, he and I hung out with his roommates, drinking beers and just talking through all my shit. He never pushed me, suggested I do something, or demanded I get my life together. He just let me be me. While he was at work I spent my days reading.

Autumn in Pennsylvania is magical. It's the cold nights, the crisp mornings, the explosive variations of reds, oranges, and yellows on the hills contrasting with the impossibly blue skies—and especially the afternoons that are bathed in an amber light that I swear is unique to Pennsylvania. I loved those days, but I knew I was in-between the old life and the new and I needed to find something else. Burke would have let me live on his couch as long as I wanted, he's just that kind of guy. Still, after a week, I knew it was time to go.

We woke up early one Tuesday morning and I flipped a coin. Heads was east, tails was west. If it came up heads I was going to go to Mystic, Connecticut because I had long held a fascination with the place ever since viewing *Mystic Pizza*. But it came up tails, so I hit the road west, destination unknown.

The sun was setting as I was coming up to the South Bend exit on Route 80. I knew I could go to The Colorado Steakhouse to get a free steak and maybe find a place to crash for the night. I went there and got a warm reception, Jean, Clint, and Gary weren't present but the General Manager J.D. was and he comped me a prime rib dinner and a beer. J.D. and I hung out at the bar and talked for hours, mostly about my time in Europe. Clint arrived and invited me to stay with him; he was living with his parents now, having broken up with his girlfriend. A waitress came over to J.D. to beg off her shift the following night, but J.D. said he did not have anyone else to cover it. I said I would do it if he wanted, I could always use the cash. He had no problem with that.

Clint's parents' house was an enormous Victorian that had a separate servant quarters wing that Clint had converted to a five-room apartment. We stayed up until sunrise drinking Becks Dark, smoking Camel Reds, and listening to Velvet Underground, David Bowie, T. Rex, and Blur.[31]

I got up around noon the next day and went to Fat Shirley's for breakfast, wrote for a while, and then showed up an hour early for my shift at the steakhouse. Gary was cooking that night, and nodded at me when I walked into the kitchen.

"Do much fishing out east?"

"None."

Gary had taught me to fly fish and was as big a fan of *A River Runs Through It* as I was. He was also that hilarious cook in the kitchen who had at least a couple of screws loose. He wore a nametag that read "In Bread," and his favorite joke started by asking waitresses if they had any hillbilly in them.

31 Clint hates when people list authors or books or bands, in case you forgot.

"You bring me a case of crabs?" he would always ask whenever I came back from Maryland. He thought this was hilarious.

"It's called a bushel."

J.D. made Gary get back to work and set me up for my shift. So as not to have to set me back up in the POS computer system, which was a lengthy process, they had me log in with the ID number of the waitress whose shift I was covering instead. I worked the smoking section, which was my favorite since, smokers are drinkers and thus big tippers. I killed it for a Wednesday night, probably clearing close to $100, which was pretty good for South Bend on a Wednesday night.

Back then, most people paid for meals at restaurants with cash. Credit cards were becoming more common, but they were not yet the norm. For every one credit card customer we had four or five tables that would pay with cash. As a waiter, you have to hold onto all the cash until the end of night. Then you would settle up with the manager, which was called "cashing out." When I went to cash out at the end of the night, rather than having $100 left over in tips I somehow owed $60 dollars. Now I am not someone who practices caution with how I spend my money, but while waiting tables I had never been short by more than a few cents. I am meticulous with where I keep my cash and always count everything out three times. I knew there was no way I could have made that big of a mistake, but J.D. checked the printout twice. I owed what I owed, so I handed over $60 that I couldn't spare. I was devastated. I probably had less than $200 left to my name after that.

Gary was cooking that night and was coming to get me for a cigarette break and overheard the whole thing. He told Jean and Theresa and they spread the news around to the staff. J.D. bought me a beer at the bar and I just sat there smoking a cigarette and staring at the mirror, reliving the entire night and trying to figure out what happened.

Theresa walked up to me and handed me an envelope.

"It's not going to make up for what you lost, but hopefully it will help."

There was about $132 dollars in the envelope. Everyone that worked that night, even the cooks kicked in. I was speechless. Theresa gave me a hug. For the first time, I thought maybe South Bend was my home.

Gary drove me to Fat Shirley's and we sat there talking about the kindness I felt in Indiana that I hadn't in Maryland.

"See how nice we are to you here? The least you could have done is bring us a case of crabs."

"Bushel."

"It's funny every time."

"It hasn't been funny once."

Gary grinned his crooked grin and took a long and loud drag of his cigarette. At that moment, J.D. burst in the door of Fat Shirley's like a man on a mission.

"I knew you would be here."

He handed me an envelope. There was $168 in it. He figured out the money mistake on the way home, turned around, and went back to the steakhouse to fix it. What had happened was the waitress I covered had clocked out after her afternoon shift and turned in that money, but it wasn't credited towards her daily total. Normally if you work a double shift, you just cash out everything at the end, but she had cashed out half way through her shift. So that was why the numbers were off and it looked like I owed $60 instead of having $108 in tips.

After a moment of vindicated relief, the realization came over me that I had to make things right.

"I got to give this money back to everyone."

"You can't. No way we'll be able to figure out who gave what. Just don't say anything ever about this."

"People thought I fucked up and they still gave me their hard-earned money. Even though they know I'm going to leave tomorrow and I might never see them again."

Gary lit another cigarette.

"You don't need to leave. Stay here, we'll go fishing."

J.D. agreed: "Why don't you stay through the rest of the fall, at least? We need help on football weekends, so at least work those. You can stay with Clint as long as you want, he's got like five bedrooms."

And so, for the next three or four months I worked occasional weekends at The Colorado Steakhouse, and then would leave and drive in a different direction each time. In one trip I went north, visiting my grandparents and family in Rockford, then up to Minnesota to visit Prof, shot over to the Badlands of South Dakota, and then back to South Bend. On another trip I went west, I visited Cousin Alicia in Missouri, Cousin Alexis in Colorado, and sent a postcard from Breckenridge to a bartender from The Hobbit Restaurant in Ocean City that I never saw again, and then back to South Bend again.

The next trip I went on was just supposed to be a short trip to visit my college friend Kerry in St. Louis. It's about a six hour drive. But after having lunch with Kerry, I decided to keep driving. I had no destination in mind. I drove until I got to Santa Fe, New Mexico, probably drawn there because of the musical *Rent*. I kept going and went to Winslow, Arizona to see the Meteor Crater, and since I was so close I figured I would go to the Grand Canyon. There's nothing to say about the Grand

Canyon that hasn't been said, and what I say wouldn't matter anyway. Some things cannot be contained by the words on a page. Go see it.

My intention was to stay at a cheap hotel by the Grand Canyon, but those don't exist, and I was running out of money. I looked on my atlas and saw that I wasn't really that far from Las Vegas. I had heard you could get cheap hotel rooms in Vegas so I drove on, arriving there around midnight. I instantly hated it. Whatever I was looking for, I knew it was not in Vegas. I left immediately and just drove until I found a truck stop in the middle of nowhere and turned off my car and went to sleep.

When I woke up I found out I was at a truck stop in Baker, California. I was completely broke, having maybe thirty dollars in my pocket, and had no idea how to get back to South Bend. I was desperate and didn't know what to do. I called my brother just because I felt the need to talk to someone in my family, and he was the only one I was really talking to at the time. I told him I was in Baker California and he started laughing.

"What's so funny?" I asked him.

"Home of the world's tallest thermometer!"

"The what?"

Tom started in on his story: "Okay dude, last time I was out seeing Kirk, who lives in LA now, he convinced me we should drive to Las Vegas for the night. He said it's an easy drive, people do it all the time. After three hours of driving, his car breaks down in the middle of nowhere. We ended up having to spend the night in Baker, California, and we had to go back to LA the next day. Instead of seeing Vegas, I got to drive eight hours to see the world's tallest fucking thermometer."

I looked around and, in the distance, I could see a tall tower-like structure that I thought could be it.

"I think I can see it."

"Yeah, if you are in Baker you can see it. Fucking Baker, California, that's awesome. What are you doing out there?"

"Nothing. Just driving."

"You okay?"

"Yeah?" I gave one of my least committal answers ever. Tom doesn't have much time for my shit, but I'm sure even he was able to tell I wasn't doing too well.

"Bro, call Kirk. Let me give you his number. I'm sure he would love to see you."

So I did. After laughing about the world's tallest thermometer, Kirk told me he was walking out the door to work, and since he wasn't going to be home for eight hours I should swing by Death Valley before meeting him. I took his advice.

I was in Death Valley for about ten minutes before big, dark clouds started to roll in. You can see the sky forever out west, and the lightning was strobing the clouds long before I could hear the thunder. It rained for close to an hour, the once-dry streambeds somehow ran with clear water, and flowers bloomed. The smell of the moment after a desert rain was sublime.

Leaving Death Valley, I drove to Los Angeles and hung out with Kirk for a few days in LA. He bought me a burger and chili fries at Barney's Beanery and took me to see *Velvet Goldmine*. When I left, he gave me $200, which was the only way I was able to return to South Bend. I found out later it was Tom who told Kirk to give me the money, as a favor to him, saying would pay him back. I know this is messed up to put in a book, but Tom most likely still owes Kirk $200.

After leaving Kirk's place I drove down to San Diego and slept on the beach for a night, then drove non-stop to Athens, Georgia just to go to Weaver D's Delicious for lunch. Their slogan, "Automatic for the People" was used by REM for the title for my favorite album of theirs. The food was great but I was seeing double. I had a friend named Claire that lived in Atlanta, so I called her up and stopped by to see her, but within fifteen minutes of being in her apartment I fell asleep on her floor. I woke up about five hours later and left in the middle of the night for South Bend.

That last trip was tough both physically and mentally on me. It's not healthy or safe to drive that long without sleep, I was being selfish and stupid. I have a strict rule about never drinking and driving, so much so that I've never had a single beer and then gotten behind the wheel of a car. But driving all the way across the country without sleep was probably as reckless as driving drunk. I'm thankful I didn't get in an accident and hope to never be that selfish again.

About this time, I realized I was taking advantage of Clint's parents' hospitality. I had been living there intermittently for a few months and knew it was time to move out. But without anywhere else to go, and without much money, I decided it was best to stay in Indiana.

I got an apartment in an old schoolhouse in downtown South Bend. It was a large two-bedroom, and had repurposed hardwood floors that were once the basketball floor for the school—it even had a section of the key lines in the corner still. Interestingly, this was the same basketball floor on which legendary coach John Wooden began his coaching career. The apartment itself had almost floor-to-ceiling windows, and those ceilings were at least fourteen feet high. There was also a huge chalkboard on the wall of the living room. It was the single coolest apartment I will ever live in. I moved in a week before Christmas.

I didn't have any furniture, so I bought a mattress that I put on the floor in the back bedroom. I had two bath towels and my clothes. Other than that, I had an ashtray I stole from Colorado Steakhouse, and literally nothing else. Clint bought me chalk for the chalkboard.

After not speaking to me since Ireland a full year before, my father showed up on Christmas Day and asked to see me. The day before, two boxes of dishware had arrived courtesy of my mother, so at least I could throw a formal dinner party for eight, as long as everyone was okay with sitting on the floor. Except, I didn't have any food. The apartment was across from an Always Open, so I popped over there for a couple of personal pizzas, a bag of Bugles, a Diet Dr. Pepper for my dad, and a cup of chalky black coffee for myself. We ate on my new dishes while sitting on the floor. My father hardly said a word to me the whole time. The only time I got any reaction from him was when I told him that John Wooden coached on the floor on which he was sitting. I thought he would be excited about that and maybe we would talk about basketball or sports. Instead, he just heaved a huge sigh and said:

"I know. You think I don't know that John Wooden coached at Central High School? Remember I lived in Indiana a long time before you did. Sheesh."

That was about it. After he wolfed down the food, he got up and left, heading to my grandparent's house. It was Christmas of 1998, and I wouldn't speak with my father again until his father died in the summer of 1999.

I don't know why my dad came to South Bend. I think he wanted to tell people he saw me for Christmas. That's the only reason I can think of for his visit. We never talked about it.

This period of time is unique in my life. From the end of that summer to the following May, I felt no desire whatsoever. I had no interest in romantic relations, no sex drive at all. I had no hunger to write, or even to read. I did read, but I was not as voracious as I had been before. I oscillated between being depressed and manic, but I also felt really empty, even in my manic moments.

I reconnected with my friend Aidar, who was from Kazakhstan and at the time was a PhD candidate in Applied Mathematics and Theoretical Physics at Notre Dame. Aidar, Clint, and I spent most of that January and February drinking at Mickey's, the blues bar that was a block away from my apartment. We would chat with a cocktail waitress named Justine, who always seemed happy to see us. Or we would go see Clint's ex-girlfriend bartending a few blocks away at McCormick's, who religiously switched the music over to Velvet Underground as soon as we walked through the door. Or we would hang out at my apartment and discuss philosophy for hours while listening to a soundtrack of glam rock and Brit pop. Clint made me a few mixtapes of hard-to-find, import-glam-rock songs mixed with some Scott Walker, Jacques Brel, and obscure Frank Sinatra songs. We smoked too many cigarettes and I occasionally smoked weed, but wasn't habitual with it. I watched *Suddenly Last Summer* about five times. When I read, it was usually poetry, especially Keats. I read Virginia Woolf for the first time, and tried reading D.H. Laurence but couldn't get into him. Clint gave me his copy of *The Hero with a Thousand Faces* by Joseph Campbell, but I didn't read it when I was in South Bend.

Clint and Aidar started coming over to the apartment every night after work. Aidar would smoke weed and dance in the reflection of the giant windows. Clint and I would write reasons to live on one side of the chalkboard, and reasons to die on the other side. We probably had thirty reasons to die (mostly sarcastic), but only five reasons to live: music, cigarettes, poetry, coffee, and Fat Shirley's (which was also on the "reasons to die" side). On my days off, I would "go hunting" with Gary, which really meant just walking through the woods with a gun, because I never shot anything. Or we would go fly fishing, even though the water was icy cold; I wanted to practice my technique and feel the rhythm and comfort of the cast.

I was content, if not happy. I was in a cocoon with people like me, people that liked to think and discuss and dream and discover. Aidar, Clint, and Gary became my brothers. At work, J.D. became my dad and Jean became my mom. They were kind and wanted me around. I had a family that liked me, and was glad to be in their lives. For the first time since I was sixteen I wasn't with a girl, so had time to gain some perspective. The last few girls I had dated showed up at night (usually drunk), then broke up with me in the morning. They knew there was something wrong with me, and it probably scared them. I think they sensed as much as I did that the person I professed to be was dying, and neither them nor I had any idea what, if anything, I would become. Even if I had the desire—which I don't think I did—I had no energy for a relationship.

Though my mom was only talking to me sporadically, and as I mentioned my father wouldn't speak to me again for months, in this time I felt like I had a healthy family life, and in an odd way I did. I was starting to understand who I was as a person. I was finding art that reflected my thoughts and feelings, that expanded my mind. While I was growing into the new me, I felt comfortable and safe. But it didn't last. I didn't realize how fragile my momentary peace truly was.

Against my wishes The Colorado Steakhouse made me a manager. I didn't want it, but I said I would do it until they found someone better.

I soon found out they weren't going to look for a new manager. Since I didn't have enough money to afford furniture, I got a second job working as an assistant for an inventor in Elkhart, Indiana, testing out things like a new type of spring and trying to figure out uses for it. I also worked in his plastic factory, using a vacuum mold to make flute cases. The Elkhart job was actually pretty fun, but the steakhouse working environment was becoming more contentious. Even though I am probably a natural manager, I did not like managing at this time. I wasn't done with my cocoon yet, I wasn't done morphing into the next version of myself.

An acquaintance of mine was released from jail at that point and needed a place to live, so I let him stay with me. He brought with him a TV and a Sony PlayStation. He had some friends that, unlike my friends, didn't want to talk and think and explore, but rather wanted to simply smoke weed and play video games. This guy was also a very charismatic liar, the kind that manipulates others easily. I'm just going to call him Jimbo, which is not his real name. I recognize now it was important for me to have met someone like him early in my life, because now I'm keenly aware of when people have such traits, and I can avoid them. But I was too trusting in those days, and the timing of when he came into my life could not have been worse. One of Jimbo's friends who smoked weed and played video games with him had a boyfriend who was getting abusive, so she moved in with us, too. The now ex-boyfriend believed that she and I were sleeping together, which we certainly were not; in fact, I didn't really even hang out in my own apartment anymore.

There were now external pressures on my utopia. Only a few months after I moved to South Bend, I became a magnet for the desperate.

Also, in those days I got little exercise, except the occasional walk in the woods. I didn't play sports anymore and had no idea where there was even a gym in town. I smoked too many cigarettes and started drinking more whiskey. The waitress from Mickey's, Justine, started hanging out with us when she wasn't working, and hanging out at the steakhouse bar waiting for us to get off our shifts. Instead of drinking being something we happened to do while exploring ideas and having meaningful conversations, drinking became the focus of the evenings. It was as if we *had* to go drinking; we were no longer comfortable going to the apartment to just hang out, because at any time my "roommates" might come home, and there could be no good conversation that could take place with those people there. It might sound arrogant, but they were kinda dumb to start with, and then they smoked so much pot that nothing interesting was going to come out of their mouths. Unfortunately, because they were so high they thought that everything they said was really smart, and therefore they felt the need to get in the middle of every conversation. Since those nights were wasted, we avoided my apartment and just went to the bar, to... well, get wasted.

One night the ex-boyfriend of my new roommate showed up at the steakhouse when neither of us were there and told a cook he was going to kill me. I bumped into the cook at a bar, who told me to watch my back. On the walk home I kept looking behind me to see if anyone was following me. I hated that feeling.

The next morning, I awoke to the sound of rain on my window. I have always loved rain in the morning. I had the full day off, so I went to Fat Shirley's for breakfast. I got a new mixtape from Clint the day before and popped it into my car's stereo. After breakfast, I went to a coffee shop right on the edge of campus called Lulu's, which I frequented during my college days. The sun had come out and the world was shiny and clean. I got an enormous coffee and tried to read, but I couldn't get into the book. I clearly remember putting the book down and sitting back in my chair and just looking around Lulu's. I saw the old poster for that year's Sophomore Literary Festival. I watched the workers behind the counter, all new faces from when I frequented the place. But they were somehow similar to the faces I would have recognized, it was as if the people I knew had been replaced by the next version of themselves. I watched people come in and get their coffees and teas, chat about their classes, and study for the upcoming finals, just as I had done when I had a purpose. I went outside to smoke a cigarette. I saw a former professor of mine walk past, but she ignored me—I couldn't even remember her name. I looked at my refection in the window. I looked old, out of place, and strange.

I felt unclean, discarded. Not by the professor or the other students who were exactly where I was just three years earlier. I felt discarded by myself. I felt as if I had thrown myself away, that I had made myself trash, and that I had wasted everything that I was. I felt like I had failed at everything, that I had let everyone down. I felt like it would have been better if I had not ever existed.

I don't remember what happened next. If you had asked me a week later what happened next, I'm not sure I could have recalled it. I left Lulu's and at some point went to my apartment, which was full of people I did not really know and did not really like. I probably went to Fat Shirley's again. I might have gone to Potato Creek, my favorite fishing spot, but I know I did not fish.

At some point I ended up on the banks of the St. Joseph River sitting on one of the "depression walls." At least that was what they were called there; they were apparently built by the Works Progress Administration for no real reason other than building them gave people something to do during the Depression. I get the symbolism, it isn't subtle.

I stared at the water for the better part of an hour. I walked onto the nearby bridge and wondered if I would die if I jumped from that bridge. I decided the bridge probably was not high enough for that. I got in my car and smoked a cigarette. I started my 1990 Chevy Lumina and thought, *I could drive it over the bridge and that would certainly kill me.* Clint's mixtape was at max volume, playing David Bowie's version of "Across the Universe." I never liked that song before, but the way Bowie sang it, the struggle in his voice, the desperation as he screamed "Nothing's gonna change my world" changed the meaning of the song for me.

He knew, that moment, David Bowie knew what I needed to hear and how I needed to hear it. He was screaming at me to keep fighting. I know this isn't what that song is about, but it was for me at that moment. In the end, art is what the individual gets out of it, and David Bowie was telling me the fight was not yet over. I yelled and clenched my fists and beat them into the steering wheel, and then my eyes teared up. I knew for sure I was nothing, I was empty, and I was alone. The tape flipped over to a new side. The next song started; it was Bowie's "Rock and Roll Suicide." It starts:

Time takes a cigarette, puts it in your mouth
You pull on your finger, then another finger, then cigarette
The wall-to-wall is calling, it lingers, then you forget
Oh, you're a rock 'n' roll suicide

I lit a cigarette. My hands were shaking, I felt like I was going to throw up. This song was written four years before I was born, but hearing it while staring at that bridge, I swear it seemed like it was written for me. The song builds in intensity, repeating the phrase "You're not alone," and with each time Bowie's voice becoming more desperate. The song ends with the lines:

Just turn on with me, and you're not alone
Let's turn on and be not alone
Gimme your hands, 'cause you're wonderful
Gimme your hands, 'cause you're wonderful
Oh, gimme your hands

I wept.

Then I smoked another cigarette, rewound the tape and listened to it again, and again, and again. Somehow I started to believe it was okay to be the failure I was, to be the trash I was. It was okay to be nothing. It was okay to have let down everyone I had ever known. I was not alone, I had David Bowie. As he kept screaming that it didn't matter what or who I had been, that it didn't matter when or where I saw, through space and time, David Bowie reached out and grabbed me by the shoulders. He screamed into my face that I was not alone, that he would help me with the pain, that he would hold my hand and tell me that I was beautiful, that we are beautiful and wonderful and that I was not alone. I could be nothing, but I wasn't fucking alone.

I should have sought help, but I didn't. I just kept listening to that mix over and over. I went to Mickey's, smoked cigarettes, and drank whiskey. I dragged myself back to work for one more week, but I was quiet, sullen, and empty. At least once an hour I thought about killing myself. Music and cigarettes pulled me out of my deepest depression, but I was not free and clear. This is when I first started conceptualizing a rudimentary idea that, if I just kept smoking, I would kill myself eventually, just really slowly. There was a dark joy in that.

My "roommates" disappeared for the weekend and I finally had my apartment back. Aidar and Clint came over, and Aidar wrote a two-page manifesto about art and beauty. I read it, and looked at Clint and Aidar.

"I'm moving to New York to start a commune."

Aidar, who remember was working on his PhD at the time, nodded. "I'll go with you."

Clint agreed to come too, and went home to pack his car. Aidar sold his car for $20 and whomever he sold it to got ripped off. I guess he told his advisor he was quitting, I don't really know. I went over to J.D.'s to quit and say goodbye. The sun was just rising, he was in his pajamas when he came to the door. One way to know how selfish I was in this period of my life is by all the odd-ass hours I would just knock on someone's door. I stood in his doorway and told him I had to go to NYC, I couldn't give notice, I had to leave right then and there. His young towheaded son, Chris, who was maybe six years old at the time woke up and came down the stairs rubbing his eyes. I liked Chris and he liked me; for a few months I was like a fun uncle to him.

"Daddy, what's going on?" he asked.

"Hey buddy," I said, trying to get up the courage to tell him I was leaving forever.

"Chris," J.D. spoke sternly. "I want you to look at this person. I never want you to be like him. Ever."

J.D. slammed the door in my face. Clint met Aidar and I at my apartment with his car fully packed, but he backed out of the trip. I said goodbye to Gary and told him to keep my rifle and flyrod. I reached out to the roommates to confirm they would take over the lease (they never paid and were evicted). I forgot to tell the inventor I was leaving, and I had one of his inventions in the trunk of my car (a unique spring he hadn't yet patented). By the time we left town the sun was setting. I drove as far as I could, but the loss of a night of sleep and the emotional exhaustion was too much to continue on. I handed the driving duties to Aidar as we approached the Pennsylvania Turnpike. Aidar was a terrible driver.

I smoked a cigarette in the passenger seat and said to Aidar that it felt like I was smoking my last cigarette ever. He laughed, and I fell asleep. I woke up an hour later to the sound of the tire beneath me exploding. Aidar had hit a concrete barrier (you know, that thing that prevents you from going over a cliff) and blew out the front right tire. He pulled into one of those emergency pull offs, and I installed the spare tire. I drove a couple of miles to the next exit, found a service station, and bought a new tire. They said it would be a couple of hours, so we walked to the diner up the street. Aidar had yet to apologize for almost driving us over a cliff. As he opened the door to the diner for me, he said:

"Dan. Breakfast is on me."

I snorted a laugh and bought a *USA Today*. We ordered coffee and eggs. I opened up the paper while Aidar smoked a cigarette and looked out the windows, admiring the springtime Pennsylvania sun illuminating the morning mist, which clung to the treetops all the way down the mountain. He nodded at my paper.

"Anything about us in there?"

I wish I had something more profound to say about this time in my life, as it was the closest I ever came to acting on my suicidal thoughts. I wish I could say those thoughts have totally gone away, but they have not; they've simply morphed into something else. I don't think about killing myself anymore, but I think about dying all the time. It's not at all the same, but I feel it is connected.

I do have a quality that tells me to keep going, no matter what. Keep pushing. Keep trying. Keep swinging. It might very well be learned behavior, I don't know. Maybe this goes back to sports, back to Little League batting practice. I really don't know for sure if anyone could say, but somewhere along the way the thoughts of self-destruction became more academic or philosophical, rather than literal. This obsession with death made life matter more. It made art matter more. It made everything matter more.

That was it for me and South Bend, it had nearly killed me. But then again, without South Bend, there was no Clint. And without Clint, there was no David Bowie. And without David Bowie, how would I have known that I wasn't alone?

LIVING IN NEW YORK WITH THOSE FUCKING YANKEES

Yes, I moved to New York City to start a commune. Mark Decker moved up from Maryland to join Aidar and me, so we rented a tiny, roach-infested little one-and-one-third bedroom apartment in Astoria, Queens. We called it The Astoria Commune, and at most we had five people living there full-time. The few times I did sleep, I slept on the floor, but not with the roaches. Roaches never sleep. We drank too much Gato Negro—a dirt cheap Chilean wine—Aidar and I smoked too many cigarettes, and we put out a newsletter called *The Warrior's Voice* where we talked about the evils of television and how it was ruining our society. Appropriately, I got a job a couple of years later working at MTV and stayed there for a decade. Life didn't wait too long to make me a hypocrite.

The first week after I moved to New York, a street bookseller in Brooklyn sold me a $2 copy of Fitzgerald's *This Side of Paradise*, which I read at the L Café when Williamsburg was just starting to be a thing. It was perfect timing, the first week you move to New York you should read *This Side of Paradise*, especially if you are a twenty-something privileged dude. I always had luck for the right book finding me at the right time, even if it was a bit cliché. When I was backpacking through Europe, someone gave me their copy of Kerouac's *On the Road*, and a week after I arrived in Dublin in December, Méabh's father gave me Joyce's *Dubliners*. While none of these are my favorite books by those authors, the timing was impeccable.[32]

At this time, a couple years before I worked in television and sold out my principles, I was a waiter at EJ's Luncheonette on the Upper West Side. My brother had just quit his job there, and a manager named Chad Rosen hired me to replace him. Chad joked that we O'Hare's looked so much alike that he bet most regulars wouldn't even notice. I had a fun time for about six months, until management told me I had to work on Christmas. So I quit. Not that I cared about Christmas, but I wanted to

---

32 *The Subterraneans* for Kerouac, *A Portrait of the Artist as a Young Man* for Joyce, and probably *The Beautiful and the Damned* for Fitzgerald. *This Side of Paradise* is really good though, sometimes it's probably my favorite. Read them all and tell me what you think.

spend it with my new girlfriend, Caroline.

I met Caroline three times throughout the summer and autumn of 1999, and even though each of those three times she completely forgot who I was, through my dogged perseverance, I somehow tricked her into becoming my girlfriend just before Christmas of 1999. The story of my love for Caroline should be its own book and I do not want to even try to tell it here. Needless to say, I was in love and I wanted Christmas off to spend it with my Jewish girlfriend. When EJ's didn't give it to me, I quit.

I took Caroline down to Maryland to meet my mother, who only called her "Méabh" three times. All of my mom's friends went out of their way to be sure to say "happy holidays" to her instead of Merry Christmas, because it wasn't political then and it was just a nice thing to do. Since my mom was still with my former boss, we didn't stay there long. Most of that Christmas and New Year's we spent in-between Brad Bebee's parents' house in Salisbury and Brad's own place in Dupont Circle. Brad had been a great friend since high school and actually gave me the money I needed to start the commune. All in all, over that holiday Caroline and I spent about ten days with Brad, but we never once saw my father. That was my choice, as I didn't know how my dad was going to behave.

After the holidays, my buddy and new commune resident Jeff Woods got me a job working for a website called Urban Box Office, specifically a channel called Indie Planet, which was awesome. Each day we interviewed independent artists all over New York (although mostly in Brooklyn). My first solo interview was for the Wordz Channel and was with author Victor LaValle, who had just written his first book, *Slapboxing with Jesus*. I interviewed him for two hours, but in my awkward nervousness I dropped my mini-cassette recorder within the first five minutes. When I played it back, I learned I'd interviewed Victor for five minutes, and then apparently we just hung out for another hour, fifty-five.

Any job where you get to hang out with Victor LaValle for two hours is a great job. At that moment in my life, it could not have been more perfect. Working at UBO while living in the commune and publishing my own newsletter was a transformative experience. I became something new, as I combined the confidence of my youth with the fearlessness of someone who had nothing to lose. In those days, Mark started to refer to me as either Dan Quixote or Charles Foster O'Hare, and I loved the implications. I was looking forward, pushing forward, trying to create something new, not just out of myself, but, out of the world itself. Combine that energy with meeting my future wife, having the support of Aidar, Mark, and eventually Jeff, and an ever-expanding group of creative, crazy, artistic friends, it was exactly what I needed in my life. And since both my brother and I were in New York we saw each other regularly and became much closer than we ever had before. That being said, I did not speak to my parents much. But I think that was necessary: I was becoming my own person, and I needed to do it on my own terms. I talked to my mom once a month or so and only talked to my dad briefly, while at his father's funeral.

Then, what happened to almost all dot coms after the 2000 peak happened to UBO. One day we were eating sushi for lunch, and the next day a sheik pulled his funding and the doors shut. We were all without jobs, but right at that time Chad Rosen had just started running the kitchen at The Gin Mill and asked me to help him get it organized.

I worked at The Gin Mill on and off for a few months and became good friends with Chad and then-manager (and later owner) Josh Cohen. Chad, Josh and I had a ritual: we'd meet every Monday and order sandwiches from Lenny's, the best sandwich shop around in those days, and sit and talk about baseball. Lenny's had a great Thanksgiving-on-a-roll footlong sub for which I was a sucker, but I always tried to get Josh or Chad to order a pastrami too, so I could—as I liked to say—"surf and turf it."

While I had lots of male friends in my life in those days, they were all either very artistic, played lots of D&D, or both. So it goes without saying that I didn't have anyone that I could talk baseball with except Chad and Josh, so I should have been happy to spend lunch every Monday talking baseball with them. The problem was, these guys, while technically my friends, were among the worst people ever, because they were Yankees fans. And they weren't casual Yankees fans, they had *season tickets*. When the O's came to town and I was working at the Gin Mill, they would let me go to games with them. This was really nice, but since the early 2000s were some dark days for the O's, it was kinda cruel, too. I went to around a dozen O's games at Yankee Stadium, and until 2012 I never saw one O's victory there[33]

I started to treasure these lunches so much that even after I stopped working at The Gin Mill, I would do my best to get there one Monday a month for the next few years. Josh and Chad became really good friends of mine and brought me back into the world of sports that I had left after coaching soccer in the autumn of 1998. Now, two years later, I suddenly had people to talk baseball with again. They even let me join their very exclusive fantasy baseball American-League-Only-Auction-Keeper League that had been going on for seventeen years at that point, and as I was the only Orioles fan in the league, they gleefully drove up the price of far too many subpar Oriole players just for me.

It wasn't too long after UBO closed its doors that the commune split

---

33 Coincidentally, in 2012 Chad was working for the Yankeess and got me sweet tickets to the game the O's won.

up. Things like that are too special to last forever, and with good reason. The newsletter ended and we all went our separate ways.

I worked at The Gin Mill on September 10th 2001. I worked late, and did not fall asleep until probably 4AM on the 11th. Mark called me from his office in Midtown waking me up right after the second tower was hit. He had called his mom, who worked with my dad. She didn't know what to say, so my dad got on the phone and talked to Mark. But my dad didn't call me, we were not talking much yet.

I lived in Woodside, Queens in those days, so walked up to my building's roof, and it was just in time to see the first tower fall. I was numb, hungover, and confused. I left the roof and walked down to my neighborhood pub, The Copper Kettle. They were not normally open yet, but the bartender opened up for me, and soon I was joined by a dozen or so regulars. I drank four or five Jamesons and then walked over the 59th Street Bridge into the city and went to the Upper West Side. I found Chad and Josh at The Gin Mill, we talked for a minute, and then Josh made a comment that none of their scheduled deliveries had arrived. I told Chad he should go to every grocery store he could and buy as much meat as possible, because he was going to run out. He left, I had four or five more Jamesons and then started walking south.

I knew I needed to help, I just didn't know what I could do. In the bar, I had heard someone mention that they were taking blood donations, so I went to the Red Cross location over on the West Side, somewhere around midtown, I don't remember exactly where. The line was crazy long. We had to fill out a questionnaire, and one of the questions stated you could not donate blood if you had lived in England, Northern Ireland, Scotland, Wales, or The Isle of Man in the years 1996-1999. I assume this was because of Mad Cow Disease, but it did not mention the Republic of Ireland, so I thought I should check. I explained my predicament to the person working the line, and she said she was going to go ask someone. I stopped her and said:

"Oh, also, can you check to see if it's okay to donate blood if you're a little drunk?"

In a lifetime of receiving many exasperated looks, this one might be the most memorable. She snatched the paper away from me, and I left.

I continued on southward until I got to Chelsea Piers. While in the blood donation line, I had heard ambulances and volunteers were gathering there, and I thought maybe I could be of help, somehow. In fact, a huge line of ambulances had come from all over the eastern seaboard to volunteer their services at the site, but since there was nothing for them to do, they just lined up waiting at Chelsea Piers. The inside of Chelsea

Piers had been transformed into a staging area for supplies and was just forming into a relief center. What most people probably don't know or remember is that most everything south of 23rd street was shut down for about a week. Restaurants that couldn't open had food that was going to waste, so they cooked it up and brought it to Chelsea Piers for the emergency workers. People were arriving from all over the Tristate Area with all different kinds of donations, clothes, food, cigarettes, and medical supplies. Everyone showed up there with something to give, except for me, who just showed up a little drunk and emptyhanded.

As I walked up to Chelsea Piers an ambulance that was full of medical supplies was unloading. I went up to the driver, grabbed a bunch of boxes, and carried them into the relief center. Once I was inside, I kept busy, carrying things for people. I noticed everyone had a name tag that had their department on it, and since I didn't know where to get the name tags, I found a sharpie and wrote "Security" right on my shirt. About two hours after I had been helping move stuff, one of the people in charge had figured out I had snuck in, but since I was willing to lift anything that needed lifting she brought me over a proper nametag and let me stay. It was pretty chaotic, and figuring out who was in charge was a new task every few hours. I stayed at Chelsea Piers for five days helping with security, administration, logistics, and housing out of town rescue workers. Eventually I had a couple of different teams working for me including a fleet of bike messengers, who liked to be known as New York's Craziest... and that is really saying something.

The first people we got housing for were a Canadian alpine rescue team that packed up their trucks and drove down the second the first tower fell. They said they brought tents and asked me if I could point them to a park so they could sleep there.

"Uh no," I responded. "We have rats the size of dogs here, hang on."

I checked with the makeshift administration to see if anyone had considered this yet, but no one had. They asked me to call nearby hotels and see if any would donate rooms. This was Wednesday and the city had cleared out of visitors. I turned to a guy who had just been assigned to me, I think his name was Don. He was either a personal trainer or dietician for famous people, and was good looking, charming, had a big smile, and was a great talker. I asked Don if he could call local hotels and see if anyone was willing to donate some rooms. He flipped out his cell phone and speed-dialed the Waldorf-Astoria. That was back in the day when speed-dial was limited to around 100 numbers.

"Hello, I'm Don ___ and I'm working with the relief effort at Chelsea Piers. We have some out-of-town firefighters here that need a room and we are just calling hotels to see if anyone is willing to donate rooms. The Plaza has donated twenty rooms to us but because of the amount of... oh you will... thirty rooms... that's very generous, thank you, we'll be sending the first group over now. They are a Canadian alpine rescue... okay thank you."

He hung up. My eyes were bulging out of my head. This guy was smooth.

"So," I said, "do you want to go with them to make sure they get settled?"

Don shook his head.

"Why don't you? I'll call the Plaza now."

Needless to say, I gladly handed over the five-minute-old housing department to Don and asked the Alpine Rescue Team to show me to their trucks.

The ride to the Waldorf was a nice respite from the relief center. I sat in the bed of their pickup truck with two firemen and directed the driver through the open truck slider window. It was the middle of the night, the streets were empty, and the air was cool. Those of us in the bed of the pickup smoked cigarettes and didn't talk much. It's crazy how everyone seemed to smoke cigarettes in those days. I thought it was strange that none of these guys had ever heard of the Waldorf-Astoria before.

When I got back to Chelsea Piers, I was sent to pick up more biohaz-ard bags from Bellevue Hospital. It was probably 4 AM when I got there. I had to walk down a long passageway lined with candles and photos. No one else was there. For anyone that's never lived in New York City, when you are in public places in Manhattan, you expect other people to be around, at any time of the day or night. You are never alone, there's always someone else moving somewhere and usually making noise. But not this night. It was just me, the candles, and the photos. So many of those pho-tos were of people smiling, laughing, and living their life surrounded by loved ones and family. Joy frozen in time. I tried not to look, but one photo after another caught my gaze. Thousands of eyes stared back at me in the flickering candlelight. It was so quiet I could hear the candles burning. New York was never supposed to be that quiet. I didn't know if the silence was respectful or terrifying. I pushed through the hospital door, where the reception attendant was expecting me and the bags were already at the desk. I wished they weren't, as I was not ready to walk back outside.

The next night was Thursday, and I negotiated with a police boat captain a way to ferry supplies down to the North Cove to set up a relief center for those working on the pile from the south and west sides[34] It took a while to be approved, and by the time we left the dock it was dark.

34 "The pile" is what everyone at the time called the area of destruction left by the collapsed buildings. Because the pile was so large, most roads were not passable, so we couldn't drive supplies around the pile to get to the far sides. There were, however, rescue workers working on every side of the pile. So the only way to get supplies to the south and west sides was to bring them by boat.

I grew up on the water, but this was my first time on a boat in New York. I wanted to reach out and touch the water like I always did as a kid, but something stopped me. I didn't know if it was a feeling that the water was unclean, or if it would seem like some kind of breach of protocol; even though we were in a little Boston Whaler, I kept my hands dry.

In the sky over New Jersey, I saw flashes of lightning. I heard we were going to get a storm, and in fact, had two boxes of coats with me just for that purpose. The captain of the boat donned his own rain coat, and said to me over the engine, "If you got one, you better put it on." I dug through the box and found one that fit. I still have that coat today.

As we reached the dock, the first thing I noticed was the putrid air. Even though I was wearing a mask, every inhalation felt like someone dragging a back scratcher through my esophagus. The fire, that would burn another 98 days, poisoned the air so thoroughly that my body was revolting with every breath. To this day I have no idea how so many people stayed down there as long as they did.

We arrived at the dock in time to unload the supplies before the storm hit. I brought coffee, water, and some hot food that was donated by a local restaurant. The rain was coming and we didn't have a place to set up. There was a coffee shop in a building that looked damaged; the door was locked, but a passing firefighter popped it open with a metal tool he had. We set up in the coffee shop. All the rescue workers wanted was coffee and cigarettes. I gave away all the cigarettes I had on me, and I promised to send more down on the next trip.

The skies opened up just as I went out to the dock. It was complete chaos there, but the closer you got to the pile, the more organized it became. I tried to find anyone in charge, but even without the lightning and the driving rain, it would have been difficult. With each lightning strike I saw a new flash of horror. I remember the building I was walking past looked like it had a steel claw of twisted girders coming out of it. At the next strike I looked up again to try and see it, but it was gone. The lightning illuminated the smoke that was being pushed around by the rain and wind. A ship from New Jersey arrived with supplies and we formed a human chain to unload it as fast as possible. The police boat captain motioned for me to come to him; he said he had to go back to Chelsea Piers, but could bring another load down in a couple of hours. I told him I would go with him, and I checked back in with the makeshift relief center in the coffee shop to see what people were requesting. Again, hot coffee and cigarettes were the only things people wanted.

As I walked out I heard one of the relief workers say she figured out how to make coffee in the coffee shop. It sounds obvious, but in a thunderstorm with no power, we didn't even consider it. I guess she got someone to run an extension cord from a generator.

When I got back to Chelsea Piers, I recruited five more volunteers to go down to the North Cove. I made sure they packed the boat with hot coffee, cartons of cigarettes, and some hot soup, since I figured people would be cold after being out in the storm. Then I went to sleep for the first time since Mark had woken me up Tuesday morning.

I stayed at Chelsea Piers until Sunday, when the realization suddenly hit me that no one was being rescued. I don't know why we believed for so long that we were working to rescue people, but really we were just solving the problems in front of us and I hadn't taken the time to really think about what we were doing. Honestly, what I was doing was avoiding thinking about what had happened. If I kept working, if I kept having some task to do, then I wouldn't have to think about all the lives that had been destroyed when those building fell. By Saturday night, I had realized we were not working to find survivors. On Sunday morning, I said my goodbyes and went home to Woodside. I lived two buildings down from a firehouse. I had to pass it to get home. They had a makeshift memorial out front, as they had lost three guys. That night I finally faced what had happened, and I cried harder and longer than I have ever cried in my entire life.

Everyone knows September 11th changed everything, but the more I hear people say that, the more trite it sounds. I had to leave the city. It was years before I could go back to Chelsea Piers.

But before I left the city, Chad, Josh, and I got one last Monday Lenny's sandwich session. Since I had left Chelsea Piers, all anyone wanted to talk about was my time there, or what it was like down at the pile, which people were now starting to call, "Ground Zero." I couldn't talk about it anymore, and Chad and Josh knew it. So we talked baseball. I remember Chad started in on how the whole country would be rooting for the Yankees now. I just rolled my eyes. He was incredulous.

"Are you joking me? Come on, the Orioles have been eliminated since July. I mean, after everything that's happened, you aren't going to root for the Yankees?"

I laughed.

"Nope."

I was lying. For the rest of 2001 I rooted for the Yankees for the first and only time in my life. But please, if you are one of the few people that has read this far, don't ever tell anyone.

OPENING LINES TO THE FIRST ISSUE OF THE WARRIOR'S VOICE NEWSLETTER (AUTUMN '99)

Today a wind blew. A young man, with speed and skill, unfolded the awning at his father's restaurant. Clouds tumbled and glided over one another. A woman laughed, unfettered. An old immigrant danced through the sunrise, leading his ancestors into the day. Mushrooms appeared. Nomadic geese cut the sky with purpose. A child was born and began dreaming. A teenager died alone. A memory inspired a romantic to sit in silence and enjoy the colors. Sun burned the shoulders of a carpenter. A word was finally understood.

Today a man cried. A woman danced. Playing a game, children invented rules, and broke them. Brave souls held their breath. A dead man smiled, so his friend cried. Boundaries were redefined. Anger consumed a love. Honesty consumed a mountain. Heartache died to freedom. A smile of a child reminded someone what it meant to be human.

In this world, beauty is alive. In this time, some chose to touch it, some chose to watch it, some chose to love it, some chose to kill it, some chose to be it, some chose to forget it, some chose to fear it, some chose to search for it, some chose to wait for it, some chose to walk away from it.

We chose to fight for it.

We just wanted you to know that today a wind blew.

Redemption and Returning to Ireland a Second Time

For my father and I, repairing our relationship did not happen quickly. It was progressive, and took over a decade or so, and since a decade is a lot to cover in one chapter, I will give you a brief overview of events here:

In the summer of 1999, not long after I moved to New York City, and before I had the apartment that would become the Astoria Commune, my paternal grandfather, Ed O'Hare, passed away. My dad called me at work to tell me the news, as I didn't have a phone and was living in a Single Room Occupancy (SRO) in Sunset Park, Brooklyn. I didn't have a suit or any nice clothes for the funeral, but a fellow waiter at EJ's named Stevie Rodriguez took me suit shopping and then took me to the tailor, telling him in Spanish to rush the job because it was for a funeral. Stevie then told me the only reason the tailor rushed it was because Latinos respect family, unlike gringos like me. Stevie was a good guy.

The funeral was in Dyer, Indiana, the town my grandparents moved to when my dad was fourteen. My dad claimed to have moved fourteen times before he was fourteen, but once they moved to Dyer, they never left. At my grandfather's funeral, I hugged my dad. We talked about funeral stuff. I hugged all my other family members, the church choir sang "Danny Boy." I don't always cry at funerals, but I always cry at funerals when they sing "Danny Boy." I read a poem I had written on the plane. My dad said the great-aunts liked the poem. Then I went back to New York.

The next day I went into Manhattan and visited with Aidar and my girlfriend at the time, Ericka. I loved to sneak onto the Lincoln Center campus of Fordham University, where there was a quiet second-story green space and garden; it was like my secret garden. I met Ericka and Aidar there for "lunch" (aka coffee and cigarettes). I talked about how my grandfather was essentially Willie Lowman, and Ericka told me that *Death of the Salesman* was on Broadway at the Eugene O'Neill Theater. It was probably 2 PM at the time, and I said we should walk over and see if we could get tickets. The three of us were broke, however, and you could not get tickets to a show like *Death of a Salesman* last minute, so Ericka said we didn't have a chance.

"Nah," I said waving my hands and packing up my bag. "My dad does stuff like this all the time. We'll get tickets."

I walked up to the theater, and discovered they had one ticket that had just been turned in, front row, left of center. The box office said I could have it for $20. Ericka and Aidar couldn't get tickets, but this was more for me anyway, and they didn't seem to mind.

I went home and put on the suit I had bought for my grandfather's funeral. I got to the theater early, so I grabbed a whiskey at Ye Old Triple Inn, my favorite watering hole in Hell's Kitchen. I had only lived in New York for a couple of months at this point, and this was the first play I was attending since moving there. I was a muddle of different emotions, but the whiskey calmed my nerves, and I went into the theater with a gentle ease.

Brian Dennehy was playing Willie Lowman. Dennehy didn't look that much like my grandfather, but he looked almost exactly like my dad. He was a physical actor, he made himself bigger on stage, and he had a thunderous roar, just like my father. Kevin Anderson played Biff, and reminded me of why I loved that show so much. He was a great Biff. The entire cast was fantastic, but Elizabeth Franz, who played Linda? Holy shit, she was incredible.

For those unfamiliar with the show, Linda, who is Willie's wife and Biff and Happy's mother, has a great, long monologue at the end of the first act about how Willie deserved better. It is the, "Attention must be paid" speech. She's begging her sons to care about their father that one hates and the other dismisses. It's what makes the play a classic, and it's heart-wrenching. It's the eulogy that would never be said, as we know Willie will die (because, the title) and yet Linda is pleading for something else. In many ways my grandfather was Willie, and my grandmother was Linda. Throughout the play Linda's blocking brought her closer and closer to me, until the final scene at Willie's funeral, where she stood just a few feet away from where I sat. I swear I could feel the heat from the lights reflecting off her skin. The closer she stood to me, the warmer I felt. It was as though I was seeing my grandmother on stage, and throughout this entire play I was experiencing a different funeral, the funeral that should have been—the honest funeral for my grandfather. I wanted to get up and hug her, I wanted to hug my grandmother again. It was one of those rare moments in life when there was no difference between what was happening inside of me and what was happening around me. I was consumed by the play.

I didn't wait by the stage door at the show. I went back to Ye Old Triple

Inn, which was packed. I got a whiskey and slammed it. A bartender with whom I was somewhat friendly came over and asked me why I was in a suit. I said I had just come from a funeral. He poured me another and told me to put my money away.

Say what you will about people in New York, they understand the kindness of a comped drink. I finished the whiskey and headed out, walking through Times Square and all the way down to Union Square. I jumped on the R train and got to Sunset Park well after midnight.

I have never forgotten this day for a reason. Before that night I had never actually seen *Death of a Salesman*, a play which I knew so well; I had only been in it. Sitting in the audience was a way to step outside of myself and look at the life I had been living and the person I had become. I thought about my grandfather, and my dad, and how even with all of their flaws, Linda was right. Though Willie was flawed, his sons were ungrateful, and he deserved better. Linda lays it bare: we're all flawed, how could we expect others not to be? My dad had been an ass, and had been cruel to me, and I assumed he wanted nothing to do with me. But the more I thought about it, it might have been his twisted pride that cause him to be that way. It might have been his flawed way of protecting himself. I decided not be the reason we no longer spoke, and it would be up to him if he wanted to have a relationship with me moving forward.

After the events of September 11th, 2001 I went back to Ocean Pines for about ten days. I stayed with my mom, but I saw my dad and we watched a Notre Dame football game together, the first one we had seen together since I was in high school. Looking back, I think it was either the Pitt or West Virginia game. My dad made popcorn and we ate Bugles, and while he was still guarded around me, things were better than they had been in a long time.

By Thanksgiving of that year, I was living in Fort Collins, Colorado with Caroline while she finished her bachelor's degree so she could become a teacher. My dad flew out to have Thanksgiving dinner with us at a friend's house. He was only there a few hours, but I liked that he got to spend some time with Caroline. He was his old affable, charming self.

The following year Caroline and I moved back to New York. We lived in the East Village with Mark in a horrifying basement apartment. Caroline started teaching in Brooklyn, while I started working as a production assistant (PA) on commercials. My dad visited us a couple of times and took us out to dinner.

Even though I was brand new to the TV industry I worked on commercials with a bunch of big name directors; including an Ikea spot for the international market with Wes Anderson, and a Sprite commercial with Joe Pytka. Working as a PA on big budget commercials is like peeking behind the curtain of the whole capitalist system. Perhaps working in any aspect of advertising or marketing lays bare so many societal incongruities, but for someone like myself who was so uneducated in that world, the lessons were stark. One of my first commercial jobs required sneaking the owner of a huge national pizza chain into a studio's back door so he could film his own commercials during the SAG strike. Because he was in SAG, he was crossing the picket line to star in commercials for his own company. In another spot a makeup company made a commercial for $300,000 and spent $16,000,000 on an ad buy to let people know they were donating $100,000 to charity. The common hypocrisies were pretty eye-opening, and even though I was just a PA, it was a pretty good education.

At this point I was loving everything New York, other than the baseball teams, of course. I made it up to The Gin Mill a few times a year for Lenny's Sandwiches, and I knew I wanted to marry Caroline, even if I felt I didn't have the money for it. My brother and I became even better friends, and I played D&D or World of Darkness with him and his group once a week. In those days I worked fairly regularly for a Production Manager named Drew Santarsiero.[35] who was one of those rare people who could talk about the Godfather trilogy, politics, art-house films, and name Scott Walker songs in the same breath. Drew played a 12-string bass guitar in a band called Hunk, and was on an episode of *90210*, which led us to call him "9-0-Drew-1-0." Man, he hated that nickname.

On one of Drew's sets, I met a fellow PA named Yori Tondrowski, with whom I would work on dozens, if not a hundred productions. Yori is a Yankees fan, but he was much more of a football guy. So he was a Jets fan, which in those days (as in most days) was pretty rough. Yori and I were grubby degenerate PAs when we met each other, but I was just working in film and television because I needed a job. Yori wanted it to be his career. In many ways he mentored me, and he was certainly the first to elucidate to me the injustice and dangers of film sets. I like to think I gained my positive reputation as a producer because I avoided putting others in the same physically dangerous positions in which Yori and I so often found ourselves. Since I had previously been employed by so many OSHA nightmares (Frontier Town, construction, kitchens),

---

35 Also a Production Manager named Kathy Hoffman who was amazing and had the best PA crew in town. In fact, every regular PA that worked for Kathy later became a producer or 1st Assistant Director, and if you don't think that's rare, you have never worked on a set before.

I needed someone like Yori around to point out all the wrongs to which we were being subjected. Admittedly, my style of producing was not so much, "would Yori complain about this?" but rather "how can I minimize the length of time Yori would complain about this?" In the end, that seemed to work pretty well.

I saved Yori's life once, but he only agreed to produce my film *Rehearsal* if I stopped telling people I saved his life. Clearly, I have kept up my end of the bargain.

There was a great moment with Yori when we were shooting a mayonnaise commercial in suburban New Jersey. We had a huge light truck that needed to back out of a long residential driveway that was on a hill, at the front end of a blind curve. We went down the road a few hundred feet to stop traffic, but the only car that came was an SUV that stopped when Yori—who was, as always, wearing his Jets hat—stepped out into the road and put up his hands. The driver lowered his window and yelled, "Jets?!?" Yori walked over to the car and saw Michael Strahan, an all-pro defensive end for the New York Giants. Yori immediately started booing the future Hall-of-Famer, telling him how this was going to be the Jets' year[36] Strahan laughed and said, "It's not my fault you didn't have a daddy that loved you. Want me to get you a Giant's hat, I think I got one back here." It was a great exchange. Since the truck took about five minutes to navigate the driveway, Michael Strahan was stuck there a while, and all he and Yori did was go back and forth talking trash. Years later, Caroline was working at *Live! with Kelly and Michael* when she got pregnant with Olive. I was at the show when she told Michael Strahan we were leaving New York because we were going have a kid. He came up and shook my hand told, us we were doing the right thing, and was so nice to me. I wanted to tell him about the exchange he had years before with Yori, but I didn't want to admit to having a friend that liked the Jets.

I was reading lots of books on religion in those days, especially Mircea Eliade's *A History of Religious Ideas*, and since I argued with Yori in the truck about... well, everything, one day we got on the topic of Islam, which I had just read about. We were sitting in the line of trucks waiting to pick up expendables (light gels, tape, sash cord, etc.—things on sets you use and then throw away) and even though I knew Yori was wrong, this was before smartphones existed, so there was no way to look anything up[37] However, we had cell phones so I got the idea to call a

---

36 It wasn't. I'm not even sure what year this happened...but...it wasn't going to be the Jets year.

37 All my editors want to know what Yori was wrong about. Everything, he was wrong about everything. But, specifically, in this case it was a complicated and nuanced debate about the organizational structure of Al-Qaeda.

former college professor of mine. Father Patrick Gaffney was an Islamicist and anthropology professor at Notre Dame, so I called information in South Bend, eventually got the Notre Dame switchboard, and then miraculously caught Father Gaffney in his office. Father Gaffney had no idea who I was but talked to us on speaker for twenty minutes, mostly explaining how Yori was wrong.

About a month later, I emailed Father Gaffney another question, and we started a correspondence (although this was most likely very annoying for him). Whenever I went back to South Bend, I would try and see him and even took him out to dinner a few times so I could ask him 400 elementary questions that I would know he already answered in the class I was in, had I been paying attention. It turns out he went to The University of Chicago and studied under Mircea Eliade, which for certain people is way more impressive than Impy growing up with Jim Darcangelo.

These crazy days were filled with sleepless nights, a constant struggle to make bills, and a relentless pursuit of the future. I was surrounded and inspired by dreamers and creators, and every conversation was an exploration of how to express ideas to others. My depression was put on hold by a million cigarettes, coffee all day, and whiskey all night. I worked on an independent film called *The Forgotten Road* with a cinematographer named Dave Ferrara. Dave and I became good friends, and he taught me to play straight pool because I liked the film *The Hustler*. He eventually brought me in to play baseball in his baseball league. While in that league I tore both my hamstrings, yet I didn't come close to sustaining the worst injury on our team. That experience is the backbone of the plot of the screenplay I am currently working on in my free time, so I'm not giving it away.

Dave loves baseball, and at least he isn't a Yankees fan. He's a Cleveland Guardians fan.[38] Whatever, nobody's perfect. He also has an encyclopedic knowledge of trivia; in fact, he is the only person I know that could have kept up with or, dare I say, even surpass my father in his prime in trivial knowledge. But unlike my dad, Dave actually put his skills to the test on *Jeopardy!*

After a couple of years working as a PA, I got hired to be the equipment room manager and key PA on the first season of *Queer Eye for the Straight Guy*. Reality TV was just finding its way at that point, and I was working 18–20 hour days with less than five-hour turnarounds.[39] Without

---

38 They were the Cleveland Indians in those days.
39 A "turnaround" means the time from when you leave work to when you need to be back. Things like eating, sleeping, and commuting need to be factored into your turnaround time.

getting the approval of the production coordinator, I hired Yori to drive the truck. When the production manager called me in to dress me down for hiring someone without approval I laid out the hours I was actually working and told her I would crash the truck if I had to drive. Since I wouldn't risk crashing the truck, I would continue to do my job only if she hired a driver. When Yori came on board, I would sleep in the truck while he drove. Yori worked two days, quit, and told me I should quit too. He was right, but I stuck it out for four episodes before I started to lose it for lack of sleep. They hired three people to replace me when I quit.

I loved working with the Fab Five[40] though, especially Thom Filicia. One day he was waiting for the paint to dry at an apartment and we were in the backyard eating lunch, and I asked him if he was excited for the show to start airing. He told me he was nervous, especially for his dad. Thom said he shared a name with his father, and while his dad was always supportive of him, it was a big deal that he would be out on national television. I didn't realize how uncommon it was to be openly gay in those days, so I had never thought for a second about what these guys were going through. Which just goes to show how clueless I was/ am as a cisgendered straight white male.

On the first shoot day we were in Long Island and I was sitting on the back of the truck smoking a cigarette. Carson Kressley came out and asked if he could have a cigarette, so I tossed him my pack. He opened it and saw it was the last one and said he would never take the last one. I insisted, telling him I could get others, not to worry about it. He said thanks and lit it; then he looked at me for a minute and said:

"If I become famous...I'm going to buy you a Corolla."

I smiled.

"Carson, you better watch what you say. You're going to be a star."

He took another drag and nodded slowly while he really thought about it.

"Yup. A Corolla."

As of my writing this, the very famous Carson Kressley has yet to buy me my deserved Corolla.

A cool moment happened when my father came to visit one weekend. Even though I had the day off, I had to pop over to the equipment room to swap out charging batteries, so I took him with me. It took about fifteen minutes to change out the batteries, so my dad got to see my

---

40 *Queer Eye for the Straight Guy* featured five on air talent dubbed "The Fab Five." They were Ted Allen (Food and Wine Connoisseur), Kyan Douglas (Grooming Guru), Thom Filcia (Design Doctor), Carson Kressley (Fashion Savant), and Jai Rodriguez (Culture Vulture).

"office." Yes, it was just an equipment room, but it had a desk, and that was the first time he had seen me have one; to him that translated to having a "real job." While I really enjoyed my time at *Queer Eye*, especially working with the Fab Five and the hard-partying crew, Yori indeed was right, I was working myself to death, so I quit.

Caroline, Mark, and I moved to Astoria, to the first floor of a small house on 37th Street between Astoria Boulevard and 28th Ave. It was a great little two-bedroom place with a huge backyard (huge for Queens, about 875 sq. ft). Mark only lived there for a year before moving out to Portland, Oregon, but Caroline and I ended up there for over a decade. That year we held our first Orphans Thanksgiving. We invited all of our friends that didn't have local families or weren't able to go home for the holiday to come over for a traditional turkey dinner. We had about twenty-five people in our backyard; the tables, chairs, and tents all came from Keith Guliner at Wits End. Even though I was just a PA in those days—the lowest guy in the production hierarchy—he thought it was pretty cool that we would have all these "orphans" over to our house for Thanksgiving, so he gave it all to us for free. Of course, once I became a producer, I made sure my production managers never went anywhere but Wits End, sending him hundreds of thousands of dollars of business. Keith didn't know I was going to become a producer one day, he was just being a good guy. Dad did not come to the first Orphan Thanksgiving.

Caroline and I got engaged that December, and my dad came up to New York and took us out to dinner, which was the only time I saw him that winter.

Just before Caroline and I were engaged I began working at *Tough Crowd with Colin Quinn*. I started out as a PA working in the cargo van with Adam Wade, or driving Colin Quinn and the writers around. It was a great gig and I loved working at Rockefeller Center. I got promoted to be payroll accountant, getting my own desk with a computer and everything.

The back problems I first had when playing lacrosse at age nineteen became pretty severe by this time, and I got addicted to Vicodin. I was eventually taking nine or ten pills a day. This was back in 2003-2004, and I remember clearly my pain management doctor telling me I could take as much as I wanted, they were not addictive. I just couldn't drink alcohol with them. So while this was my "dry year," I was high all the time. He also gave me a total of nine epidurals over an 11 month period, and I was taking three muscle relaxers a day, too. Even that heavily medicated, nothing seemed to be working.

As my addiction reached another level, I started to become paranoid, hoarding food and prepping for the apocalypse. Caroline rightly called me out for my behavior and once I realized that it was the pills, I quit cold turkey. I survived, but the back pain got really bad again; for the first time in quite a while, I wanted to die. This time it was not because I thought it would be better if I had never lived, but because the pain was making any enjoyment of life impossible. Finally, Caroline called her father in exasperation, who reached out to his good friend Donald Fagen, lead singer of Steely Dan, whose wife Libby had recently had back surgery. He gave me the name of her surgeon, which I thought was a waste of time. I'd seen seven surgeons over the last decade who'd all told me the same thing: nothing could be done. But to satisfy Caroline, I went to see this new guy.

He examined me for about ten minutes and then asked to see my myelogram. I told him I had no idea what a myelogram was, so he sent me to Dr. St. Louis[41] the following day to get the myelogram done. Three weeks later he operated on my spine, removing a piece of hardened cerebral spinal fluid which all of the previous surgeons had no idea was there, because they never did a myelogram. Finally, the extreme back pain was gone from my life, hopefully forever.

I told Tom that for my bachelor party I wanted to canoe on the Pocomoke River in Maryland with Tom Westcott like we had when we were kids. Tom talked to my dad, and they planned a party at my dad's house after the canoeing, with Tom Westcott, George Zaiser, and other teachers and coaches from WCS, plus a couple of my friends from college. We watched the Notre Dame game and I stayed up talking to Zaiser until five AM about art and life. At seven, we left for the Ravens tailgate with Kevin McNulty and Lee Reilly, and on the way got the news that my maternal grandfather passed away. Dad flew out for his funeral, he always went to funerals.

Caroline and I got married in upstate New York, and a month later *Tough Crowd* was canceled. I was still recovering from my back surgery, so we didn't do a big Thanksgiving that year for the first and only time while we lived in Astoria. We didn't get a tent or anything and only about seven people came. I remember it was pouring rain. I didn't have my strength back yet, so Dave Ferrara came over and cooked. He made a really good garlic soup, which I had never had, before or since. My dad came this time, but he ended up spending most of his time with Tom at a bar because Tom was going through a divorce.

Still, even though he wasn't there long, I had just seen Dad at my

---

41 Solidly good Dr. name. Also would be a great name for a trombone player in a funk band.

bachelor party, my maternal grandfather's funeral, and my wedding. He wasn't yelling at me, he wasn't grumpy. He wasn't avoiding me, he was showing up. He talked with Tom and I, and, more importantly, he was listening.

That January, I started working for MTV. Jessica Borovay, who I had first worked with in commercials—and who then hired me to work at *Tough Crowd*—had brought me in to work as a PA on her first MTV shoot. At first I refused, but acquiesced after she agreed to my terms that Yori would be my truck buddy. I was dreading working for MTV, but it turned out to be a really fun five-day shoot with a bunch of stories I probably shouldn't tell.

I met Jessica's boss, Meg Sudlik, in the bar after the last day of the shoot; and I told her I was going to quit working in production because I thought I was too smart for it. She thought I was hilarious, even though I kept protesting that I was serious. She actually hired me then and there, and I told her since I had never worked at any job for more than a year, she wouldn't have to live with her decision for long. Meg said she was likely to fire me before the year was up, anyway. Naturally, I worked for her ten times longer than I worked for anyone else. I moved up the ladder very quickly working for Meg, going from PA to producer in less than a year. I'm a huge pain in the ass to bosses, and even ones who were my good friends generally couldn't stand me for too long. To this day I'm not sure how Meg kept me around for as long as she did.

The year I started working at MTV, Notre Dame began its football season playing at Pitt. I called Dad about fifteen minutes before kickoff to see where he was watching it. He was at home, so we spoke through part of the first quarter and then again in the second half. It became a ritual after that, for us to talk on football Saturdays. I know this is a cliché! Clichés only become clichés because they happen all the time, so they are hard to avoid in real life. But yes, when my dad and I couldn't really talk anything else, we could talk about sports. I'm sure as a reader you saw that coming, but as someone going through this life, I sure didn't until it happened. Thank goodness for clichés.

Of course, after football season ended it would be a long time until we had much to talk about again, but that spring Dad gave me a call and started talking baseball with me. We hadn't talked baseball in years, but I guess I mentioned my fantasy baseball draft that was upcoming, and it must have rattled around in his brain a bit until sometime after opening day, when he realized Nick Markakis was on the Orioles. Dad called and asked how Nick Markakis was doing, and told me he saw him when he was with the Shorebirds, the O's A-level farm team that played in Salisbury on the Eastern Shore.

Up until that point, I never had a conversation with my dad about the minor leagues at all, and the Shorebirds were founded after I left the area. I found out he attended a bunch of Shorebird games, so we started talking about the different players he'd seen who had made it to the bigs. His favorite was Calvin Pickering, who stood six-foot-six and was pushing 300 pounds. Pickering could hit the ball a mile, but was so slow he would get thrown out at first base from right field all the time. I'd never heard of him, since his brief stint in the majors was when I was in Europe, and I didn't follow baseball while I was there.

Now that Dad and I had baseball and football season taken care of—and since he always kept me in the loop with Mike Brey and the Notre Dame men's basketball team—we were pretty much back to talking all year. This is when I first discovered that Dad was a Yankees fan. I will tell you why in a later chapter. About this time, I hired Tom as a Production Assistant, and he liked the gig so much he quit his job as a waiter to be a full-time PA. When Tom called Dad to tell him this, Dad didn't seem to understand how I was able to hire anyone. Tom explained to him that I had a "real job" and was in charge of a bunch of people, so my dad found out when my next shoot was and then coincidentally planned a trip to New York. He literally invited himself to set.

The shoot happened to be a Pepsi spot for the VMAs, with Soo-Hyun Chung directing. She was one of my favorite directors to work with. She was the type of crazy person that I loved, the kind that dreamt crazy, rather than act crazy to hide their insecurity at being unable to dream. Her idea for this spot was an opulent, glittery stage inspired by *All That Jazz* where various people would sing a karaoke version of Fall Out Boy's "Dance, Dance." We cast about thirty people for this thirty-second spot, knowing we would use at most twelve in the final cut. Since we had far too many people, we started figuring out how to group them together. About that time my dad walked in and I asked him sit in a director's chair in video village (the place where producers and clients sit to watch what the camera is recording) while Soo-Hyun and I tried to work out the cast parings. Soo-Hyun gave me a how-dare-you-not-introduce-me-to-this-man-that-is-cleary-your-father look, so I introduced them. Soo-Hyun shook his hand.

"Hi, nice to meet you," and then, turning to me and not pausing for a second she said, "We're putting your dad in this spot."

She gave him a sombrero and some maracas. Even though he had never heard of Fall Out Boy and had no idea what song he was singing, he wouldn't have been able to sing it, anyway. So instead he just made a funny face, shook the maracas, sang "Dance Dance," and, of course, made it into the final spot. That is how my dad ended up on MTV.

Later, I sent him a DVD of "his" commercial. When WCS was back in session he made every student that made the mistake of walking past his office come in and sit down to watch "his" commercial. He would always say to them:

"Now, have you heard of MTV?"

"Yes, Mr. O'Hare."

"Oh good." He'd pause for a moment. "Have you ever been on MTV?"

"No, Mr. O'Hare."

Super quickly, "Oh really because I have!"

Then he would show them the spot. He never reported if he impressed any students by this fact, but, honestly, I don't think he cared.

After that, my dad and I were good. We had a great relationship. It had been a decade since I dropped out of school, but slowly—because I put him on TV, and we talked about sports, and did Thanksgiving—we rebuilt our relationship. I think part of his anger towards me had more to do with his fear of me ruining my life by dropping out of college and becoming a drifter. I think him coming to set and seeing me as a producer and being married and comfortable made him content, or at least less afraid for me. He saw that I was capable and able to succeed on my own.

Of course, the external plot is never the whole story. There was more going on inside my dad than what was shown on the outside. My dad was going through his own mental health journey, but he just kept it to himself. I can only speculate on what he discovered in those days, what struggles he went through, where he sought help—if he did at all. He was drinking pretty heavily during that time, despite never being much of a drinker before that. Maybe that was his solution? I will never know. I'm glad he let me back into his life, even if I don't know why he decided to have a relationship with me. At the same time, he never made peace with his brother.

Dad came to every Thanksgiving we had in Astoria except the first, and the Thanksgivings grew in size until we regularly had over fifty people every year. Fitting fifty people in that backyard in late November was not the easiest task, but with the help of our neighbors, Peter Hodson and Carl Hansen, we erected an enormous multi-tent structure that kept out wind, snow, rain, and even had a fireplace inside—though Keith at Wits End got a little annoyed that I started returning the tents smelling like a campfire. The Orphan Thanksgiving became a bit of misnomer, as people traveled from all over to attend. Clint came from Indiana, my aunts came from Arizona and Indiana, and even Méabh and her husband Richard came from Ireland. After my mom broke up with the terrible guy she left my dad for, even she started to come to Thanksgiving. It became a pretty big party. It was the only time all year that the entire family was together again. After every Thanksgiving, my dad would call me and thank me, always saying the same thing:

"You managed to do it. You did the impossible. You managed to bring the family together again. I'm so proud of you."

It was the best thing he ever said to me, and he said it every year.

In 2009, Kevin McNulty planned a family reunion in Ireland. Again, we are one of the few people of Irish descent in Maryland not related to Kevin McNulty, but nevertheless we went to his family reunion. Dad bought us the tickets. I let Méabh know we were coming, and her parents said they would love to have us over for lunch.

It was my first time back in Ireland since 1998. The moment we got off the bus at the hotel, I breathed in deep. It was like smelling the pillow of an absent lover. I felt like I was finally home again. I couldn't believe I had spent so little time in this place, but still felt so comfortable.

I'm sure my dad was a little nervous as he walked into Méabh's parents' home, given what had happened before. But Méabh's father greeted Dad with a warm handshake, her mother hugged him, and we had a truly pleasant afternoon. As we were saying our goodbyes, my dad walked out of the house first. Méabh's father turned to his wife and said:

"What a lovely man."

"See," Méabh's mom said. "I told you that you should have let him in for a cup of tea."

I just laughed. Clearly no one had forgotten anything in the eleven years I was gone. While nothing had been forgotten, it seemed all had been forgiven. It was a great trip with the McNulty clan, but it was a really important trip for the O'Hare family. My dad and I were finally together in Ireland. The bridges had been repaired, the fences had been mended. While I didn't think of it at the time, all that healing can be traced back to the Eugene O'Neil Theater, Elizabeth Franz, and Arthur Miller.

ANXIETY VS. DEPRESSION AND THE LIES I TELL

Speaking as someone who has had both anxiety and depression, anxiety is, without a doubt the worse of the two. Again, I am not a mental health expert, so please, please, please: if you are dealing with any mental health issues, ask a professional for help. And if that professional is not helping, find another one.

I have had depression issues since at least adolescence. I was likely bipolar when I was younger, but as I have aged I appear to have grown out of my manic phases—probably because I just don't have the energy anymore. All kidding aside, I never really had that big of a problem with my mania. I enjoyed the euphoria associated with it, as well as the general excitement of what I felt as passionate madness. My dancer used the term "wildflower fever" to describe a similar feeling, and I adopted that term to describe what I now know was mania. In those manic days people would look at me, smile, and call me crazy with as positive a connotation as that word could allow. Depression, on the other hand, elicited the opposite response from people, as most people recoil from sullen behavior. When I first experienced depression, I had a difficult time hiding it. Throughout my life I came up with a bunch of methods for dealing with depression, such as compartmentalizing it within myself, or hiding it from others. I developed tools to mitigate the severity of my depression, including self-medicating, mostly with cigarettes and alcohol. For anxiety, not only did I not have any tools to deal with it, I wasn't even able to recognize anxiety for what it was.

Here is an abbreviated list of some of the things I was able to do while experiencing a moderate bout of depression:

- Sleep fifteen hours a day
- Watch the same film over and over again for fifteen days in row
- Read poetry
- Write poetry
- Listen to depressing music
- Make the greatest "depressing music" mixtapes of all time

- Eat far too much food
- Cook far too much food
- Go for walks/drives/journeys
- Play Madden, Civilization, or World of Warcraft
- Smoke cigarettes
- Drink alcohol
- Think about the meaninglessness of existence... read philosophy, write philosophy, talk about philosophy... anything really with philosophy

Now, here is an exhaustive list of all the things I could do while experiencing a moderate bout of anxiety:

- Drive myself to the hospital (barely).

At one point in my life, I thought it was terrible to be depressed and want to sleep fifteen hours a day. Then I experienced anxiety, and I couldn't sleep because I thought that if my eyes closed, they would never open again.

As I mentioned, when I was depressed, I thought about suicide. And again, I still think about my death all of the time, but that doesn't mean I think about committing suicide. However, when I was really depressed, I certainly thought about committing suicide many times. With anxiety, I never considered suicide once, since I believed I was already dying, and that thought paralyzed me.

If I'm anxious, I can't write. But even when I was in the deepest throes of depression, I could write for days without sleep.

It's hard to understand depression or anxiety if you haven't experienced them, because everyone has been sad or nervous in their life, and those words are synonyms. I think a popular misconception about depression is that someone is merely sad, and they let themselves continue to be sad as if it is a choice they are making, or some moral failing. This stems from our moronic adherence to the laughable and unscientific concept of "free will." Anyway, that is not how depression works.

Most people don't think *about* thinking, so this might get a little confusing, but here goes anyway: I'm going to go out on a limb and assert that most everyone has a voice inside their head. This voice, which we refer to as our "thoughts," creates a near-constant string of words, which is how we "hear" ourselves "thinking." The voice is usually understood to be of ourselves, "who we really are." It's our honest self, our true self. When someone says, "penny for your thoughts," they want to know what that voice is saying. And I think people have varying degrees of control over this voice. There are two things to keep in mind here: first, sanity is a sliding scale, and the more control you have over the voice, the more towards sane you most likely are. Second, we think in words with this voice—not in colors, shapes, or sounds. One can think in colors, shapes, sounds, but I'm going to focus on the voice thoughts, the thoughts we put into definable words.

I can usually control this voice when I concentrate, so when that happens, I think about what *I* want to think about. Then I can be creative, and can fantasize, dream, and organize. When I concentrate, my voice can be full of positive affirmations, telling me that I'm a great person, am smart, honest, hilarious, good to be around, and am a benefit to society. However, when I don't concentrate, that same voice tells me I'm a piece of shit, and that I'm worthless, and have wasted my life. My existence means nothing to others, and I've only made the world worse by living in it. I don't know if most people experience this, but this is what my brain does when left to its own devices.

When I'm in the grip of depression, I'm not able to control the voice at all. Even if I concentrate I will have no control over my thoughts. Can I write when I'm depressed? Absolutely, but I can't form the story a way I want it, I don't get to decide its outcome or even its tone. If you go back and read things I wrote in my early writing days (please don't), during the worst days of my depression, the stories all spiraled pointlessly until they ended. There was no humor, no joy, no catharsis, and no reason. It was a depressed person transcribing the words of depression.

The notion that you can "control" depression by mere desire, or that you have some choice in regarding your inner voice is frustrating laughable to someone going through this. One does not choose depression. I'm neither a psychiatrist nor a neurologist, but I do spend an inordinate amount of time thinking about thinking. I wile away my hours actively exploring my thoughts and challenging my mind. I learned to control my dreams, meditate every day, and do therapy once a week. I actively think about the brain all the time. If I could control the voice, I would. After all, I like thinking that I am awesome as I *am* a narcissist.

While I couldn't control my depression, I could live with it. I found lots of different tricks and strategies to mitigate the worst of it. The most common one was whiskey: I found that if I drank, I felt better and the depression subsided. Of course, the next day I felt worse, until I started drinking again. I also smoked cigarettes as a way to focus and calm my thoughts, as well as to get a tiny pleasure from the hit of nicotine. Obviously these are insanely unhealthy coping methods, as they were killing me, but they were my very misguided way of dealing with my situation. I also found ways to hide my depression from others, but I had to, as my generation is still not as accepting of mental illness as the younger generations are.

I'm not there yet with anxiety. I'm working on finding healthy ways to cope—the meditation helps, and the therapy helps. Reading fiction really helps sometimes, but I have to be careful about what I read. One of my favorite novels that I read in the past five years was *Normal People* by Sally Rooney. I tore through it in a day. After that, I was so excited to read her first novel, *Conversations with Friends*. Everything was going fine until I got about two-thirds through the book and suddenly became really anxious, and had to put the book down. This is a testament to Sally Rooney: she is such a good writer that the story consumed me, and I put myself into it completely. While her characters went through mental distress, I did as well. I was about to have a panic attack, so I put it down and opened *Murder on the Orient Express*. And you know what, that worked. My anxiety faded.

I believe I have a bad mix of personality traits for anxiety. While I'm a curious person, and am generally an optimist, I often tend to dwell on worst-case scenarios, especially those relating to health or safety. This is a problem, as whenever I have a twinge in my chest, I think for a moment it must be a heart attack. And while I'm very aware of emotional cues from other people, I have a crippling amount of empathy. I don't want others to be in pain, as that causes me pain. So when I have a twinge in my chest I also envision my daughter being heartbroken that she has no father, because I died of a heart attack. Thinking this causes me physical pain. Also I'm an addict, and a drunk, having a hyper-addictive personality. The years of smoking and drinking have taken a toll on my body, and I think I am more likely to die of a heart attack thanks to those bad habits. I blame myself for my past mistakes that will steal the future happiness from my daughter, and thinking this causes me to feel physically worse. By now, the twinge in my chest has turned into a full-blown panic attack. All of these thoughts happen so quickly that my conscious mind doesn't have time to keep up.

When I first dealt with anxiety, I reached out to my friend Len Foxwell, who had been open with me about his issues. Len talked to me for over two hours that first night, and he told me, "Anxiety is the curse of the active mind." He was right, but for me, "Anxiety is the curse of the active mind when given no focus." When allowed to wander and investigate every stimulus that flits around our brains, anxiety can grab hold of us and not give us space to breathe. If I am focused on a specific task, like writing a book, I don't give my mind the space it needs to become anxious.

Okay, so anxiety sucks, right? But let's not forget about depression, because in the end, there is a good chance that anxiety fed or caused my depression. I need to step back here and talk about it. Depression is difficult to talk about, but not emotionally—it should be clear by now I have no problem talking about emotions. It is hard to talk about logically and conceptually.

I think I was fourteen when I first started to experience depression. That would have been 1990, and society didn't have a thorough understanding of mental illness. In those days, I assumed if someone was crazy, they wouldn't actually know they were crazy. In my 10th grade English class (taught by the wonderful Erin Drew), I argued that King Lear was not crazy precisely *because* he thought he was going crazy. I really believed crazy people completely lost control of their faculties. It turns out that such a thing is only one type of crazy. In very gross and most likely outdated terms, mental illnesses can be divided into neuroses and psychoses. Using massive generalizations here, neuroses are rooted in reality, while psychoses are not. Psychosis is when you have schizophrenia, hallucinations, or delusional behavior, but is generally recognized by the person not understanding they have the problem. For instance, a schizophrenic might hallucinate that a tiger is stalking them, and even if it's explained to them that there is no tiger and they are hallucinating, they will still believe there is a tiger. Neurosis, on the other hand, is anxiety, depression, OCD—basically any mental illness where the person can understand they are experiencing that problem. But as a fourteen-year-old, I didn't have that kind of understanding; I thought crazy people only had psychosis.

Bear in mind that I was a healthy teenaged boy, athlete, actor, and politician, and was generally well-liked. Thanks to sports, I got a high daily dose of dopamine. Yet even with that dopamine, I started to become very interested in self destruction. I thought about suicide, and the way I started to think about it was to argue with God about suicide.

Here's the deal, I've cut four very long chapters out of this book.[42] One about racism, one about how we do not live in a simulation, one about free will, and one about God and Last Rites. I get it, you picked up a book about sports and now you're enduring this idiot talk about arguing with God which couldn't possibly be what you had wanted. Still, I need to give you a tiny bit of context here, so I am going to briefly talk about God and free will because it relates to the fourteen-year-old me struggling with the idea of suicide.

42 You're welcome.

Before I was fourteen, from the first moment I was conscious, I loved God. I had that true faith that seems so easy in youth. I spoke to God often, and I believed God answered me; I heard what I knew was the voice of God in my head. One day, when I was perhaps thirteen, that voice stopped, I no longer heard God. Shortly thereafter, I began to argue with God, but He continued to not respond. I was Catholic, so the God with whom I was arguing tended to fit the image of the things the Catholic Church taught. Eventually I stopped believing in God altogether, probably while in my mid-twenties. I miss having God in my life, even a God I was angry with, or a God that disappointed me. I would do almost anything to really believe in God again, as I miss having that certainty in my life. I often wonder if I would have ever had anxiety at all if I still believed in God. We'll get back to God in a bit.

I also don't believe in free will, as previously noted. Of course, I believed in free will when I was younger, because we are all trained to believe in it. Free will is generally defined as the ability to act at one's own discretion without the necessity of fate. It is bound very tightly to what I believe to be a very misconceived notion about the individual. Why do we believe in the concept of the individual? Because it's easier, not because individuals exist. We are multispecies organisms; as roughly 39 trillion organisms make up an "individual" human. This is not an exaggeration. Some of these organisms affect our behavior, like how hungry we feel, or how risk-averse we are. One example of this is *toxoplasma gondii*, one of the most common parasites in the world, the presence of which increases the chances someone will have schizophrenia, have bipolar disorder, get in a car accident, or attempt suicide. We are only starting to scratch the surface of the effect those 39 trillion organisms have on the "individual" but it's clear that there is no such thing as an "individual" that is independent of other organisms or that exists in a vacuum.

Most modern scientifically-minded people who argue that free will exists point to quantum mechanics. I don't want to get us off track, but nothing that would be considered "will" happens at the quantum level. The electrochemical activity of our brain appears to be governed by good old-fashioned Newtonian causal physics, and thus believing there is free will requires supernatural belief. God could have gifted humans free will if one was so inclined to have faith in that, but there is no scientific basis for it.

However, there have been multiple scientific studies that seem to show that disbelief in free will causes an increase in antisocial behavior, which is—maddeningly—both an argument against free will existing while also an argument for promoting it within our society. That leads us to the only ethical position which is to believe that free will only exists in ourselves and nobody else, even if we know full well it really does not.

The problem I have with the belief in free will is that you don't get to decide the things that are most important in your life. Many people that believe in free will would concede that one can't decide if something tastes good or not. It's a feeling, a stimulus that works at a subconscious level. But then take it a step further: do you use free will to decide who to love? Do you use free will to decide to believe, or not believe, in God? And if you use free will for those, can you start or stop believing in God or loving someone just by your own choosing?

Free will and God are two important things when it comes to the big lie that in many ways defined my life. Again, this all started around the time I was fourteen and I began to think at length about self-destruction.

So why did a smart, private school, God-loving, middle class, cisgendered, straight, white male who was good at sports want to destroy himself? Why did I have a voice telling me that I was worthless, that I was awful, that I was trash? When we think about this contradiction, this is where the "magic" (for lack of a better word) of depression or mental illness manifests. "Chemical imbalance" is a phrase I hear all the time now, but not so much back then. "Child of abuse" would be a bit of a stretch, as most kids were likely getting similar treatment and they were not thinking about killing themselves (or at least they have never admitted such to me). James Hillman author of *The Soul's Code*, might argue that my soul was conflicted because I was not leading the life that it wanted, but I'm not convinced that something like that is possible. I don't believe in souls, although I did when I was fourteen. Perhaps the mere belief in the soul is enough to create that conflict, but I doubt it.

While I had a negative voice that berated me, I also had a voice telling me I was awesome, was great, and was a special person destined for special things. This would actually fit neatly in Hillman's model, if I believed in souls. These disparate thoughts resulted in very intense conflict within me. I don't know why, but the more I hated myself, the more I professed to love myself. I have never read much about adolescent psychology, but I imagine that when people go through puberty, they start to construct the adult they are going to become, and that construction involves a decent amount of destruction as well. I suppose I had a lot inside of me I wanted to destroy. So I wanted to destroy myself, but I did not want to die. I still believed in God, but I was questioning that more and more. I was angry at God for not allowing me into heaven if I killed myself, and I was angry at Him for not speaking to me anymore.

Thus, I created a lie. I desperately needed to talk to someone about what was happening in my mind, but I didn't know how. I also didn't want anyone to lock me up in a looney bin, which I assumed would happen if I admitted what I felt. I created a lie about a friend who killed himself. It allowed me to talk about suicide without actually talking about *me* committing suicide. Oddly enough, it turned out to be a healthy way to deal with what I was dealing with. I am sure no therapist would suggest this route, but again, I'm still here thirty years later, so I there may be something to it.

I told almost everyone I know this lie, although it was not well-constructed: I assume most people knew I was lying, but other than my mom, no one ever called me out on it. My mom investigated it with the police department and then told me she thought I fabricated the whole thing. This instigated one of the worst fights we ever had, as I was upset that she didn't seem to care why I made it up in the first place.

My dad had a totally different way of addressing the situation. He never asked many questions about it, and never brought it up until almost a year later. We were coming back from a Phillies game, we were still on Route 13 in Delaware, just south of Dover. He told me the story of what happened between him and his brother Mike.

As he told it, Dad was finishing his last year of seminary away at Wawasee Prep, and Mike wrote my dad a letter saying he'd found evidence that my grandfather was having an affair. This was right before my dad went home for break, so when he came home he and Mike talked about it. Mike was all worked up and demanded that my dad confront their father with the "evidence." Now my dad didn't tell me what the evidence was, but he did say it was not necessarily convincing. It was open to interpretation, but Mike was so agitated that my dad felt it was better if he talked to my grandpa about it rather than his brother.

So my eighteen-year-old dad confronted my grandfather with the evidence that he was having an affair. My grandfather was a former WWII bomber pilot, a traveling salesman, and was in many ways exactly like Willie Lowman. There might very well have been another woman, and I don't think I will ever know the truth. But my dad confronted my him, and instead of confirming or denying it, my grandfather told a story about a pilot with whom he had served in the war. It wasn't a very long story, and I don't remember the pilot's name, but my dad did. The pilot had become depressed and felt like he had disappointed his family, but instead of doing anything about it, he killed himself. His family was heartbroken.

My grandfather's reason for telling this story is suspect. It seems to me that he was telling my dad that disappointing his family is something that he didn't want to do, but at the same time, killing himself would be way more disappointing. He explained to my dad that no matter what, nothing you are facing is ever worth killing yourself over. My dad told me this story as a way to get at that idea, without outwardly saying it was about me. In this case, he really seemed to understand what I was going through.

I know what you are thinking: *What did that story have to do with the affair?* I thought exactly that when I was fifteen, and still think that today. I have never been able to reconcile the two things, and I don't think Mike or my dad could, either. Dad hinted at that when he finished the story: he related how he went to Mike and explained what happened, and Mike blew up at him. He said my dad should have pushed my grandfather more, and that Dad was letting down Grandma by not sticking up for her. And that's when Mike and my dad stopped talking, for the rest of their lives.

Lots of family members said that I reminded them of Mike, so maybe we were more alike than I realize. Maybe my dad noticed this. Mike was the Biff of his family; my dad was certainly more like Happy. I might have been Dad's second chance at a relationship with his brother. Maybe I'm reading way too much into it.

My father had anxiety and depression. He was certainly manic, too. I don't know how much he realized was going on in his brain, or if he realized he had issues, or if he admitted it to anyone if he did. Mike committed suicide between when my dad had the stroke and when he died. I told my father what happened, but I don't think he understood. If it had happened before my father had the stroke, I don't think he would have understood then, either.

Becoming a Prophet

During the winter of 2011-2012, I was still working at MTV and living in Queens. In those days I was frequenting a blog called Camden Chat, which is a SB Nation site where fans can discuss all things Baltimore Orioles. While I still had Josh and Chad up at the Gin Mill, they rooted for the fucking Yankees; my next door neighbor Peter loved talking baseball, but he preferred the Mets, so it was pretty hard to find anyone to talk with about the Orioles. But at Camden Chat, I found an entire community of fellow Birds fans, and logging on to the site became part of my daily routine. And we wouldn't only discuss all things Orioles, but would also debate food, music, films, lots and lots of politics, and various members' love lives. It was a magical space on the internet ruled by Stacey Long, who decreed that being respectful to one another was the first and most important commandment. She was quick to ban trolls, and had the total support of so many of us wayward O's fans who were tired of cruel people and looking for a place where we could argue about whether Miracle Whip was better than mayonnaise, or whether Mike Mussina belonged in the Hall of Fame. The rule was that an individual needed to be kind to other individuals while disagreeing, until they established a rapport, after which they could talk about each other's moms all they wanted. Except for Stacey's mom, we were never allowed to talk about Stacey's mom.[43]

Up until January 2012, I never spoke up on the site, I was a lurker. I went there for the articles and would skim the comments, but I was always too afraid to post anything. I don't have the confidence to talk to strangers online; I prefer face-to-face communication. I only went there to get some inside scoops and laugh at the gentle teasing amongst the users.

The Orioles had just wrapped up their fourteenth consecutive losing season. Even so, I was sure they were going to be good in 2012, I just had a feeling. I figured some of the Camden Chat regulars would have the same feeling, but they did not. So I decided to poke my head up in the

43 Thanks Fountains of Wayne for ruining everything.

chat. I brazenly claimed the Orioles were going to win ninety games in the next season. It was February, so what harm was there in saying this now? The season was still a couple of months away from starting; people would probably forget I said it. Besides, everyone here seems to be so kind to one another. Why not inject a little bit of positivity into a gray February day?

I learned my lesson. Since I had been lurking for a while, I felt like I knew these people, but since I had never posted before, they had no idea what to make of me. At first everyone thought I was being sarcastic, that I was a troll. But once they realized I was serious there were lots of different reactions. The kindest among them laughed at me, but most derided me. Everyone called me crazy. Stacey said that if they won ninety games, she'd buy me a Maserati. It became a joke that would not die. My name became synonymous with delusion, insanity, foolishness, and Pollyannaism.

So, I did what any sane person would do: I doubled down, big time. I wrote a five-page "fanpost" complete with charts and stats that I cherry picked from dubious sources to make my prediction seem possible. I got really drunk and searched for any data that might support my wild assertation and ignored any other data that conflicted with it. I titled the post, "The End of Suffering" and opened with a quote from Shakespeare's *The Tempest*, probably because I was drunk. I was drinking very heavily in those days, and I don't think I ever wrote a word while sober. Anyway, I won't submit you to the entire lunacy of the manifesto, but I will give you a taste:

> *I have suffered with those I saw suffer. I look on with pity at the faces of the children who don't understand payrolls and prospects, who just can't understand why their team always loses. I see their tears and hear their sobs. And yes, their cries knock against my very heart. But it will all end this year. Redemption is at hand.*
>
> *Perhaps I am mad. Perhaps I am a fool. I have been called much worse and am sure I will be again. But maybe, just maybe, I speak the truth. Maybe this year everything changes. Maybe this year we care more about the players than about prospects and payroll. This is the year the Yard will fill again with laughter and smiles. This is the year the specter of a proud past will be shaken free and the echoes of bygone glory will be drowned in the living cheers of present victory. This is the year that the suffering will end.*

Long story short, it became a big joke on the blog that I was insane (which, I clearly am), that I was a fool (also valid) and that I was wrong. Have these people even read Shakespeare? The fool is the only one who always tells the truth.

A big issue people had with my prediction was their belief that Chris Davis would never make it as a big-league slugger. They called him a 4A (AAAA) player (which will be explained in the next chapter). He struck out too much, didn't walk enough, and didn't hit enough home runs to be a factor. One of his scouting reports said that he had the raw power of Thor, so I said let's name his bat *Mjolnir* and stand on Eutaw Street with a bright orange target. They had a problem with me saying he was going to hit twenty-six dingers. I think I started referring to him as "Thor" during spring training. Later on when he crushed a home run, the "THOR!!!!!!" exclamation on the game threads was prevalent.

As any baseball fan worth their salt knows, that year the Orioles won ninety-three games in the regular season and made the playoffs for the first time since 1997. But as almost none of you know, I attended their 90th win, and was on TV celebrating a Chris Davis homer with my dad. Literally there I was on television, celebrating my victory over everyone who'd ever doubted me, while I hugged my father, and some random dude that I met on the internet who went by the handle "Wieters Wieners."

It really was one of the greatest nights of my life. A few months later, when the dust had settled, I wrote about it. You might think that was a common thing I did, because here you are reading a book I wrote, but at the time, I didn't write that much, I was devoting most of my creative energy to films. And I don't think my father had read anything I'd written in years.

However, on my birthday I snuck out of my office in Times Square and popped over to St. Andrews Pub for a few glasses of whisky and then came back to the office and wrote the single thing my father liked the best out of everything I ever wrote. It was called "The Way Home," and I'll let you read this one:

The Way Home
January 3rd, 2013
(published as a "fanpost" in Camden Chat)

"The world is so empty if one thinks only of mountains, rivers & cities; but to know someone who thinks & feels with us, & who, though distant, is close to us in spirit, this makes the earth for us an inhabited garden."

—*Goethe*

It was just after 7am on September 29th 2012 when I drove onto the Bay Bridge going home. Home. It had been fourteen years since I have thought of the Eastern Shore, or even Maryland for that matter, as my home. But as the sun rose over the bay, and a low mist clung to the opposing shores, I sped over a bridge I had traveled so many times in my wandering youth. This route was once so familiar to me but now it was almost as if I was having déjà vu, traveling a familiar route for the first time, the fog and memories creating a theater of light upon the estuary. I remember ducks flying low under the bridge. The air was cool, but not cold. I had a gas station coffee that tasted like burnt chalk. I was listing to "Coles Corner" by Richard Hawley and I tried to sing along to the music but I couldn't. Because I started crying.

Okay, I may have been in a "fragile" state due to having a drink or two the night before. But that morning was just one of those mornings that I know I will never forget. Even if so much of the night before was a blur, the quietude of that dawn, the stillness and comfort of my entire being stretched out each moment pressing it deep into my memory. This world was just so damn beautiful.

By the spring of 1998 I had dropped out of college, become estranged from my family, and was basically homeless, living in my car as I drove without any direction around the US. I was considered "lost" by all who knew me then. I didn't care about baseball, or anything other than poetry, philosophy, coffee, and cigarettes. It was a dark time in my life when I learned how to be truly alone, a valuable lesson that made me the man I am today. I remember writing in a journal then, "I am a man without a home, a man out of time. Perhaps the only place left for me is New York." In May of 1999 I moved to New York, and believed I would never live in Maryland again.

But on that September morning in 2012, I drove down Rt. 50 heading home. I stopped at a roadside fruit stand to get an apple. When the proprietor innocently asked me how I was, I explained that the night before the Orioles won their 90th game of the season, as I predicted they would. I crunched the apple as I told him the tale of "my" struggle, being called crazy, becoming a prophet. He looked at me and said, "Me too! I said they were going to win 90 this year too!"

I wanted to tell him that he was wrong, that only I predicted this. I thought for a second to ask him for some kind of documentation proving that he believed this. Perhaps a sealed letter he mailed to himself that I could open for proof. But instead I just said, "Great!" and meant it. Because it was great. Everything was great. I went to my home, the first place I could really call my home, and that night cooked a steak and listened to the O's game on the radio out by the fire. Steve Johnson started, Thor and Manny hit homers, Thor even stole a base, and the Orioles won their 91st game and were one day away from clinching their first playoff appearance in fifteen years. I was happy, really truly happy. It wasn't about being right, or other people being wrong, it something else entirely. It was victory against despair. In those days I felt as if everything was organized in such a perfect fashion, even the words of others had helped form my narrative. From Stacey's "10 Best Things About Being an Orioles Fan" to Mark's "Torch Still Lit," the signs were all there. Something special had happened, some great play had unfolded throughout the summer and we were all spectators and we were all players. I had painted a mural of gods, battling on the side of the righteous versus the moneyed scientists who lacked imagination. It was good versus evil, faith versus science, heart versus money, youth versus experience, hope versus despair. This became my narrative.

But really, let's be honest, it was just a bunch of big kids playing a game. And that is why I love baseball. It can mean so much, and mean so little, all in the same moment.

Had It not been for Camden Chat, had it not been for all of you who make this site so special, this year would have just been another year for me. I may have bought the farm still, and the Orioles still would have won over 90 games, but I never would have been a prophet. I never would have been at win #90, never had the morning with Richard Hawley and the Bay Bridge, and never had the sense of redemption. Had it not been for Mr. Jonathan Britton (Wieter's Wieners) there's no way I would ever be on TV hugging my father. Had it not been for Stacey challenging me, had it not been for Andrew and EME, and really most people calling me a lunatic, had it not been for the tension and conflict of the site throughout the entire summer, the debates of run differentials, the stat guys versus the stat deniers versus the stat apologists none of this would be possible. Had it not been for the doubt and fear, for the creeping belief, the faith and the denial, this journey would have been without flavor. In fact, there would have been no journey at all. It was all of us, together, that made this season something so special. Everything was heightened, everything mattered so much.

My father taught me everything I know about baseball. He has been a lifelong Yankees and Cub fan. He taught me to love the Orioles even if he didn't. He took me to games (and Charles Village Pub before the game), and he got me Cal's and Eddie's autographs, bought me a crab cake sandwich and an Orioles hat and program and taught me how to keep score. Most importantly, he taught me about the community of baseball. He always spoke to the people next to us, the other fans in Charles Village Pub, even people on the walk to and from Memorial Stadium. Now I understand, he was not teaching me to love a sports team, but rather, to love the land of my birth, my home. It was somehow fitting that he was there with me at the culmination of this journey. This year, I rediscovered my love of Maryland. This year, after fourteen years of self-imposed exile, I finally came home.

So I just wanted to say thank you to all of Camden Chat. Without you, the moments that became so momentous for me never would have happened. Without this community, the narrative would never have been written. This year, I finally found my way home, and in the end, it was all of you that showed me the way.

There lots of Camden Chat inside baseball in there that you wouldn't understand, and neither did my dad. He didn't get all those references to people or other articles. He just knew it was an affirmation that something he did in his life had stuck with me. Something he did had mattered. He printed it out and gave it to his friends, and sent it to his family. He was truly proud of it. "The Way Home" spoke to him more than anything else I had written, and he told me so. It was the last time the two of us had a real long conversation, which was about a year and a half before his stroke.

One month after I wrote it, Dad told me he was retiring from WCS and moving to Florida. He moved there for a woman who did not love him, who left him the day after he had the stroke. She didn't even go to the hospital with him, even though she was with him when he it happened. I will never mention her again, she's the other woman. *Death of a Salesman* is such a good play.

I suspect every final baseball game you see with your father matters. It just so happens, I never saw another baseball game with my father.

"The Way Home" was the last thing I read to my dad, after the priest who gave him last rites had left, after all his other visitors had left. In fact, they were the last words I said to my father, other than "I love you," and "It's time to let go."

CHRIS DAVIS AND THE AAAA PLAYER

Like most sports, professional baseball is organized into several different leagues. It includes independent teams and semi-pro leagues, but when most people talk about professional baseball they are referring to the Major League Baseball (MLB) a.k.a. "the majors," "the show" "the big leagues." MLB is the oldest sports organization in the U.S. and has a great deal of power over the game of baseball. The MLB also oversees the Minor League Baseball (MiLB) which consists of four different levels.[44] Those levels are: Single-A, High-A, Double-A (AA), and Triple-A (AAA). Within the Orioles organization these would be the Delmarva Shorebirds, Aberdeen Ironbirds, Bowie Baysox, and Norfolk Tides, respectively. There is no such thing as "AAAA."[45]

But, in the winter of 2012, there was a prevalent belief on Camden Chat that Chris Davis was an AAAA player: someone who dominates in AAA, but struggles in the Majors. This is actually pretty rare; most AAA players that are too good for that level go on to be at least decent major leaguers, it's a natural progression. That being said, there is a very small percentage of players that are stuck between too-good-for-AAA and not-good-enough-for-the-majors status. One of my dad's favorite minor leaguers, Calvin Pickering, is an example of a classic AAAA player. He crushed minor league pitching, but just couldn't put it together in the majors. Chris Davis also raked in the minors, but struggled so much in his first couple of seasons with the Rangers that they deemed him expendable, trading him to Baltimore in 2011.

As I have already stated, I believed Davis wasn't going to be stuck as an AAAA player. Why? I can't answer that question without being brutally honest, even though I know it's going to come across as rather arrogant. The fact is, I knew what it was like to be an AAAA player. Not in baseball, mind you, but in my creative life. I'm one of those people who

---

44 There's also Rookie Ball, which plays a short season, and international Rookie Ball, but let's not confuse things.

45 I've only heard it pronounced as "four-A" but it would make sense to call it "Quadruple-A". You're going to get AAAA though and decide for yourself what your brain wants.

has too-high an opinion of themselves, to the point where they believe they are destined for something greater. I'm an optimist when it comes to my own life, and I'm an optimist when it comes to the Orioles.

Optimism and the concept of the AAAA player are starkly at odds with one another, however. I didn't want anyone to be an AAAA player for the same reason that I haven't quit writing, even though I know that very few people will ever read my words. I want to believe that there is always a path for talented people to rise to the level they deserve. There is no AAAA, those people are lost in between. I don't want to be one of those people. It's this belief that pushes me to keep trying, and a belief that I believe my father and I shared.

I remember one Sunday back when I was eight or nine years old, I was at St. Luke's Church in Ocean City sitting through Mass in a pew next to my dad. He had the missal open while pretending to follow along, and I glanced over because I noticed he was writing something. He had slipped the weekly church bulletin in the missal and was drawing shapes all over it. I looked closer and noticed he was drawing five or six wide crosses. Each cross had little uniform dashes radiating out from its interior angles. To a casual observer, this would look a little insane, but I found it strange and somehow beautiful.

A month later, my father was building the set for the WCS production of *Jesus Christ Superstar*. In those days there was no dedicated performance space, so all of the shows were staged in the tiny multipurpose room where we ate lunch. In that little space, he created a stage that was itself a cross, with seats on two sides, almost as if he was creating a theater in the round—or at least, in the half-round. The entire musical was performed on a large cross. It was far more creative and inspired than any other staging he had done. It wasn't Broadway, but it was not your typical Berlin, Maryland high school production, either.

Twenty-some years later, I made a feature film for $100 called *Rehearsal*. I wrote it in ten days, filmed it in seven, and I was drunk most of the time while working on it. It's probably one of the better things I have ever made. In the film, the main character, Tim, is putting on a play and in one scene he explains his staging to his imaginary friend/ghost/muse, named Gissel:

GISSEL: What does it say, your stage?
TIM: The end of immortality.
GISSEL: Does that make sense?
TIM: As much sense as the beginning of immortality would.

Tim goes on to explain how the stage tells its own story, and in this case, the stage is a metaphor for the world in which we live; it's not subtle, but as I've already stated, I'm a blatanist. There is no question that part of this scene was inspired by my father drawing those crosses in the missal. In fact, the scene itself opens with Tim writing something and drawing, later revealed to be a bunch of crosses.

Rehearsal was accepted into a few festivals, and I am very proud of the film. It was the best feature film ever made in seven days for $100, but that doesn't win you any awards or accolades. The film even talks in a roundabout way about how no one is going to see it, since I'm postmodern and all. I have seen hundreds of no-budget, bad independent films, and I would say *Rehearsal* is better than most. I put more thought, care, and ideas into it than all of those other films. Does it deserve distribution on Amazon, Netflix, or some other streaming service? Did it deserve to open in theaters, or even get a straight-to-video distribution deal back in the day? Absolutely not. It was a no-budget, self-indulgent independent film—an AAAA production by an AAAA director.

To be clear, I'm not talking about being rich or famous. There is a huge gulf between a published author and a famous author, just as there exists a huge gulf between an MLB role player and an All Star.

A creative person comes to this realization with difficulty, and the first time I really explored it was in *Rehearsal*, when I addressed the difference between finishing something and being successful at something. "I'm not the best, I'm not even in the top thousand, but I'm not a failure" is one of Tim's assertions. This was to justify me making a film that I knew almost no one would see, and works just as well regarding me writing a book that almost no one is going to read.

If I'm really writing this book to understand myself, then I have to look at the source of my motivation to keep writing. It's not about my need to be creative--that's something I assume everyone has, even if most people bury it or allow it to somehow be fulfilled by work, video games, fantasy football, or whatever. I'm talking about pursuing the futile path towards oblivion over and over again.

The concept of the AAAA player isn't only something that exists in baseball. In the musical *A Chorus Line*, Cassie Ferguson represents the AAAA dancer. She's too good for the chorus, but can't get a job as a soloist. Apparently the role was actually based on the life of Donna McKechnie, the actress who created the role of Cassie on Broadway. Right before her solo, Cassie confesses, "The truth is I never even came close and nobody has the guts to tell me." McKechnie went on to win a Tony Award for that role.

Baseball is cold, because success in baseball is measured only in numbers. Art is more complicated. In the memoir *The Art of Asking*, Amanda Palmer writes about how she came to terms with imposter syndrome, or as she called it, "the fraud police."

> *There's no correct path to becoming a real artist. You might think you'll gain legitimacy by going to college, getting published, getting signed to a record label, but it's all bull shit, and it's all in your head. You're an artist when you say you are. And you are a good artist when you make somebody else experience or feel something deep, or unexpected.*

When my father retired he moved to Naples, Florida and joined The Naples Players, the local community theater. He performed in four plays with them, and I was able to see him portray Feldzieg in *The Drowsy Chaperone*. He was magnetic on stage. At 68 years old he was alive with an energy I had not seen in him for years, and I could tell he was finally doing something that was special to him.

Maybe I'm looking too deep into something that wasn't there, or projecting my own issues onto my dad. It's telling that my dad told me about a year before his stroke that performing with the Naples Players was a dream come true, and he wished he had retired sooner.

That isn't to say my father didn't do good things in his life. He influenced many students and had many positive effects on the lives of others. He sparked creativity in people, including me and my brother. He created the sports program at WCS from nothing, inspired generations of students in both the performing arts and athletics, and was well-liked, just like how Willie Lowman had hoped Biff would be. Just like Happy Lowman.

Holy shit, I just got why his name is "Happy!"

But anyway, this chapter is supposed to be about baseball, so let's get back to that. Back in 2012, Chris Davis got off to a solid start, but all of the doubters still applied the AAAA moniker to him. "Small sample size" was the phrase used to describe his early success. Davis went into the May 6 game against the Boston Red Sox with a .326 average (for those that don't know baseball, that's really good). That game ended up going to 17 innings, and I believed changed the fortunes of both teams involved. Davis was the designated hitter, was 6th in the batting order, and went 0-8 with five strikeouts and grounded into a double play. So he was really responsible for nine outs. It was one of the worst performances by a designated hitter, ever. And yet, it was the game that many fans point to as when they started to believe that the Orioles could actually win ninety games that year, and it was the game that ended the complaints that Chris Davis was AAAA. It was the game in which Davis became a legend.

It was the last game of a six-game road trip. The O's had taken two of three from the Yankees before facing the Red Sox. The first game of the series on May 4 went thirteen innings, with the bullpen throwing eight of those innings. The O's won, but their bullpen got used too much. Jason Hammel pitched well on May 5, but the pen still needed to eat a couple of innings to secure the win. Tommy Hunter started May 6, but only managed to make it 4 1/3 innings. The bullpen was tired, and yet it was called on to pitch another 10 2/3 innings to preserve the tie going into the 16th inning. Meanwhile, Chris Davis was having the worst game of his life at the plate, he looked totally lost. So what did legendary manager Buck Showalter do? He told Davis to pick up a glove and warm up, he was going to pitch.

When Davis took the mound, everyone knew that the game was over, the O's were going to lose. The Red Sox had one of the best lineups in baseball, and Davis wasn't even a pitcher. But what was Showalter supposed to do? He was out of pitchers. The first Red Sox batter up was Jarrod Saltalamacchia, who struck out swinging on an 83 mph slurve.[46]

What just happened?

Next up, Will Middlebrooks hits it a mile, but mostly up in the air, and Adam Jones settled underneath it for the easy out.

Close call, but we just might get out of this inning.

Then, Marlon Byrd hit it to 3rd baseman Wilson Betemit, who committed an error and allowed Byrd to reach first.

That's it, the game is over now. That was our chance.

Then Red Sox leadoff hitter Mike Aviles lined it into the gap, and it rolls all the way to the wall.

That's the ballgame.

BUT WAIT!

Centerfielder Adam Jones picked it up and fired a perfect laser to cutoff man J.J. Hardy. Hardy had a cannon for an arm, and his throw was on line and beat Byrd by a step. After a collision at the plate, catcher Matt Wieters held on to the ball, and with a shit eating grin, showed it to Byrd.

In the top half of the 17th inning, the Red Sox turned to their own designated hitter to pitch, Darnell McDonald. Adam Jones crushed a

---

46 A "slurve" is a mixture of a slider and a curveball. It's gripped like a curveball but thrown with the velocity of a slider. I'm not sure Davis meant to throw a slurve, but that's what it looked like to me.

three-run homer for the O's, but that was just the top of the inning. Davis had to come back out and pitch another inning to secure the win, and had to do it facing the top of the Red Sox batting order.

The first two guys reached, one on a single and one on a walk. Davis looked gassed, but no one was going to pick him up or bail him out; it was his game to win or lose. Next came Red Sox cleanup hitter Adrian Gonzalez, who less than a month earlier had signed the second-largest contract in Red Sox history. Two men on, no outs, and one of the best hitters in baseball was at the plate. Fenway was going nuts, and the fans were on their feet, clapping and stomping.

At the plate, Gonzalez got two quick strikes. Davis breathed a heavy sigh, and then chucked the ball home. He threw a splitter change up that died right at the plate. Adrian Gonzalez swung... just over it. He struck out.

The Fenway crowd collapsed in shock, completely deflated. Two pitches later, Darnell McDonald grounded into a double play to end the game.

The Orioles had won, and the legend of Chris Davis was born.

While this crazy instance where Davis pitched didn't mean he wasn't an AAAA player, something changed in him that day. Or, better put, something changed in the perceptions held by those watching him that day. It was as if the pressure was taken off him and he was able to simply bask in the glory of being the winning pitcher in the strangest game of the weirdest year in Orioles history. I don't really know if this is accurate, but it really *felt* like something had changed. I think it was Pickle's Pub, right across from Camden Yards, that put up a "Chris Davis for Cy Young" banner. It was fun. After fourteen years of losing, Baltimore baseball was fun again. It was because of Buck Showalter, Adam Jones, J.J. Hardy, Matt Wieters, and Chris Davis. He was no longer AAAA—he belonged.

Davis went on to hit thirty-three home runs that year. The following year, he led all of MLB in home runs, RBIs, and total bases, and was third in the MVP voting. My dad started referring to him as "Your man, Thor" or "Your buddy, Thor," and would text me every time Davis hit a home run or had a good game. My father, the Yankees fan, even rooted for Thor over his beloved Yankees.

While I know it's presumptuous and maybe even ridiculous to say so, I think my dad and I would be considered AAAA players in life. Whenever I tell stories, people always say, "You should write a book!" But when I do write a book, only about seven people end up reading it, because I'm an AAAA writer. If I wasn't AAAA, if I was an All-Star, or even if I was a regular Major Leaguer, I would have something much pithier to say to wrap up this chapter.

But obviously I don't. I don't say this for the sake of pity, but rather honesty. If I'm going to look deep, I have to explore my insecurities, moral failings, unwarranted arrogance, and even my most selfish thoughts. I'm slightly comforted in the fact that only about seven people will be annoyed at me for this vanity. And I would be lying if I said I wasn't slightly hopeful that someday there would be a May 6, 2012 game for me.

WATCHING TWO BRAINS

In the days after my father's stroke, my perception of the brain and my understanding of its dominion over our personality changed drastically. Prior to his stroke, I believed that the individual used the brain as a tool to think and do math and stuff. Somehow, the individual was more than the sum of its parts; and the brain, while immensely important, was just one of those parts that helped process the unknowable stuff that really makes us who we are. In my defense, I was an athlete and coaches constantly said things like: "Give 110%;" "Games are won by those with more heart;" and, "Pain is just the brain trying to fool us into giving up." The idea that we are much more than our brain is hammered into us conveniently when we are most tired, which, now that I think about it, is a little like *The Manchurian Candidate.*

It's frightening how fast our perspective can change in a crisis, in contrast to how we are so resistant to change in our daily lives. I have this theory that most people believe in the permanency of the individual once we pass puberty. I'm sure this comes out of some perversion of the Christian ideal of an immortal soul, but it's probably just laziness. Most of us don't believe we change much, because we have a concept of the individual and think that somehow the individual is well-defined. This line of thinking states that, while we can change our clothes, our haircut, or we can gain or lose weight, we can't fundamentally change who we *really* are.

You would think that social media would have exposed the flaw in this thinking, but it strangely hasn't. At this point, we have all been disturbed by someone we really liked in high school or college posting some horrid thing on social media. Instead of assuming that this person has actually changed, most of us think something to the effect of, *I guess that's who they really are,* or *I can't believe they were always racist and just hiding it from us all these years.* This isn't confined to casual observers— scientists have for years believed that personality traits become fixed in childhood, or are largely attributable to genetics and rarely changed through life. However, recent studies have shown that personalities do change throughout our lifetimes, often gradually. Which is why if we are friends with someone and see them once a week for thirty years we don't think they have changed much, because the change is incremental. However, if we don't see someone for 30 years and then they come back into our lives, the change seems pronounced to us. Suddenly we can't understand how they can hold such opinions about politics or religion or whatever, because we weren't present for the gradual evolution of those opinions.

Sure, you'll say, *opinions can change but that doesn't change who we really are.* This would suggest that we are something other than our external personality. When we think about someone, we unconsciously separate the person from their actions even though it actually makes no sense for us to do that. As an example, let's say we have a concept of a person named Susan. We know Susan, we have become friends with Susan over a few years, and we like Susan. We have created the character of Susan in our mind, but that concept belongs to us, not Susan. For lack of a better term, we create a "soul" for Susan. In our minds, there's the real Susan (the soul) and Susan's actions (her personality). So, if our friend Susan goes out one night and acts like a drunk asshole, you might say, "I didn't like that person" or, "That's not Susan." But think about what this implies: it suggests Susan has become a different person for a short period of time. To make it far more dramatic than necessary, your mind's implication is akin to Susan being possessed by a demon for that night, and her soul (which keep in mind, is *your* construct) was not in control of her actions. But how do you know Susan's soul? You can only do so through interacting with her external personality.

The fact is, it's simply easier on our brains to think of people as individuals rather than realize what we really are: constantly-changing, multispecies ecosystems with a proper name. The entity known as Daniel, Danny, Dan, Dan'l, Sleeper, Danimal, and "that worthless piece of shit" isn't just a single organism at a single point in time. There are roughly 10,000 different species that exist in and on my body—not different organisms, different species. There are roughly 39,000,000,000,000,000 different organisms that live in and on my body—and again, that's not an exaggeration. There is a great book by Rob Dunn called *Never Home Alone* that scratches the surface of all of the different and largely-unknown lives that exist on, in, and around us. These organisms effect our decisions, and the makeup of these organisms is constantly changing.

For example, after living with Caroline for about a decade, I came to always know what she would want for dinner. I usually got home before she did, and would either cook or order in *exactly* what she was craving, without ever having to ask her what she wanted. I attributed this ability to either latent psychic powers or deep connection of true love, until I read about a study that showed married couples shared fecal microbiota. Suddenly, it made sense to me: the reason I knew what "she" was craving was because "I" was craving the same thing. But in reality, it was our shared gut microbes craving it. I excitedly told her that I wasn't a psychic, we just had the same shared microbes! Her response? "Gross."

Our microbiome is constantly changing, but that's just part of our physical person. There is also the emotional aspect of our person, which is affected by diet, exercise, hormones, various bacteria, sunlight, the style of architecture in which we live, etc. Most of these variables are constantly changing. Then there is the rational person: being exposed to different art, different philosophy, different music, different friends, different experiences, and so on will drastically change who we are.

We are constantly consuming new information, and even though we try to conform that information into our preconceived notions and prejudices, we still change. The notion that we don't change is wrapped up in the concept of the "immortal soul," which is somehow separate from the body. Many cultures share this concept, or something like it. For instance, the *atman* in Hinduism is the "real" self, or the innermost essence that doesn't die with the body. Jainism believes in the *jiva*, which is the immortal essence of every living thing. The *jiva* can neither be created nor destroyed, but has always existed. The ancient Egyptians believed there were many different parts that made up the soul, and the *ka* (the essence), *ba* (personality), and the *sah* (spiritual body) were separate from the *khet* (physical body). Most animist religions—far too numerous to mention—have a concept of a soul that is separate from the body. Plato said the *psyche* is the essence of the soul, and it continues to think after the body dies. Aristotle connected the soul to the body, but he also asserted that the active mind is immortal. René Descartes outlined what is now referred to as Cartesian dualism, or the Cartesian soul, which claims that the mind can exist outside of the body, and that the body does not think. This concept dominated Western thoughts on the soul for centuries, and is still prevalent in modern thought about psychology and personality.

In *The Soul's Code* (which I highly recommend even if I disagree with the premise), Hillman claims that at a young age our soul knows our vocation. He calls it the Acorn Theory. You see, an acorn contains all the information necessary to grow into an oak tree, and *only* an oak tree.

He envisions the soul as the acorn and extrapolates that to assert the actor's soul knows it must be an actor, the writer's soul knows it must be a writer, etc., and anything that gets in the soul's way is met with conflict and strife. He reinforces this notion that we are always who we will be, and that the internal force of our personality is far stronger than the external forces of the universe. I'll admit, it's an elegant and tempting philosophy in which to believe.

That is, it's tempting until you have to cope with someone who has massive brain damage from a hemorrhagic stroke. Overnight, their personality changes. The reason the personality changes is due to physical brain damage, no one can deny this. But it creates a conundrum: in a healthy body we believe that the soul is dominant. In an unhealthy body, we believe the body is dominant. Why? When my father said terrible things after the stroke, people would say, "That's not him, that's the stroke" or "That's not him, that's the brain damage." But where did his soul go?

One of the reasons I became so fascinated in the brain at this time was because I was watching own my daughter's brain develop. From her birth until she was three months old, she couldn't sleep unless someone held her. It got very challenging, especially for Caroline, who was with her twenty-four hours a day. Because Olive was so tiny and I was so large, I wouldn't allow myself to fall asleep while I was holding her. I wrote to stay awake, which is when I wrote the first poem of this book. Or I watched any movie or TV show I could to help keep me awake. When Olive was three months old, Caroline's father suddenly died, and somewhere in the process of our driving to Philadelphia and then flying to Montecito, CA my daughter somehow learned to sleep anywhere. She slept in the car seat, she slept on the tray table in the plane—she no longer needed to be held.

After that, the time I spent with her was while she was awake. And it felt like every day she would have a new level of understanding of the world around her. She never paid any attention to the television, but when she was about four months old, I had the TV show *Chuck* on, and when the opening credits started she stared at the television as if it was the hypnotoad. As soon as the credits were over, she looked away. Now, the opening credits of *Chuck* are animated, so perhaps she liked the animation. But the thing is, she didn't watch *any* TV at the time, animated or otherwise. The next time the opening credits came on, she snapped to attention again, and as soon as they ended she again looked away. She heard the music, and associated the music was with the cartoon she wanted to see. I found this fascinating.

In the eight or so months before my father's stroke, I lived in a state of daily amazement at the power of the brain and the incredible beauty of the mind, and its relationship to the concept of the self. I would not say it was a preoccupation, but it was a pleasurable pastime for me to think about how thoughts come into our lives and are shared. The growing little mind on display before me kept unlocking more and more possibilities.

I wish I'd taken more notes during this time, but I wasn't journaling like I once had. Luckily, I did write a few things down just before and after my father's stroke. I wrote this first piece just a month before, when my daughter as about ten months old:

On every moment we leave a string. An invisible thread is touching everything we contact, everything we sense, everything that senses us. Every step, every kiss, every tear, every taste, every dream, every echo, every breath, everything is tethered to us.

While we move, the strings quiver. We each unconsciously resonate in the world. But we can touch these strings, pluck them, strum them. Our memory is gathered in harmonies constantly changing with distance, played with skill by some and frustration by others. Some artists weave strings that never existed before the audience arrived. Some send strings into the abyss of the future, hungry to create a song they are certain they somehow know. Maybe they are just following the path so many strings seem to desire. Or maybe magic is.

Each string is from our spirit, from our body, from our "ourness." It is physical and without form, symbolic and literal. We wander through a constant and unknown web of this universe every minute, strumming innumerable strings, creating a violent and inaudible euphony. When we touch another, the threads together weave, when we hear another new overlapping lines are created, when we remember another the music is as much ours as theirs. Our memory, our requiem mass is a collection of the songs they taught us to play, a collection of the music that they brought into our life.

We are not one. We are not "a." There is no singular, no individual, no object alone. We are connected to everything through everything and everything through us. Still, every sound is unique. Every moment on every string has its own music. Some may find some music more beautiful than others. Some may think they hear no music at all.

But they are wrong. There are no places, no names, no individuals that belong to the universe. There are no islands, no isolated thought, no unwed moments. There is no I. There is only music.

And then a month after the stroke:

> *There is an evolutionary benefit to the creation of tertiary mental representations once self-awareness is attained, because with self-awareness comes awareness of birth, death, nonexistence, the concept of justice, or the idea of balance and perfection... in effect, reality. But there is no such thing as perfect "justice" in "reality," because there can be no separation between cause and effect even if a concept of "free will" is inserted into the justice equation.*
>
> *Reality is impossible to define. Because it doesn't exist.*

Looking back now at these two pieces, I see that it didn't take long to break my brain. The beauty and wonder that came from the fascinated moments of early fatherhood were crushed by the harsh reality of facing the sudden personality change in my father due to his illness. What broke my brain exactly? Seeing that my father's soul was gone, but his body remained. Possibly even worse, what was left behind had so many of my father's memories, so it could fool me for a while into believing that it was still my father. Looking back, it was clear there was a distinct change in me the moment I realized my father was not coming back; and even worse, the new person he had become was not going away.

WHY MY DAD WAS A YANKEES FAN

My father never lived in New York, but he was a lifelong Yankees fan. He was also a Cubs fan, but that makes sense, as he had lived in the Chicago area during his formative years. The only place on the East Coast he ever lived, until retiring to Florida at age sixty-seven, was Maryland, but he certainly was not an Orioles fan. I feel the need to explain this.

My dad was the son of a traveling salesman. As I noted, my grandfather, Ed O'Hare, was a bomber pilot in WWII, and we know he flew at least thirty-six missions. Ed's brother was named Matt, so was the namesake of my father. This Matt was also a pilot that flew for the Air Force for thirty-some years. One of Matt's claims to fame was transporting the Presidential press corps for Nixon's visit to China. Thus he piloted the first American plane to land in Communist China, since the press arrived before the President, so they could document his arrival. Anyway, getting back to Ed: when he came back from the war, he started having kids and selling potato harvesters.[47] My father was the first born of Ed and Mary's kids.

My father was born in North Dakota, where my grandfather was from. My great-grandfather was Doc O'Hare, who was an Irish doctor in a Polish town, and an abusive drunk. I don't know my great-grandmother's name, but she was Norwegian, and my grandfather always loved to remind people that he was half Norwegian, because he loved his mother more than his father. I mean he never said these things, but read between the lines people.

My grandmother was Mary Reardon, and she was part of the Ryan family clan from Delevan, IL. They were all farmers, and all good storytellers. One of the favorite family stories dates back to the 1880s, when a group of rough-looking characters came by the house one day. They were riding horses and were looking for some food for themselves and their animals, and a place to bed down for the night. Great-grammy Ryan (as she is known to everyone in the family, but I think she would be my

47 Insert Irish joke later.

great-great-great-grandmother) said they could stay in the barn but they had to be quiet after 9 PM. But apparently these toughs got into some whiskey and were hooting and hollering after their curfew, so great-grammy Ryan went out to the barn in her nightgown and screamed at them to be quiet, threatening to get a switch if they didn't go straight to sleep. They got quiet real quick.

By morning they had left, but there was a note left behind that simply read, "Thanks." At the bottom was a scratchy signature that looked like it said "J W James," and three gold coins sitting on top of the note. The family is positive that great-grammy Ryan scared the hell out of the James Gang.

Shortly after my father was born, Mary and Ed started moving around. They moved within North Dakota a couple of times, then to South Dakota, Minnesota, Colorado, Iowa, Illinois, and eventually to Dyer, Indiana. Mary then supposedly said if they moved again, she wasn't going. So they stayed in Dyer, in the same house, for the rest of their lives.

Can anyone guess why my father was a Yankees fan from the knowledge presented? That's right, because he lived in Denver, Colorado when he was ten and eleven years old. While there, he attended every home Denver Bears game he could. The reason my father was a Yankees fan is that the Denver Bears were a New York Yankees minor league affiliate, and many of the players on those teams ended up on the great Yankees teams of the late '50s and early '60s. My dad said he used to go to the field for batting practices and he talked to the guys that would later go on to win the 1958 World Series: Don Larsen, Marv Thornberry, Bobby Richardson, Norm Siebern, Tony Kubek, Ralph Terry—just to name a few.[48] He followed these players' careers, seeing them win or play in World Series after World Series, and that alone was probably enough to make him a Yankees fan. You root for people you are familiar with, and he was familiar with the Yankees, and they were really good.

But I think there is something more to my father's Yankees fandom than just these guys that he knew were really good at baseball. But for this, we need to enter the realm of conjecture.

As you know by now, my father was a natural storyteller, and loved the stories of sports. If you asked my father what his favorite film was, he'd probably have said *The Graduate*. It wasn't true, but he said this because he was tired of explaining what his actual favorite film was. Remember, my dad always wanted to be well-liked, and liking a movie that no one had seen or heard of wasn't a path to being well-liked. His

---

48 Fun fact: Whitey Hertzog and Tommy Lasorta were also on those teams.

actual favorite film of all time was *The Loneliness of the Long Distance Runner.* If you have seen this film and knew my father, it would probably surprise you that it was his favorite. If you haven't seen it, it's about a tough kid who gets sent to a reform school for breaking into a bakery. He's a great runner, so he gets to leave the school to practice running. He finds freedom in the running... but I won't spoil it for you, so watch it. Needless to say, this is not a Hollywood film in any way. Most people wouldn't even consider it a sports film. But it's a damn good story. Good stories give you the option to think about them long after they have finished.

My father moved roughly ten times before he lived in Denver. He lived there longer than he had lived anywhere else up to that point. Not long after the family moved to Dyer, my dad went to boarding school. He had no place to consider home. So in these future Yankees players, he had heroes he looked up to whom he actually knew. He used to say, "I had real conversations with them, like they were just regular people." Of course, they later became irregular people; they became elite world champions. In rooting for the Yankees, he rooted for a greater narrative, one in which he connected to something from its origin to its culmination. He rooted for a good story.

This is one of the great things about the minor leagues: you get to witness the beginning of greatness, and be involved in the story from the beginning. I think this is also something my father loved about teaching. To be witness to and, in some small way, be a part of the foundation of what will become a lifetime is special for anyone. But for a storyteller, it's the absolute lifeblood of existence. Without the uncelebrated or humble beginning, then the pinnacle of massive achievement will be given less context. The story is not the baseball smashing into the light at the end of *The Natural*, it's everything that happened up until the moment Roy Hobbes swung and the bat connected with the ball.

My father was never an Orioles fan. Yes, he took us to Memorial Stadium and Charles Village Pub, would buy us Orioles hats, and got Cal and Eddie to sign autographs for us. But he never rooted for the Orioles, and he certainly had never rooted for them against his beloved Yankees. But in 2012 he did. Why? Certainly because of me, because of the narrative I created around that year, but I believe there was another reason.

The Delmarva Shorebirds started in 1996, the year my mother left my father. I don't know if he went to any games that summer, it was pretty chaotic in our household. Once it became an Orioles affiliate in 1997, I know he went occasionally because he saw Calvin Pickering, and

Pickering was there in 1997. Eventually the Shorebirds were managed by Ryan Minor, who was the son-in-law of a good friend of my father's, so he would go to lots of games with this friend. My dad was impressed by Nick Markakis and blown away by Dylan Bundy. He often reported to me what players he liked the look of, but there was one above all others: My dad loved Manny Machado. He reported, "He's a man among men," which was one of my dad's favorite sayings. He knew from the moment Manny stepped onto that field that he was going to be a star. But more than that, because my father went to games with Ryan Minor's father-in-law, they would wait to talk to Ryan after the game and would therefore he got to spend time around the players. Just like he did with the Denver Bears in his youth, he got to talk to these future major leaguers and have real conversations with them, like they were regular people. He got to see Manny Machado as a nineteen-year-old kid goofing off, having fun, and just doing normal things like grabbing food, carrying his own bag, and getting on a bus.

There was one story about Manny that my dad often told: one time he was standing in front of the team bus talking to Ryan Minor, when the team was just coming out of the clubhouse. They were running late, so a few of the coaches were trying to get the players to hustle onto the bus. A table was set up with a bunch of pizza on it and some plates and napkins. Manny Machado came out of the clubhouse and stood looking at the pizzas. He put his bag down, opened up a pizza box, took an entire pizza out, folded it in half, and just devoured it in like seven bites. Not a slice, an entire large pizza.

Just a year later in 2012, Manny got called up to Baltimore, and the Orioles started winning. My dad started rooting for the Orioles, even when they were playing against the Yankees. He told me he had never once rooted against the Yankees until that season, and he said it was because of me. But I suspect it was because of the stories. It was because of the redemption of Chris Davis, who had been given up on by so many and yet I believed in him when few else would. It was because of Buck Showalter and the gravitas he brought to the team. It was because anyone could recognize that the leadership Adam Jones showed on and off the field was a once-in-a-generation treat. It was because of players like Miguel Gonzalez, who came out of nowhere like in a baseball comedy. And finally, and maybe most importantly, it was because my dad knew Manny Machado could inhale an entire large pizza in seven bites.

Deep down, I want to believe that above all else it was the story itself that my father loved. Frankly, the Yankees in 2012 were boring. Sure, they were good, but they were mostly mercenaries. The Orioles were misfits, outcasts, and kids. My dad stood a few feet away from Manny Machado while Manny did goofy teenage things, and the next year Manny was winning games against a dynasty for which my father had rooted his entire life. And yet he chose to cheer for the kid.

That's the beauty of the minor leagues. And that's the beauty of baseball.

DREAMS

Shortly after Carlos Castaneda died, I read *The Teachings of Don Juan* and became fascinated by "his" concept of the four natural enemies to a man of knowledge: fear, clarity of mind, power, and old age. I had no issue with fear, I didn't have any real power (other than being tiresomely charming), and I was young, and so those three enemies didn't bother me. But clarity of mind was a real villain in my life. I briefly became convinced that logic prevented me from seeing things as they really were and thus I needed to explore my dreams more.

For those that don't know, Castaneda was a con man "anthropologist" who was really into drugs, especially peyote. He most likely didn't do any of the field work he claimed to have done in order to get his PhD, but he was a pretty good writer and his dissertation—while probably fiction—is a really enjoyable read. Prior to my making a small study of religions and philosophy, and absorbing the writings of Mircea Eliade, Joseph Campbell, and Clarissa Pinkola Estes, reading *The Teachings of Don Juan* first expanded my horizons past my existentialist and Catholic worldviews. While I never tried hallucinogens, I became convinced there was more to learn in my dreams than in my waking life, but there was a problem: at that time in my life I never slept.

I know plenty of people say they "never sleep," and that means they stay up late and wake up groggy to an alarm five hours later. But that's not what I'm saying. When I say I never slept, what I meant is that, in my early twenties, I slept on average two-to-three hours a night. I didn't have enough time to actually dream—or if I did, I didn't remember my dreams at all.

This era of sleeplessness contrasts with my era of sleeping sixteen hours a day, which I also would do when I was depressed in my late teen years, and especially when I first went to college. When I did that, my dreams were full of nightmares, and no matter how much I slept I felt uneasy. This persisted for my entire first semester, and it wasn't until I started exercising again that my sleep hygiene improved enough to get a restful night's sleep without having awful dreams. At the time,

I attributed the nightmares to emotional issues, but in retrospect, poor diet and lack of exercise were the most likely culprits.

Many years later, after my father's stroke, I learned that he had suffered from night terrors most of his life, and had terrible sleep hygiene issues. It got so bad that he needed to sleep with the TV on all night to keep from screaming. I don't know if this could be genetic, but I did mention that my father rarely exercised, so there may be a correlation between the two.

Anyway, after reading Castaneda I decided to improve my sleep habits, as well as to learn more about what my dreams meant. The problem with this plan was that Castaneda isn't the only charlatan in this space. Searching the internet for the meaning of dreams was probably not the best use of my waking life, but I did at least pick up a couple of neat tricks that eventually allowed me to control my dreams.

This may not be universal, but the way I learned to control my dreams was to start with an *intention* as I went to sleep. I worked very hard to envision what I wanted to dream about. Then, once in the dream, I forced myself to look at my hands. I looked at my hands, counted my fingers, and made two fists; this allowed me to realize I was dreaming and thus I could begin to explore the dream. I didn't always dream about exactly what I wanted, but I was hyperaware of what was happening in the dream and would have solid memories of what occurred after waking. Even when I was drinking pretty hard, if I didn't pass out and instead focused on my intention before going to sleep I could gain some control. Still, this is much more difficult if you're drunk.

I enjoyed this ability for years, up until 2018. In that year, I was making a documentary about racism and was trying to meet a deadline for the Ocean City Film Festival. Our editor dropped out last-minute, so I needed to learn to edit, something I'd never done before in all my years of working in film and television. Whenever you learn a new task—especially when you're older—it really messes with your dreams. Added to that was the horrific subject matter I was dealing with, and for some reason I lost the ability to control my dreams. Even now, three years later, I've yet to get it back.

It turns out that this was a good thing, because this whole journey through anxiety started with a dream the night of my 44th birthday. My father had passed away eight months before, and as I stated, I was dealing with health issues that I thought were related to a heart attack or a stroke, but were diagnosed both times as a panic attack. Then on my birthday I had this dream:

I was driving my daughter to Worcester Preparatory School because I was supposed to play Willie Lowman in the opening matinee of *Death of a Salesman*, except we had not rehearsed and I didn't know my lines. I went into the gym, which was also the auditorium and the space where we held my father's memorial. My dad was sitting in the front row talking to people. I told him that we were not ready to do the play, and that I didn't know my part. He said we would be fine and handed me a book which just said "Theater" on the cover. He told me my lines were in there, and that Scott Mumford would help me with them.[49] Then I gave Olive to a classmate I had not seen since we graduated and went into the locker room to learn the lines with Scott. I kept flipping through pages of the book, but I couldn't find *Death of a Salesman*. I remember being at least halfway through the book and only being at Euripides. I gave up in frustration and Scott and I went outside to the parking lot to get some fresh air and clear our heads. By the parking lot was a big puddle of water. I told Scott I was surprised that the puddle was still there, it had remained since "that funeral." He asked what funeral I was talking about, but I couldn't recall. I said he had to remember, that funeral last spring, in April.[50] He could not remember, either.

I woke up and knew it was time to go to therapy.

I remember that dream as if I had it yesterday. I also remember dreams I had when I was a teenager, as clearly now as when I woke up from them. Of course, I don't remember *all* of my dreams—most I forget a day or two later, or sometimes in the first moments of being awake. One dream I had at fifteen was seeing my name on a tombstone with my date of death. I had only lived to twenty-one years old; this dream really affected me. I have come to think that, in some way, the person I was really did die at twenty-one years old, and a new person was born. But either way, I'm still here.

I also want to address a couple things in this chapter. First, I am not recommending reading Castaneda. By all means, read whatever you want, but he is not required reading at all. Second, people have said we

---

49 Scott is a good friend and one of my father's favorite students of all time. His senior year was my freshman year, so we played lacrosse together for one season. He also coached lacrosse at WPS for 20+ years. But the funny thing about him helping me with my lines is that when Scott was in my dad's shows he could never remember his lines. For instance, Scott played Pseudolus in *A Funny Thing Happened on the Way to the Forum* and the first line in that show is supposed to be "Playgoers, I bid you welcome. The theatre is a temple and we are here to worship the gods of comedy and tragedy." But the joke was Scott would say, "Playgoers... " and then ask for the rest of his line.
50 My dad died in April, but his memorial was in May.

can't read in our dreams, or that we supposedly can't do this-or-that in our dreams. But I read all the time in my dreams. I have read in my dreams since high school at least, as I remember reading the opening lines of "The Sleeper" by Edgar Allen Poe on a gravestone in Mystic, Connecticut (which at the time I had never been to):

> *At midnight, in the month of June,*
> *I stand beneath the mystic moon.*
> *An opiate vapor, dewy, dim,*
> *Exhales from out her golden rim,*

I have never forgotten those lines, even if I can't remember the rest of the poem.

I have come to believe that part of living the examined life means delving deep into our dreams and trying to gain knowledge or guidance from them. The dream I had on the night of my 44th birthday told me I was not dealing with grief, and even a casual decoder of dreams knows that showing up to a performance without knowing your lines is a common anxiety dream.

When I woke up from that dream I called Tom and told him about it. He laughed pretty hard when I told him Scott was supposed to help me with my lines. Then I told him, "I think I need therapy." He was silent for a few moments, and then said:

"I think that's a good idea."

THERAPY

We are not alone in this world. You are not alone.
What kind of dummy are you that you think you are alone in this world? I mean, you didn't invent language. Your thoughts are in words, right? Someone taught you those words. Even your deepest thoughts are a shared experiment with hundreds of generations of human beings that created that language. You are the beneficiary of culture, and since we are essentially a global society now, you are potentially the beneficiary of the wisdom of *all* cultures. You are not out there by yourself. You are not alone.

There is a great moment in the *Hardcore History* interview with James Burke I previously mentioned where he tells a story about calling a professor who had written a book on Medieval English history. There was a footnote about the idea that the invention of the stirrup lead to the foundation of feudalism, which caused Burke to realize that everything connects in ways we do not always acknowledge. Burke wanted to use that idea for a TV show, so he called up the historian and asked permission to take this idea. The scholar laughed and said, "I stole it, you steal it, that's how this works."

Burke was stunned; he could not believe what he had heard. He said, "You stole it?" to which the professor replied, "My dear boy, you don't think we are born with ideas, do you?"

We are not alone. Cast out of your mind all those stupid movies where some macho character says, "This is something I gotta do by myself." That's just a storytelling device, it's not real life. In real life, you don't have to do things alone. There are people who want to help, there are people who have been *trained* to help. Just as physical therapists, dieticians, and car mechanics have been trained to do their jobs, therapist have also been trained to help. If you are struggling with your own mental health, you should see a therapist.

Don't get me wrong: not every therapist will be the right therapist for you. You might need to shop around a bit. It's okay to try one out, and if it's not working, try out another one, just as you would with a doctor, a physical therapist, or a mechanic. After all, if you don't like your mechanic, that doesn't mean you should therefore let the wheels of your car fall off. Find the mechanic that is right for you.

For years I chose to not do therapy because I was selfish and dumb. I believed therapy was a cop-out, that it was a weak choice by a weak mind.

It's really easy to make excuses to not do therapy, but it's not a strong choice to not do therapy. It's not brave. For at least twenty years, I made those excuses for why therapy wasn't right for me. Meanwhile, I was drinking myself to death. That wasn't courageous, it was stupid.

I am not alone, you are not alone, we are not alone. Please, seek out therapy. No one has to do this alone.

THE GENIUS OF RACHEL BLOOM

As you know, I tried lots of different methods to treat or cope with my anxiety. Perhaps most importantly I started doing weekly therapy. In the past I had tried therapy only once, during the summer before I moved to South Bend for the second time. It ended with me throwing a check at the therapist and leaving, but after I had a child, I knew I didn't have the luxury of being that selfish. I should have been in therapy much sooner.

There is no singularly right way to deal with depression, anxiety, or maintaining one's mental health in general. There is no one smart way, strong way, or brave way. I used to think medications were wrong, therapy was wrong, and that both were weak. I was wrong. I was close-minded, misinformed, and weak.

Eventually through therapy I got my first few diagnoses. Depression was a given, I had known that ever since I had listened to the Bare Naked Ladies song, "Brian Wilson."[51] Anxiety was a given, being obvious after the second panic attack and the dream the night of my 44th birthday. But I knew something was physically wrong with me, and I felt like it was related to my heart. I had weird pains all over my body, I just didn't feel right anymore. That's when I got the diagnosis of Somatic System Disorder.

That was it! I had solved it, through the help of my therapist, and my struggles with mental health ended. I won. Me, 1 – Mental illness, 0. I could finally move on, what's next? I hope you enjoyed this book and thanks for reading...

Oh shit, it's back.

This is basically the roller coaster I've been on while working through this. Just when I think I have it solved, some new weird feeling from inside my crappy body starts, and it exhausts me.

---

51 BNL does not get enough credit for talking to jocks and frat boys about mental illness, domestic violence, societal pressure on genders, and other progressive ideas. As my good friend Kyle once said, "They talked about depression using major chords, who else was doing that?"

Another way I deal with anxiety is by reading novels and watching TV shows or films. The ones that deal with anxiety are a little triggering, like *Conversations with Friends* or *Ted Lasso*, but they are still important depictions of common mental health struggles. There is one I have not talked about until now because it deserves its own chapter, which is *Crazy Ex-Girlfriend*. Created by and starring Rachel Bloom, it's a four-season postmodern musical dramatic comedy about dealing with mental illness.

I get that all people don't like musicals. If you are one of those people, I'm sorry. I love musicals (thanks, Dad!), so for me this show would have been great even if I wasn't on my own wellness journey when I discovered it. I'm not going into a long, drawn-out, self-indulgent explanation as to why a TV show is wonderful, though. Let's be honest, you have read enough self-indulgent explanations already. But I do want to talk about one episode while trying to not give anything away about the story arc. In the twelfth episode of the last season, "I Need a Break," there are a couple different storylines that would be very difficult to understand if you haven't seen the whole show up to that point. Go watch three seasons and twelve episodes and come back to this, I'll wait.

Cool. By the way, that Greg thing, right? Also, how great is Darrel? Okay, the reason I love episode twelve is because in my life, I have had a tendency to blast through things and take everything to extremes. Back in early 2012, while playing basketball I tore my Achilles tendon and wore a boot for six weeks. After I got the boot off and was cleared to go back to the gym I told to my boss Meg that I was going to the gym the next day. She said, "Okay but please remember... moderation." Then, without a hint of irony, I told her I was going to be the most moderate person ever.

I have a problem with getting things out of the way and moving on to the next thing. I am much more of a sprinter than a long-distance runner. Dealing with mental health is not a sprint. In *Crazy Ex-Girlfriend*, Rachel Bloom's character Rebecca Bunch did the work, but she moved on to the next thing. After finally getting a diagnosis that matched her, going to group therapy, doing individual therapy, changing her self-destructive habits, doing her workbooks, and getting healthy, she believed she had conquered her illness. She was good; she even started dating again. But she stopped going to therapy, stopped going to group, stopped doing all of those things. And she was doing well until suddenly she wasn't. The foundation she had built up through her hard work vanished, because she had not bothered to maintain it. Through a very difficult episode, her character finally gets more help and says something that really resonated with me:

"It's like I've done squats every day for a year, and now I just want to eat donuts for the rest of my life and never go back to the gym, but still have a great butt forever, you know?"

Just like that, a musical comedy show got through to me with the one thing that I have understood perhaps my entire life, or at least since my father threw 200 balls at me on the lacrosse field to teach me how to hit a baseball: there are no short cuts for being good at something. There are no short cuts to getting better, or in this case, healthy. Sure, some people might be lucky, but if you want to be good at something, you have to work at it. You gotta keep taking cuts, you gotta keep swinging.

A couple days after I watched this episode, I talked with my therapist. Things were good. He told me it was okay if I wanted to stop therapy. I thought back to the episode I had just seen and told him about it. I asked if we could just do therapy every other week, and that is what we now do. It is a damn good thing we do.

The following week, I took the time I would have been in therapy and tried to write, but my mind spun in too many places. Instead, I tried meditation to focus and slow my mind. It didn't work. I could not get rid of the same thought: I was healed, I was fixed, and yet my father had died. I could not let go of the fact that I had wanted him to die.

Yes, I hated the life he was living, and hated when people called what he was doing "living." While for years I had told myself that it would be better for him if he died, I had to face the crushing and horrific truth that I wanted him to die because it would be better for *me*. I selfishly wanted my own dad to die, and he did. I manifested it in my mind; I had hoped for it, had wished for it, and if I still prayed, I would have prayed for it.

Somewhere in my mind I had created a thought and folded it away just past my conscious mind. It waited until I was feeling good to surface. I'm glad I didn't stop therapy, because right after I thought I was better, I suddenly couldn't get rid of the idea that somehow, beyond any logical progression of thought, that I had killed my father.

FEAR AND GUILT

I was afraid of the dark until I was twelve years old. In the winter, this was a fear I faced nightly while coming home from the basketball courts. When I finally decided to head home, I would run through the dark woods as fast as I could. I learned where the holes in the ground were, could sense where the sticks and vines laid, and almost instinctively knew where to let my feet fall. I was so afraid of the dark that, as I sprinted, I kept my eyes up and focused on the amber and blue lights always emanating from our TV room. I hated my childish fears, I hated being afraid of anything.

One moonless night in early summer, I walked out of the house with the intention of going to play basketball, but the lights at the courts were off. A shiver went through me as I felt the darkness. Ocean Pines has long resisted calls for streetlights, and with its heavy canopy of old trees is still notoriously dark at night. But on that night with fewer homes around and with no moon, the darkness was oppressive. For those that grew up in the city, suburbia, or even in small towns, true darkness is not something you have ever likely experienced. In the city you might learn to fear the shadows because of what could hide within them, but night in Ocean Pines is too dark for shadows. People that grew up one town over such as Ocean City or Berlin will speak of Ocean Pines at night as a frightful place because of the depth of that darkness. With no sky and no streetlights, there is a heaviness to the night in Ocean Pines which I have never experienced anywhere else.

But in those days, Ocean Pines was all I knew. This extreme absence of light was what I assumed everyone else thought of as "dark," and I knew it was childish to be afraid of the dark. I hated my cowardice, so I went inside and got a flashlight, and instead of going to the basketball courts I decided to face my fear. With the comfort of the torch, I walked through the park, past the boat launch, and into the woods between the boat dock parking lot and the St Martin's River. Back then there were no jogging paths through there, and no houses visible, but there was a long-abandoned logging road that I knew, which I followed into the deepest part of those woods. It was the darkest and most remote place I knew, a place that even if I yelled as loud as I possibly could, I doubted anyone would be able to hear me. I wanted to be truly alone.

I took three deep breaths, and then shut the flashlight off. I could see nothing. As soon as I shut off the light, the woods became a city of noise. My eyes couldn't adjust to the darkness, as under the cover of trees and without a moon, there was absolutely no light at all. I could see nothing, not even my own clothes, or body. I put my hand in front of me, palm inches from my face, and yet I couldn't make out its form. Almost worse, at first I could hear nothing over the desperate screeching of nature in the summer. Without vision, the sounds became overwhelming. As the forest around me got louder and louder, my heart raced faster and faster, begging me to run home like I always did.

But I stood still; I would not run, I would not sit, I would meet this fear on my own two feet. After some time, the noise became less chaotic. The mad, sexual screams of a million insects fell into a rhythm that my heart slowed to match. I still couldn't see my hand in front of my face, but my eyes had adjusted to the darkness—there was an almost silver sheen to the void.

I don't know how long I was there, but most likely it was about an hour. I refused to leave until I was no longer afraid. Darkness would have no dominion over me. I decided to walk home in the dark, but after seven steps I tripped on an exposed root and fell. I turned on the flashlight; while I was convinced I had conquered my fear, I was smart enough to not twist an ankle out of pride.

The most common fears people have are usually listed as:

- Public speaking or other social phobias
- Snakes, spiders, or other bugs
- Heights
- Flying
- Enclosed spaces
- Open spaces
- Drowning
- Storms
- Needles
- Dogs

Not a single thing on that list frightens me. Most of these things I love (dogs, thunderstorms, public speaking, flying, open spaces, shit—I even like needles.)

I tell you this because I want you to know how uncommon fear is in my life. I'm the asshole who breaks the rules because I'm not afraid of the repercussions. A part of this is because of my large size, and a part of this is because of my societal privilege; but a part of it is because I just lack the wisdom, decorum, or intelligence to know when I should follow the rules. For instance, I'm a big strong male and I love crying. If I don't cry at least once a week, I get cranky. I think it's pretty well known that I will cry all the frigging time. Anytime a small creature or person makes a sacrifice in a book, film, or even cartoon, I become a blubbery mess. In *Braiding Sweetgrass*, Robin Wall Kimmerer tells the story of Sky Woman, and there is this muskrat... I can't even type it without crying. I was inconsolable for a solid minute after reading a story that most people will likely breeze past. Sacrifice of any kind gets to me, but that's especially true when it's made by someone small. Another trigger is when someone faces insurmountable odds and still fights. *The Abyss, Don Quixote, The Iron Giant, Braveheart*—Even fucking Bing Bong in *Inside Out* will leave me sobbing. I'm a sucker for all of that Hollywood schlock.

I don't fear death, I respect it. I recognize the power and importance it gives to our lives. People choosing to die for others moves me in a way I cannot elucidate. I have spent so much of my life thinking about death, and fascinated with the very idea of it, that at times the concept has even been a comfort to me. My anxiety has very little to do with what I understand about death, or at least what I understood about death before my father's stroke. However, my anxiety has everything to do with my father's death.

The scariest film I've ever seen is *Jacob's Ladder*. The most hair-raising moment is when Elizabeth Pena's character leans into Jacob's face and she is either a different person, or has transformed into a demon. Jacob screams "Who are you?" That moment, of all the moments in that film, scares me the most; in fact, it truly haunts me and has been a source of many nightmares. Jacob was losing his grip on reality, and that is the fear I know above all others. It is the fear I cannot conquer. I am terrified that my reality will be stolen from me.

In Victor LaValle's masterpiece *The Changeling,* a character retells the original Rapunzel story. The character explains how it is not a children's story, but rather a story that allows parents to put their fears into words. LaValle writes, "The new fears are the old fears and the old fears are ancient," and indeed they are. Parents still fear that whatever they choose to do for their child will be wrong. However, there are new fears that are not ancient. There are new fears that only exist in this era.

My father should have died the night he had his stroke, when he was placed in a medically-induced coma. Had he had the same stroke in 1915, he would have died. But he had it in 2015, so the doctors operated on his brain. The doctors made me choose whether or not to do the surgery, but who would choose not to? In that situation, who would choose to let someone die? From that day forward, Dad was on a minimum of twelve daily drugs that kept him alive just enough to eat, shit, and take more drugs. He couldn't walk, couldn't use the toilet, couldn't even watch TV. There is no ancient equivalent for this; there was no ancient fear of this existence. This is not just a new fear, it's a new reality, and one that I'm guessing is far too common now. Once my dad went on the medication to keep him eating and shitting, it would have been murder to take him off his medications. No doctor in the country would be allowed to do it, and even if they were, who would give consent?

I believe without a doubt that my father's reality was stolen from him on the night of his stroke, and the last three-and-a-half years of his life were a waking nightmare. So, if I believed that, then wanting my father to die would be wanting his torture to end. His death would be a blessing, right?

I think those that knew him, loved him, and visited him in the nursing home all wanted him to die, but none more than I. Without my father dying, I couldn't move on with my life. Once I gave up the hope that his brain might repair itself, his existence in that state became my torment. Whenever I received a phone call from the nursing home, before answering I had a glimmer of hope that he died in his sleep. I'm fully aware that many caregivers have sacrificed much more and that I'm a piece of shit for feeling these thoughts, and I most likely shouldn't be sharing them in a book. But I'm not thinking about repercussions. My goal for this book is and always has been honesty. And while I would like to think I had let go of every part of the Catholic religion, I am certain there is one part of that creed from which I will never find deliverance: guilt. Guilt for agreeing to the surgery, guilt for hating his existence in the end, and guilt for hoping every day that he would die.

My anxiety comes from two things that both have to do with my father's death. First, that I will live my longest unconquerable fear, that I will lose my reality. I can't get over the memory of my father's terrified eyes when he couldn't process where he was and what was happening to him. I'm afraid I will live the rest of my days in that kind of waking nightmare.

Second, because of my selfish lifestyle choices long before Olive was born, my smoking and drinking will catch up with me. Like my father, I will have a stroke and technically survive it, and my daughter will have to watch some other version of me die slowly for years. My anxiety when I feel a twitch in my chest or have a sudden headache is not that I have spoken my last word to my daughter, it's that I have spoken the last meaningful word. I fear the person that will occupy my body will say terrible things to Olive, and those will be the last things she hears me say. I fear this version of me that will be created by a burst blood vessel and will be speaking to her from that point forward. They won't be words of love, they won't be how I feel today, and they won't be how I would always feel, if the soul was real and eternal. It will be words of a failed body reanimated by medicine. She will hear these words that are not mine emerge from my body and they will hurt her, and she will learn to hate me. She will want me to die.

This fear is so deep in me that it causes physical symptoms. My anxiety causes chest pain and headaches. Even before I could name it, I could feel it. This is not an ancient fear, there are no fairy tales or cultural wisdom that can assuage the mind. This is not a fear of death, as in a story like Gilgamesh lamenting the loss of Enkidu. This is a new terror, a terror for our time, and as much as I have loved death, myth, and philosophy, I find myself completely unprepared to face it. My only solution, my only way to go out into the darkness and to meet this fear standing on my own two feet is to write this book. I do not want to die, I do not want to live forever, but I know now that most of us don't get to choose a moment of great sacrifice as our death. Even if we are not cowards, some of us will die a thousand deaths. I won't let those words, the words of someone else, be the last words I speak to my daughter.

I know who I am. I love forever. That is the one thing that has never changed about me. Once I love, that feeling cannot be erased from my heart. So no matter what happens to me, no matter what future person or words that illness or drugs create out of this body, my daughter will know that the only truth that has always existed in me, that has made me who I am, is that once I love, it is forever.

I will always love her.

SOY HABER IGLESIA TODO OIR NO DINERO ACA NINA CIRCA ROTO OTRO TODAVIA TU YA

If you can translate this, I promise to explain. If you can't, don't bother. It's not as important as I'm making it out to be in my head.[52]

I was named after my father's best friend from high school, Dan Crotty. Thankfully, Dan has always been a great guy, and I'm proud that he is my namesake. Dan Crotty lived in Fresno for most of our lives, then he moved to Los Angeles. He was always a true friend to my father. I never remember my father and Dan fighting over anything; conflict never entered into their relationship. He was like the fun brother Dad never had. He liked sports, theater, and films, just like my dad. For as long as I could remember, they would talk at least once a week.

Dan is a huge baseball fan, and was the first person I knew who played fantasy baseball, back before it was played on computers. We always talked baseball together, and he was always hopeful that it would be the Cubs' year, no matter how clearly that it wasn't going to be the case.

There is another reason I want to write about Dan, which I will get to in a moment. While I won't be able to tell all of Dad's stories about Dan, I have to tell at least this one:

My father and Dan went to Catholic boarding school together at Wawasee Prep in Syracuse, Indiana. After high school they went to different colleges, my father went into the seminary at St. Meinrad, and Dan went to Loras College in Dubuque, Iowa.

In the spring of 1967, my father was just about finished with the second semester of his sophomore year when he was put in charge of "hospitality" for guest speakers coming to campus. This was for the American Heritage series put on by students, so was basically their Sophomore Literary Festival. I am unsure what hospitality entailed, but the way my dad put it, he showed speakers where the guest house was and how to

---

52 This was a nonsense phrase my father would say all the time in Spanish class in high school. It confused his teacher and others, but Jim Betustak still remembers it to this day. If you take the first letter of each word it reads "Shit on Dan Crotty".

get to the dining hall. There was one speaker—I believe it was Michael Lawson—whom my father described as a, "Black radical." According to my father, he gave an interesting and passionate talk and then invited my father back to the guest house. Apparently he invited others as well, and someone had brought some alcohol. Depending on when my father was telling the story, there was a beer or a small glass of wine or a scotch "near" him, or maybe he had it in his hand, or maybe he actually took a sip. Either way, as much as that portion of the story changed through the years, the next part did not.

While all this was ongoing, Dan Crotty called the campus office and said he needed to talk to Matt O'Hare; it was an emergency. Immediately, six students were dispatched in different directions to alert the campus that Matt O'Hare was needed for an emergency. Finally, someone told them that he was at the guest house with the Black radical speaker.

A student burst through the door and discovered my father at a party with alcohol, which somehow in college in the late 1960s was against the rules. I feel like *Animal House* lied to me. Anyway, Dad rushed with the student back to the waiting telephone to find out what the emergency was. It turns out Dan had just been to the movies and wanted to talk with my dad about the film he'd just seen. Not long after my father hung up the phone, he was kicked out of school for drinking.

There were times when Dad told this story that he tried to imply that because the speaker was a Black radical, he was somehow a victim of racial injustice. I don't think he really worked this out in his mind, but this was certainly an undertone when he told it.

Nonetheless, Dad always told this story about Dan Crotty. Dad was proud of it—not because he was proud of getting kicked out of college, but rather of having a good story. He also got kicked out of his next college, and that story was probably far more fiction than fact.

Throughout the fifty-plus years of their friendship, Dad and Dan met up all around the country, usually for sporting events. I think they went to seven or eight NCAA Men's Basketball Final Fours, and countless Notre Dame football games. Dan came to visit us a couple of times when Tom and I were growing up, and when we were in high school the family traveled to California to visit him. When I lived in New York, Dan would occasionally come to town and always meet up with Tom and I to take us out to dinner at Becco, or at least meet up for drinks. I am certainly closer to Dan than any of my father's relatives.

When my father had his stroke, Dan was one of my first calls.

Even though Dan lived three thousand miles away, he ended up being one of the first people to see my father in the hospital after his brain surgery.

Dan is now retired, so it's not as if he is rich, but he would fly out to Maryland regularly to stay for a couple of days and just sit by my dad's side. I want to be clear, Dan had no other reason to come except to visit my father. He was never visiting someone else in the neighborhood on these trips, which were no small feat—they were a sacrifice for him.

Dan came out for my father's 70th birthday. Once we got my dad mobile enough to transfer him to a wheelchair, Dan came out just to take Dad to a bar for a Guinness. The Irish Penny in Salisbury was the last bar my dad drank in, for a shared beer with Dan, Tom, and myself. My father's brain was too damaged for that beer to become a memory for him, but he would have liked to know he shared his last beer with the three of us. Dan came out once to watch a Notre Dame football game on TV with my dad, even though Dad couldn't follow it, nor really even see the TV. He would sit in the nursing home with my dad for hours, relaying news of people they knew from the good old days, even if my dad couldn't follow what he was saying. Dan talked about the Cubs, the Yankees, the Bears, and Notre Dame basketball. He sat there with my dad and told him it was good to see him. His loyalty amazed me. I lived less than thirty minutes from my father, and I would go see my dad twice a week. But I never enjoyed it—going to see him was never anything I did because I got some positive feeling from it, it was a duty and nothing more. There is no way Dan Crotty got any joy from flying across the country for the hours and hours it takes to get from California to Salisbury, renting a car, and then driving to a hospital or nursing home to hang out with a shell of his former friend. This was a massive sacrifice, and yet he did it, repeatedly.

People might shrug this off, but I want you to take a minute to really think about this. Think about who in your life you would do this for. For whom would you carve out time, spend money you don't have, deal with the hassle of multiple airports, go to nowhere, Maryland and sit in the stink of the "memory care" unit while your friend can't even summon the spark of humanity that you have always known? Would you still do it, after they look at you with confusion, maybe not even recognizing you, but certainly not understanding where you both were or why you were even there? Would you still do it, even though when looking at your friend, you are looking down the barrel of your own mortality and frailty? Don't think about doing it just once, think about doing it multiple times. And each time your friend gets worse, yet you keep coming, even though there is nothing left to visit.

We casually throw around words like "duty," "loyalty," "sacrifice," and "honor." Those words have lost meaning because politicians and companies have co-opted them to sell us bullshit. But just stop and think about what they mean, and think about who you would do this for, what Dan Crotty did for my dad. Think about who you know that would do this for you.

That's how many true friends you have.

SHARYN

My mother's name is Sharyn O'Hare, and I don't want to write about her in this book, since it's about baseball, lacrosse, and my dad. She was and is an important person in my life, and was the second person to read the first draft of this book. She'll likely be one of the first people to read the final draft of this book. She's a great mom and is very supportive of everything her sons do, and she's a fantastic grandmother. I'm glad Olive has had a chance to really get to know and love her Mat-ah.

Mom was always better at listening than my father was, and because of that, I always had a better relationship with her than I had with him. For instance, when I moved to Ireland, she asked if she could come over and visit, and I said no because I wasn't settled yet. She respected my wishes. But a couple of months after I was settled, she asked again and I said yes, and we had a lovely visit. She met Méabh's parents, we went to the Aryan Islands, and had a wonderful time together.

Even when I wasn't really getting along with my mom, we could usually get together for a cup of coffee or dinner and have a semi-pleasant conversation. She is much closer to her family than my father was to his, and as a result I'm much closer to her side of the family than I am to his side. Within the last few years she's gone back to Ireland with Caroline, Olive and I, and she took us on an amazing trip to Lithuania to rediscover our lost family that we wouldn't even have known we had if it wasn't for all the genealogical sleuthing she did to figure it out. She was an excellent Realtor who built her career from nothing to be one of the most successful in her area. She was a newspaper columnist, a politician, and served on a handful of boards. She was instrumental in building the Ocean Pines Veteran's Memorial, for which she also worked to compile a book of war stories and helped make a documentary. She really is an incredible person and deserves a book in her own right.

Like all sons, I have a million embarrassing stories about my mom, and they are super funny. But I'm not going to share any of them with you. It has become evident to me that in the few times she came up in this book, she hasn't come across in a very good light. This is because the major conflict in my relationship with my father happened after she left my dad.

My mother and father never got along after that. The only time they would be in the same room were funerals, weddings, and Thanksgiving dinners. My dad never got over her leaving him, and that's just the way it was until he had the stroke.

Even though my dad had spent two decades being pretty grumpy towards my mom—whether rightfully so or not—after his stroke, my mom was there for him every step of the way. She was at the hospital with him, scouted nursing homes for him, helped him get into assisted living, and bought him clothes, furniture, and snacks—everything he needed. Even though they had been divorced for eighteen years and barely on speaking terms that entire time, she was there for him when he needed her the most. It was pretty amazing.

I haven't talked about this in the book, but there was a short period of time after the stroke when my dad was able to walk a little with some assistance and a walker, and he could sort-of make a little bit of sense when he spoke. He understood he was rehabbing an injury, though he couldn't always remember what the injury was. He wasn't able to go to the toilet himself, was incontinent, and wasn't very mobile without help, but he wasn't as bad as he ended up being the rest of the three-and-a-half years until he died. It was a very short window of time, maybe lasting for a month, and was about five months after the stroke. This was the time I alluded to when Dan Crotty flew out and took dad for his last beer, a pint of Guinness at the Irish Penny.

One day during this time, Tom happened to be at the nursing home helping dad try to charge his cell phone. After his stroke, my dad constantly asked to have a cell phone, even though he never figured out how to call anyone on it. Usually he just ended up breaking them, and I think we went through ten burner phones before we stopped the experiment. Like many things we tried it was a very frustrating experience. Right at the moment my brother was trying to plug the charger into the outlet behind my father's bed, our mom arrived at the nursing home and walked to the left side of the bed.

Since my father had what's called "left neglect" if you stood on his left side he couldn't see you, and couldn't hear you, either. So if you wanted to be seen by him, you had to go to the left side of the bed (his right side). But, the left side of the bed was where the outlet was, so Tom was also over there, effectively trapped between the wall, my father, the dresser, and my mother.

Mom reached down and gave Dad a hug and pulled some new

clothes out of a bag that she had bought for him. My father really liked this; he liked being taken care of, and he didn't like the nursing home, so I guess somehow the idea came to him that maybe, if he played his cards right, my mom might take him home. Keep in mind, Tom is on his knees plugging in a charger, trapped.

It was at that moment that my father decided to try and hit on my mom. Tom was desperate to try to get away. He finally got the charger plugged in and was about to tell my mom to please get out of his way when my father evacuated his bowels into his diaper. Tom described the smell as "violent." My mother, saint that she is, calmly listened to my father try to hit on her, offered some kind words to reassure him that he was going to get better, and then went to get an orderly to assist with the diaper, thus allowing my brother to escape.

Tom describes this as one of the worst moments of his life, I see no reason to doubt him. But to an outside observer, while it might have been one of the worst moments of my brother's life, and one of the lowest points of my father's life, it was perhaps one of the best moments of my mother's life.

They took a circuitous route to show it, but I have no doubt in my mind that there was always love between my parents. There was plenty of hate in there, too, but always love.

Kevin Gates Reading the Sports Page

Remember when I first mentioned Kevin Gates—the coach I met at Impy's camp that had the Batmobile? Anyway, we finally are getting to Kevin Gates.

Like I said before, Kevin never coached me, not even in that camp. He played at Salisbury State with Impy, and after graduating he became an assistant lacrosse coach at Notre Dame. He coached the year before I went there, so had left by the time I arrived. I have wondered if, had he still been there he would have reached out to me and convinced me to continue playing, but that impossible to say. I didn't really know Kevin in those days.

Kevin left Notre Dame and went to Shenandoah University, where he started their lacrosse program from scratch. He coached there for five seasons and then went to SUNY Delhi, where he again started a lacrosse program. In 2003, after Kevin had been coaching at SUNY Delhi for five seasons, my father convinced him to teach PE and coach for WPS (formerly WCS as you may recall). It turns out that Kevin was the last men's varsity lacrosse coach my dad ever hired, leading the Mallards during my father's last decade as the athletic director. He was a good coach at Worcester; he won the most games there of any lacrosse coach in school history, and many of his players went on to play in college. Scott Mumford was one of his assistant coaches for thirteen years, and Kevin had multiple former players coach under him as well, which is always a sign of a good head coach. I got to know him in passing, but we never had any long conversations. Even though he's from Long Island, he seemed to be a nice guy, but was clearly a Yankees fan. So he certainly was not someone I wanted to talk baseball with.

But like I said, I didn't really know him, and I had absolutely nothing to do with Worcester Prep or lacrosse in those days. I hadn't picked up a stick since I coached at St. Joe's in South Bend in 1996. At this point in my life, lacrosse—the sport that once defined me, the game I had spent literally thousands of hours practicing—was now nothing but a distant memory.

My father retired to Florida in 2013, and in 2014 Caroline and I moved down from New York to Salisbury. In December of 2014, Olive was born. In November 2015, my father flew up for Thanksgiving and was staying with acquaintances in Ocean Pines when he had his stroke. I arrived at the hospital around 11 PM and stayed there for the night until they admitted him. I called my brother in the morning to get the word out that Dad had had a stroke and we did not yet know if he would survive.

The next eighteen days are a bit of a blur. I was at every shift change to ensure the information about my dad was correct when it passed from one nurse to another. I brought snacks for the nurses every time I showed up, because I didn't want to be a pain in the ass, and I wanted to ensure that my dad got the best care possible. Our family met with the brain surgeon, who recommended surgery. I resisted because of the likelihood of more damage being done, but the rest of the family felt we should take the chance. In the end, he most likely would have died if we hadn't gone through with it.

Had he died then, it probably would have been better for everyone, especially my father. But the surgery was successful, at least in that he did not die. My father was still completely out of it, and he slept most of the time, but for the first time the doctor allowed visitors. Kevin McNulty came down from Baltimore and was the first non-family member to see my dad. Dan Crotty flew in from California, and Tom Westcott and Barry Tull both saw my dad in the early days.

And then there was this guy Kevin Gates. Kevin came every day to check in on my dad. He brought the sports section of the paper, and read the entire thing to him, even though my dad was usually unconscious. Not only would he read him the stories, but he would do a running commentary on them, for no one but my unconscious dad.

When a bad thing happens to a loved one, hopefully lots of friends will reach out to the family and ask what they can do. The problem is, the family doesn't even know what needs to be done, each crisis is something new. No one in my family had had a massive hemorrhagic stroke before, so we were busy learning about how the brain works, talking to six different doctors and a dozen nurses, doing our best to notify people, figure out my dad's finances, and plan the next steps for him. When my father was moved from the ICU to progressive care, I had to meet with a hospital staff worker to plan where my father was going to go next. It was so bureaucratic and confusing. This was the extent of my conversation with the hospital worker:

"So Mr. O'Hare, what is your plan for your father?"

"I don't know. You mean after progressive care?"

"Yes."

"My understanding was that the room after the progressive care was just a regular hospital bed."

"Usually it is. It depends on how he responds to physical and occupational therapy."

"Okay, but he hasn't gotten those yet, so how will I know how he will respond to them if he hasn't gotten it yet?"

"I understand, but we need to know you have a plan."

"My plan is to have him go to a regular hospital bed."

"And after that?"

There was a long pause, as I was so confused.

"I don't know. Will he be okay to go home? A rehab center? A nursing home? An assisted living facility? He just got out of surgery three days ago."

"Of course. So what is your plan?"

"Well, will he be okay to go home?"

"I don't know."

Another long pause.

"Do you expect me to know?" I asked.

"I'm sorry, I know this is hard for you. We just need to know what your plan is."

"Okay, if you have to put something down just say our plan is for him to go home."

She frowned.

"I don't think he's going to be able to go home."

"Okay, well let's put down what you think he'll be able to do."

At the next shift change, I did not bring her a snack.

That's just one example of what the family went through. Not to mention I had a wife and baby at home, a job, and was working on a local political campaign at the time. You get stretched thin very quickly. The one thing there really doesn't seem to be much time for? The person in the bed, the reason you are going through all of this madness in the first place.

So while lots of people might ask what they can do, it's hard for the family to even think of things that friends can take care of. Some people who are good at crises understand this, but most people—myself included—do not. When Kevin McNulty came down he took me to lunch. I tried saying I was too busy, but he would not have it. He knew I needed to get out of the hospital, and he was completely right.

When Kevin Gates read the sports page to my dad, he was doing the one thing he could do, which was also the one thing I didn't have the time nor emotional energy to do. He was trying to connect to the human being he'd known and loved, even if that human was unconscious. He didn't come only one time—he came day after day, after school, on weekends, and even over Christmas break. This was the kind of dedication that we didn't see from anyone else.

Of course, this didn't happen forever. My dad regained consciousness, and was moved to a rehab center and then an assisted living facility. Lacrosse season was coming up, and Kevin was busy with his family, but he still stopped by and saw my dad at least twice a month. He probably visited dad more regularly than anyone else at the school during that first year after the stroke. I became friends with Kevin and found out he was looking for an assistant coach for the upcoming lacrosse season. Feeling indebted to him for the kindness he had shown my father, I told him that if he couldn't find anyone better, I would come out and coach for him.

I really had no interest in getting back into lacrosse, but I wanted to be of whatever help I could. I had been away from the game for far too long, and I thought I would be so bad at coaching that I brought along a friend of mine, Hoffy Hoffman, to help, too. I actually pushed for Kevin to hire Hoffy and not me, but Hoffy would not have it. Hoffy bought me a stick and basically dragged me back to the school where I had not coached since 1998, back when my father was refusing to speak to me.

From the first practice, I loved it. The kids were great, and the game had not really changed that much. It was a blast coaching with Kevin, Hoffy, and Bob Conklin.[53] Eventually even Scott Mumford came out of retirement to run the box for a few games. It was the first time I shared a field with Scott since my freshman year of high school, which was pretty special.

I coached for two years at Worcester Prep with Kevin, Hoffy, Bob, and Scott. I told the administration that I was only there because of Kevin, and if Kevin left, I would go too. So when they chose not to renew Kevin's contract after my second season, I did as promised and left the program. The school asked me to come back to coach, but I'd made a promise to Kevin and intended to keep it. Kevin got a job coaching at the Virginia Episcopal School in Lynchburg, while Hoffy became the head coach at Stephen Decatur High School in Berlin. Hoffy asked me to join him, but I couldn't go to Stephen Decatur. I assumed there would be too

53 Bob Conklin was on the first Salisbury State College lacrosse team ever and is an Eastern Shore lacrosse legend. He has been a lacrosse coach for over 40 years, and I think he knows everyone that has ever coached or been good at lacrosse on the Shore.

much goofing off, but really it was because I don't think my dad would have approved, living or dead.

Dad passed away April 20, 2019. I took that year off from lacrosse, but the next year I got hired as an assistant coach at The Salisbury School. Because of a lack of interest from student, The Salisbury School hadn't even fielded a lacrosse team for a couple of years before I was hired, so we were rebuilding the program from scratch. The first thing I did was call Kevin Gates and tell him all about it. We talked for an hour about lacrosse and building a team without a foundation, something he had done twice as a college coach. Right before we got off the phone, he said to me, "Remember, it has nothing to do with wins and losses. Twenty years from now you are not going to remember the wins and losses. It's all about relationships. That's what matters."

That season we went 1-9, and it might be my favorite team I ever coached. I talked to my brother Tom after the season ended, and I was telling one story after another about my team. Then Tom said something that really hit home:

"You're like a different person when you coach. You need to do more stuff like this in your life. You sound so much better than you did before the season started. You are so much healthier."

The following year, I returned to be the assistant coach at The Salisbury School. But because of a work conflict, the head coach had to quit the team mid-season. So I took over as head coach on April 20, 2022, three years to the day of my father's death. And who was our opponent that day? You guessed it, it was Worcester Prep, on the very field on which I had played lacrosse during high school, the field where my father had taught me to hit a baseball. The field that my father built.

Kevin McNulty came down from Baltimore for the game. That was the day I found out his brother-in-law was the head coach for Worcester Prep. I told you, lacrosse is a pretty tight fraternity. Hoffy couldn't be there, but called me both before and after the game. My mom was even at the game, just like when I played in high school.

I talked to my players at halftime about how I had been thinking recently about what the word "legacy" means. I told them about my dad building that field. I told them how he brought high school lacrosse to the Eastern Shore. I told them how in high school I claimed that field as my own, how my blood fed the grass that grew there. I told them that they were now a part of my father's legacy. I've never had players play as desperate and as hard as they did. We didn't win the game—we had no chance from the opening whistle—but my guys got every second out of that game, they never let up for a moment. And they would have run through a brick wall if that's all it would have taken to win the game.

After the game I called to Kevin Gates. I told him what had happened, and what I said at halftime to the guys. He was silent for a bit and then finally he said, "Your dad would have loved this story." I just smiled. The mention of my dad made me so happy. For once, I could talk about my father and not be sad.

After all these years away from the game, after the death of my father, after losing the relationship with my alma mater entirely, after struggling with grief and depression and anxiety, I finally realized something: my life had always been spent trying to find something real. It may have started when my dad cast me as Biff Lowman, but more likely that it started much earlier than that. I thought the thing I was looking for was just over the next horizon, like when I looked at those autumn sunsets with a hunger to run, a desire to move, an urge to fly into another life. It was as if there was a hidden secret that I needed to find, and if I didn't find it, I would die. That autumnal madness caused me to speed through different lives that I never fully lived. All the books I have read, all the drugs I have relied on, all the spirits consumed, all the self-examination of the supposed "life well-lived," and what did all that lead to? After all of the drunken declarations and pseudo-philosophical meanderings of mine, claiming that I was living a life spent seeking some shred of truth or beauty—what was the single thing I found to be most true?

What's the truest thing I know?

That returning to the place where I had already been and coaching the sport I had always loved made me feel clean again.

In the end, I have one person to thank for that: Kevin Gates.

A LETTER TO MY FATHER
(September 9, 2020)

I took Olive to Crisfield today. It was just the two of us. She's five-and-a-half years old now. We got a greasy crab cake sandwich and fries, most of which I ended up eating; she just ate ice cream. It reminded me of the places you took us, and the greasy food you probably ended up eating while I just ate ice cream.

We walked out to the pier and I showed Olive the Chesapeake Bay. She said, "Just like in *Hamilton*!" There's a line in *Hamilton* when Alexander Hamilton meets up with Lafayette in the Chesapeake Bay. She's five and a half and has almost every line of that musical memorized.

You would have loved *Hamilton*, I'm sure of it. I know you weren't the biggest fan of hip-hop music, but you weren't a fan of rock music either, and yet you loved *Jesus Christ Superstar*. So I think you would have loved *Hamilton*, too. You certainly would have loved Daveed Diggs. He goes big. I remember when you said, "People in the back row pay for tickets too." He's the kind of actor that acts for the back row, your kind of actor.

The other day I bought Olive her first lacrosse stick. She can't catch yet, but she's not bad at throwing. She's learning how to get her back hand down to scoop up the ground ball. Every team needs someone who isn't afraid to go get a ground ball, and I don't think she is going to be afraid of much.

Olive loves the stage. She ran up on stage at the Blue Dog Café when she was only four years old and sang every word to "I Know Things Now" from *Into the Woods*. Granted, the piano player was playing a Christmas song at the time, but Olive doesn't need an accompanist, anyway. Her skill at hitting notes is yet to be determined; hopefully the O'Hare tone-deafness will skip a generation. Whenever I am on a stage, she will run up onto it. When I was running for office, she used to sneak up behind me during speeches and upstage me. Or she would run at me in the middle of a speech and jump into my arms, just to make sure she got everyone's attention. She helped with bucket-asks at the National Folk Festival, speaking loudly into the microphone. I wonder where she gets that from? The second your memorial was over, she ran on stage to give me a hug, and then she just danced up there for a while. Your granddaughter is a ham.

I'm seeing a therapist now to deal with my anxiety and grief, the same therapist you saw after your stroke. He recommended a book to me called *The Soul's Code*, by James Hillman. I'm sure you probably met Hillman once, buying a hot dog in the Midwest as some Forest-Gumpian historical event happened in the background. *The Soul's Code* was written in 1997, which I think was after you had stopped reading. You would have liked the book, as it argues for the existence of an indelible spirit. It says this spirit is in us from birth and is not of our own creation. The spirit has a vocation it must realize, and struggles to live its own life against whatever societal pressures we experience. I don't know how much I believe in all of that, but when I look at Olive, I see a spirit bigger than the both of us combined.

Maybe this is just what it means to be a father—I don't know yet, and I don't know if I ever will. But I do know you would have loved seeing Olive grow up, would have loved to see her on stage, and would have loved hearing her stories.

I hate how you died. Not your last breath—that was a relief for both of us, and I was glad I was there with you, holding your hand. I hate the three-and-a-half years that you were in a fog, only breathing and eating thanks to pharmaceuticals, and kept scared and confused by brain damage. After the first 18 months we knew there was nothing that could be done. But sometimes I still had hope. I wish I was strong enough to have let you die, I wish I was strong enough to have killed you when you asked. But I didn't want to go to jail, and I didn't want to lose my family. But I hated every day that I saw you tortured. And I hate how I wanted you to die.

I'm struggling right now. I'm struggling to remember the man you were before the stroke. I've been speaking to your old friends from high school and college, and I even got in touch with Carmen Fisestra, who said you two hadn't spoken since college. We spoke for three hours. He's sorry you two didn't catch up when you were alive, but he was really proud of you. He read your obituary and the comments on it, and could tell how your life had an oversized impact on the community. He said nothing he ever did would have that kind of impact on so many people's lives. I told him how proud of him you always were. I told him how you used to record shows he worked on and pause when you saw his name in the credits, and then you would tell us the story about how you two had a ventriloquist act in college where he would pretend to be the dummy. He thought that was great.

You always said I was too sensitive, and maybe you were right. But I'm sad all the time now. I know you wouldn't want that. Tom made a shrine to you in Tom's Tavern. He toasts you all the time. He says the shrine is like you getting to be at his parties. It's his way of keeping you alive. He's writing something now, a screenplay that I think is tangentially inspired by you. You would love that, too. Grandpa always said Tom should be the writer and I should be the actor. I'm still writing a play, the same damn play I've been writing for twenty years. Maybe if I ever produce it, I'll act in it. One last time, for Grandpa.

I'm trapped in my brain. I don't want my daughter to ever be this sad, to have to watch me die for years, or watch me slowly slip away. I don't want her to see some undead version of me. I know we can't control death, but I guess I wish we didn't try so hard to keep people breathing when they aren't actually alive.

I'm glad you rooted for the Orioles at least once against the Yankees. I'm glad you got to see me coach lacrosse. I guess the only silver lining of your stroke is that those few men—Kevin McNulty, Dan Crotty, Tom Westcott, Jack Hughes, and Kevin Gates—refused to leave you alone when you were lost. They showed me how people should behave when a friend is all but forgotten to the world. And by that example, Kevin Gates brought me back to the game of lacrosse.

Stepping back on that field after a two-decade absence was a release from all of the baggage from my early twenties, from all of the battles you and I had left behind and decided not to address again. Baseball might have brought me back home, but coaching lacrosse on the same field on which I last played made the past real again. I know I won't be here long, there are too many sunsets to chase, and too many horizons to explore. At least I was in the right place to say goodbye to you. I just wish that goodbye hadn't taken so damn long.

Dad, I have so many regrets and I can't shake them. I'm going to try to write down some of your stories for Olive. I'm going to put together a book for her, and I think she's going to know her grandfather through this book, since she didn't get to know you when you were alive. I'm going to tell her about the bad times, too. I'm going to be honest. She needs to know it's okay to let people down, to be flawed, and to fail. I wish I had known these things earlier. I'm sorry if I can't remember more stories, and I'm sorry I didn't write them down sooner.

Olive is here now, I think she knew I was crying. She ran into the room and told me a story she just made up to make me feel better. She's five-and-a-half and she's the star in a world of her own. I so wish you had a chance to really know her. I have a feeling she is going to places where you and I couldn't go. She's not Biff, and she's not Happy, and she certainly isn't Linda. I think maybe this family will finally be free of the curse of Arthur Miller.

I hope you know that I think about you all the time. I don't ever make the choices you would have, unless that choice is to *tell a story*. I certainly got my long, rambling, pointless storytelling from you, there's no denying that.

I guess all that's left to say is, thank you. Thank you for being my first coach and my first teacher. In the end, I guess you were the one that taught me the most important lesson of all. Standing on an empty lacrosse field, holding a baseball bat, fouling off pitch after pitch, always keep swinging. Never let one go by, wait for the right pitch to drive. Just keep swinging and stay alive. Right? Just stay alive. That's all we can ask of one another: just stay alive, until it's finally our time to go.

Just stay alive.

Acknowledgements

Writing a self-published memoir is terribly unfair to everyone in your life. It's really a horrible way to tell a story, because you are guaranteed to leave out so many wonderful and influential people along the way, and without a doubt those will likely be the only people that will read the book anyway. The ones you include most likely don't want to be included, or remember the past differently anyway, so no matter what, I expect I will either disappoint or frustrate everyone I know with this work.

There were a few very influential people in the creation of this tomb who need to be singled out. Primarily Brent Gold, an acquaintance from Camden Chat who was the first person to read the very-rough first draft. He took a loose collection of stories and, with a thorough edit, turned them into a semblance of a book. In the process became my friend, and it's likely I would have given up if not for his encouragement.

I must thank my best friend, Mark Decker, who did the final edit. He has an absolute gift for language, and if anyone finds this book readable at all it is because of Mark, not because of me.

Thanks to Aaron Rosenberg for the encouragement along the way, guidance through the process, and for putting this book together in the end. Without your expertise, I would have been lost.

Thank you to all of the early readers of the book, especially those who gave me helpful notes, like Clint McIntyre, Chad Rosen, Carmen Finestra, and Ewan Turner. And of course, thanks to Tom, Mom, and Caroline.

None of this would be possible without everyone in my life, because that's all it is, a collection of my experiences. But I never would have written it—or anything really—without being in love with Caroline. All I need to know.

APPENDIX

MATT O'HARE'S OBITUARY
Written by Dan O'Hare April 20th, 2019
(the same day Matt died)

Born October 4th, 1946 in Dickinson, North Dakota, Matthew Reardon O'Hare passed away on Holy Saturday April 20th, 2019. Preceded in death by his parents Edward Coleman O'Hare, Mary Ellen (nee Reardon) O'Hare, and his siblings Margaret Ellen (Peggy) O'Hare and Michael Shannon O'Hare. Matt is survived by his siblings Bonnie Carol O'Hare, and Harold Edward O'Hare (both of Dyer, IN), Matt's sons Thomas Matthew O'Hare (NYC), and Daniel Joseph O'Hare, his Daughter-in-law Caroline Amelia O'Hare and Granddaughter Olive Helen O'Hare (all of Salisbury, MD), his former wife, Sharyn O'Hare (Ocean Pines, MD), brother-in-law and sister-in-law, Phil and Sherry Guarino (Rockford, IL), Niece Alicia Guarino-Hrebik (Tony Hrebik) (Rockford, Il), Nephew Adam (Jessica) Guarino (Machesney Park, IL).

If you are reading this, there's a good chance Matt O'Hare was a character in your story. He was a villain in some, a hero in others, but most likely comic relief in yours. Matt was a rare character: weird and authentic; always out of place on the Eastern Shore; and yet an entrenched figure of the community here. His mind was a trap for the trivial, while his heart and soul were devoted to the competition of sports and the raw emotion of theater.

He embellished out of need (if it made a good story), relished a lie if it would guarantee a laugh, and it is believed he coined the phrase, "hyperbole is an art form of my people." While he staunchly refused to participate in St Patrick's Day ("Unlike them, I'm Irish 365 days a year!"), he was instantly enamored with anything green and Gaelic, especially if it involved The University of Notre Dame.

If you met Matt casually, you might think he attended Notre Dame, but he didn't. He studied at two different seminaries, being kicked out of both of them by priests who would go on to be Cardinals in the Catholic Church. He was really proud of this, so I feel it needs to be mentioned. While most of his stories were at least partially untrue, this one isn't. Or if it is, he had a bunch of people in on it, which is also possible.

Far more than Notre Dame though, he loved Worcester Country/Preparatory School. Matt dedicated his life to the school and its students. He built the Athletic program and Theater Arts program at WCS/WPS and was immensely proud of everyone that participated in those programs. As Athletic Director, he attended every game he could, including games of former students who were playing in college. Likewise, he went to see former students in plays or performances at every opportunity possible. It seemed like almost every night of the school year he was a spectator, supporting his current or former students.

And here's the thing: he wasn't merely in the stands or in the audience. You knew he was there. If you were playing sports, that bellowing voice from the sideline was unmistakable. I can still hear "Every Corner is a Goal!" echoing from a distant field. If you were on stage, you knew that first pause for laughter was going to have one laugh just a little louder and just a little longer than the others. Even if you didn't know he was there before the curtain opened, it wouldn't be long before you did.

But the audience wasn't where he was most at home. That was always on stage. Although he didn't perform on an official stage in the years between leaving college and his retirement, he was performing in every room he was in. He could make his voice like thunder, and he did often. Whether for fun or for fury, his roar was all too familiar to everyone who knew him. It was his most distinctive feature, as the large man with a large voice got a large amount of notice, which is always what the consummate actor craves. He commanded attention in most of the rooms he was in, but he always went out of his way to make everyone feel welcome in those rooms.

This may be why, unlike most people, Matt loved public speaking. He used any excuse to get in front of a microphone, even if it meant having to become an art auctioneer for a night. He was a member of Toastmasters, but he had perfected his craft long before joining that organization. His advice was always, "be funny, be short, and be sincere." That's probably why he was a sought-after keynote speaker. To say he had the gift of gab is an understatement, as he really relished getting behind a podium and talking to anyone about anything. He once even spoke to a convention of nuns, opening with a joke about Jesus getting stung to death by wild bees. He claimed some of the nuns fell out of their chairs because they were laughing so hard. There's cause for skepticism, as we've all heard the joke by now, and while it's funny, it's not *that* funny.

In retirement he dedicated most of his time to acting with the Naples Players in Florida. I got to see him perform in *The Drowsy Chaperone*, in which he played a cigar-chomping, loud-mouthed, angry producer. Afterwards, when I asked him how he came up with the character, he replied: "Well, I bought a cigar."

There's no question that Matt O'Hare will be missed by his friends and family. But as people have noted, his impact will be felt in this community for a long time. He touched many lives and got a lot of laughs. And that's what he loved. Maybe, as a favor to him, you could tell a friend one of those stories or jokes that he told too-many times. Feel free to embellish if it makes a better story, as you know *he* would. Or maybe get up somewhere and give a speech. Keep it funny, short, and sincere—just remember: being sincere doesn't necessarily mean it has to be truthful.

Please join us for a celebration of Matt's life at Worcester Preparatory School on May 18th at 11:30 AM. In lieu of flowers, please consider giving to the Matt O'Hare Scholarship here www.cfes.org/DONATE which will be given yearly to a current WPS student that excels in Performing Arts and Athletics.

Made in USA - North Chelmsford, MA
1345737_9781892544179
12.13.2022 1500